In hell the only guarantee is justice...

GEHENNA

...and the only way out is down.

A NOVEL BY

PAUL THIGPEN

CREATION
HOUSE
BOOKS ABOUT SPIRIT-LED LIVING
LAKE MARY, FLORIDA

Creation House
Strang Communications Company
190 North Westmonte Drive
Altamonte Springs, FL 32714
(407) 862-7565

Unless otherwise noted, all Scripture quotations are from
the King James Version of the Bible.

Quotations from Friedrich Nietzsche are from
Beyond Good and Evil, translated by Marianne Cowan
(Chicago: Henry Regnery Co., 1955), pp. 79, 80, 82, 85, 86.

The quotation from Mary Baker Eddy is from
Science and Health, With Key to the Scriptures (Boston:
Trustees under the Will of Mary Baker Eddy, 1934), p. 237.

The characters portrayed in this book are fictitious unless
they are historical figures explicitly named. Any resemblance
to actual people, whether living or dead, is coincidental.

For Leisa, Lydia and Elijah

GEHENNA

The Vestibule   The Neutrals

CIRCLE 1 (SHEOL) The Virtuous Pagans

CIRCLE 2   The Lascivious

CIRCLE 3   The Gluttons

CIRCLE 4   The Hoarders and Wasters

CIRCLE 5   The Wrathful and Sullen

CIRCLE 6 (SEMINARY OF DIS) The Heretics

CIRCLE 7   The Violent
RING 1 : Violent toward Others

RING 2 : Violent toward Self

RING 3 : Violent toward GOD

CIRCLE 8 (MALEBOLGE)
   The Fraudulent
PIT 1 : Seducers & Panders

PIT 2 : Flatterers

PIT 3 : Simonists

PIT 4 : False Prophets

PIT 5 : Grafters

PIT 6 : Hypocrites

PIT 7 : Thieves

PIT 8 : Evil Counselors

PIT 9 : Schismatics

PIT 10 : Falsifiers

CIRCLE 9
(LAKE COCYTUS)
The Traitors

REGION 1
Traitors to Family

REGION 2
Traitors to Country

REGION 3 Traitors to
Friends

REGION 4
Traitors to
Benefactors

UPPER HELL
CIRCLES 2-5
SINS OF WEAKNESS

MIDDLE HELL
CIRCLE 6
SINS OF THE INTELLECT

LOWER HELL
CIRCLES 7-9
SINS OF MALICE
(Injury and Fraud)

——— AUTHOR'S NOTE ———

The road to hell, so the old saying goes, is paved with good intentions. Writing a book about hell ("Gehenna" is its name in the New Testament) holds a similar peril: The best of motivations can still get you in trouble. Folks may assume that you're a morbid killjoy or else a gleeful fire-eater who loves to see people squirm, both now and in the hereafter.

Worse yet is a *novel* about hell. Some folks tend to read a book like this as if it were non-fiction. They see it as a precise and explicit statement of what the author believes to be the truth about a hidden part of reality, instead of seeing it as a book-length parable. But that's as much a mistake as reading Jesus' story of the Good Samaritan as if it were a map of the road to Jericho.

In light of those tendencies, let me say some things clearly now, before you start to read:

1. I don't enjoy thinking or writing about sin and its tormenting consequences. But our culture's moral compass has become so skewed that the time seems right to do it. In fact, I'm not alone in this concern: Recent polls have shown that a surprising number of Americans are thinking and talking these days about the possibility of final justice for the wicked in the afterlife.

And no wonder — they don't have to look far for candidates. I could have clipped a hundred news items from the daily paper to paste in these pages, and you'd have hardly noticed the difference. Dante Alighieri, the Italian Christian poet who wrote a similar tour of hell called the *Inferno*, said nearly seven centuries ago: "I found the original of my hell in the world in which we inhabit." I guess there's nothing new under the sun after all.

2. In this book I'm by no means offering a map of what I believe hell is like. The Scripture provides no details about the afterlife; it only hints darkly at the terrors of judgment. So I'm simply presenting here an extended parable based on some of the biblical texts and the ancient traditions of the church. No doubt my pictures of Gehenna are pale and tame next to the terrifying reality.

Why, then, should I write even a parable about hell? For the same reason Jesus told the story of Lazarus and the rich man — to create an imaginative vehicle for getting across a few uncomfortable points. "As an artist," Augustine once said, "God makes use even of the devil."

3. This work is not intended to take a final position on two important questions that have given rise to sharp debate in some circles these days: First, what is the eternal fate of those who never had a chance to hear the gospel while still on earth? Second, are the damned tormented forever, or are they finally annihilated?

These matters have been argued almost since the church began, and I don't pretend to offer any authoritative answers. Instead, my purpose is to open up the current discussion a little further by getting our imaginations as well as our reason involved in the debate. No doubt the argument will continue until faith becomes sight and we learn by personal experience what that terrible final judgment day will bring.

4. This book isn't intended to condemn those who have committed the sins it describes. If you find yourself somewhere in its pages, keep in mind that I find myself there too. We all stand in need of grace. If we've confessed our sins to God and received His forgiveness for them through Jesus Christ, they are covered by His blood. My goal is correction rather than condemnation.

5. Finally, I fully expect that no reader will agree with everything written here, because no two people will weight the seriousness of various sins in exactly the same manner. Any given

scene in this work will probably seem overly harsh to one person and too lenient to another. The infernal "architecture" described here simply reflects in its broad lines the central ethical tradition of the Western church, a tradition that has convinced me of its reasonableness. Maybe you too will find much of that tradition convincing — and the rest of it worth thinking about further.

In the way of acknowledgments: I freely confess having borrowed the moral topography of hell from Dante's *Inferno*. That medieval book's remarkable insights into fallen human nature still have the power to convict its readers today. Any similarity, however, between this novel and other contemporary works drawing from Dante must be attributed solely to their common ancestry in the haunting vision of the *Inferno*.

Special gratitude goes to my wife's mother, Bonnie Ghetti, and to my friends Tim and Jewel Howard for lending me their homes as places of writing refuge; to my good buddy Ronnie Lang, who encouraged me faithfully for over a year to get this book written and provided an enthusiastic sounding board for ideas; to Walter Walker, Debbie Cole and Shelly Duff, fine editors and friends at Creation House; to the friends and family members who covered us in prayer; and most of all to my wife and children: Leisa, Lydia and Elijah. Without Dad around for two long and tumultuous summer months in the wilds of Central Florida we call home, they braved strep throat and skin rashes, rattlesnakes and relatives, so I could get away alone to write.

Paul Thigpen
August 1992

*Do not be afraid of those who
kill the body but cannot kill the soul.
Rather, be afraid of the One who
can destroy both soul and body in Gehenna.*

— Jesus Christ

*Hell is the final guarantee that
what we do matters.*

— Anonymous

ONE

It was June, and it was Georgia. The dog days had come early, all at once in a pack, sweating and snarling and showing their teeth.

Hours had passed since the sun had finally given up the ghost, bleeding down around the dark roof lines of old, grimy tenements and new, mirrored towers. You'd have thought the streets would be cooling off at last, swapping icy neon for sultry sun; you'd have thought the proud night would show a little mercy, even if only the scornful kind.

But a sauna in the dark is still a sauna, and though a Dixie sauna may reek of magnolia and mint julep, you can't help but smell the sweat too. On a mean street in the broken heart of Atlanta you can smell much more: whiskey and cigarettes, make-do toilets, vomit and sometimes blood. Even the mosquitoes gag and stay away.

Of course, I had no business being on that particular street in the first place, it being late and I being alone. But the best library wasn't in the friendliest neighborhood, and I guess I was too busy reading Milton's *Paradise Lost* while I walked till I was lost myself.

Where I stood, three streets tussled in a wrestling match, with no clear winner. All of them were "Peachtree" something-or-other, but it didn't matter. Within a few blocks they'd exchanged names and addresses anyway, like the drivers in the last fender-bender I'd seen at rush hour.

No map, no signs that made any sense and nobody on the street I'd dare to look in the eye, let alone ask for directions. I was lost. Lost as a Bibb County sow in a big-city slaughterhouse, and twice as scared.

Daddy never had wanted me to come here. To him, living in the city was a poker game where you bet your life playing with crazy drivers, druggies, gangs and muggers. "The stakes are just too high," he used to say. "Move to the city, and you'll die in the city."

Look, I used to tell him, you can die in the country too. What about Cousin Bubba? Choked to death last Christmas Eve on a chicken bone, watching a late-night John Wayne movie, right in his own living room in Unadilla.

Daddy and I never had seen eye-to-eye on it, never thought we would. So I'd packed my bags way back in '69 and anteed up to the big-city game, crazies and all, finding a little hole of an apartment and getting into school. Three degrees and ten government loans later, here I was, still in school but teaching now, still in the city but eating grits, talking one minute like a scholar and the next like a good ol' boy, with one foot in the field of theology and the other in a field of collard greens. I was a cultural half-breed.

Life in the big city had grown on me. But this particular night I began to wonder if maybe Daddy had been right after all, rest his soul. The night before, ten white boys had doused an old black man with gas and set him afire, just because he was black. Now Atlanta was boiling, and there I was in the middle of the stew. I thought I'd stay close to the library and be home by dark, but I hadn't planned on getting lost.

I looked up to get some kind of bearings from the skyline. Were those the cathedral spires over there? I looked down again for another street sign.

Then I saw them, and they saw me.

On this street I stuck out like a peanut in a bowl of raisins: pale skin, decent clothes, a book under my arm instead of a bottle. I'd have given anything just then for those country rags I'd thrown away so long ago — better yet, for the gun Daddy used to keep in his Chevy pickup and had tried to give me back then when I first went off to school. But all I had now was Milton, and the half-naked gang of three that had their sights on me weren't looking for poetry.

They crossed the empty, four-lane street and closed in on me. My back was up against a tall wooden fence choking on snarled vines of kudzu.

Never in my life had I been so sorry I was white. Every racial joke I'd ever told sat in my stomach like chunks of ice, and my words were ringing in my ears.

They came with foul-mouthed taunts, steps slow and even, the stalk of hunters sure of their prey. No hurry. They wanted to give enough time for the terror to burn white-hot and brand my face, a relished sight that made the kill sweeter and fed their lust for revenge.

Bloodshot fury smoldered in their eyes, glazed over by the white smoke of crack. The leader spit on the sidewalk and laughed.

"It's your turn now, white boy. Now we get the goods, and you get the grave."

The worst nightmare of a white country boy in the big city, even a country boy who'd lived for years in the big city. I could see it all: They'd take my wallet and my shoes — the ones Daddy had left me — then leave my book and my body.

Tomorrow, I thought, my classes will be canceled and my students will lie out in the sun sipping Cokes and reading the sports section of the *Atlanta Journal*.

Tomorrow my brothers will swear revenge, clenching their teeth and their guns and muttering. "Daddy told him it was coming," they'll say, "living in that hellhole city. But he wouldn't listen."

And me? I didn't know where I'd be by then, or if I'd be, or even why I'd ever been. Just a number in the police report on the *Journal*'s last page, a stat in the urban planning department at Georgia State. Maybe the old hometown paper would at least print my name: "Thomas Travis, 42, a native of Waycross, was robbed and murdered on an Atlanta street last night. Survived by his three brothers..."

They were close now. I dropped Milton, shut my eyes and

11

pressed back hard against the wall to brace. The board was loose, and I fell through. Then the cats decided they'd played with the mouse long enough.

I scrambled through a half-open door in the deserted building behind the fence under a blistered sign that read AUTHORIZED PERSONNEL ONLY. In the stifling dust and dark I knocked over rusty office furniture and crunched the broken glass on rotted carpet, searching wildly for another exit by the light of a sputtering red neon sign next door.

A second door, this one closed and bolted. But it fell off its hinges when I pulled, opening onto a stairway down.

Rats sprang out, fled across my shoes, squeaked curses at me. I hate big-city rats even more than big-country rattlers, but my predators had reached the outside doors, laughing like demons as they came. I plunged down into the blackness and hoped the rodents would be more scared of me than I was of them. Two stairs, three stairs at a time, splinters in my fingers from the cracked handrails, down on damp concrete, a sharp left through a broken glass door, then left again through an endless hall that smelled like a sewer.

They were on the stairs now, screaming obscenities, the leader barking orders to spread out and find me. My heart pushed past my throat and pounded at the door of my sinuses.

Another sharp left, and I was in a room full of musty look-alike volumes, abandoned on ceiling-high shelves and in twisted stacks on the floor.

A bat out of nowhere flew by me like a bat out of somewhere else, clipped my left ear, made his own escape route. As I ducked I saw down low, behind a pile of bureaucratic fodder, what was left of a cellar doorway, its corroded hinges and doorknob lying on the floor. My only hope. I couldn't see even a few feet inside, so I lowered myself one step at a time. No rails, splintered or otherwise.

The first stair was loose, the second was gone. The third was termite leftovers, and waiting for me. It held me just long enough to play the trick, and then I dropped like a fishing weight.

"God help me!" I shouted as I fell, but I nearly swallowed the words as I gulped the dusty air.

What should have been seconds felt like hours. Blackness swam all around me as I fell, and all inside me when I finally hit.

When I came to, slowly unwinding the black wool shroud that had buried my last thoughts, I could feel my cheek lying against a rough surface in a shallow pool of something warm and wet. At last I lifted my head and opened my eyes, but I couldn't see much.

Just enough to know that whenever and wherever I was, it didn't look like June or Georgia.

TWO

Long ago that Yankee general Sherman coined the phrase "war is hell," and I suppose that, being an old devil himself, he was in a good position to draw the comparison. At any rate, he and his boys sure made an inferno out of Atlanta, torching her glory and scattering her tears and ashes all the way to the sea.

But that Southern phoenix rose up again, weaving a new nest on top of the old ruins, and I guess she just got into the habit of building in layers. When I was a boy, I went to see the shops and bars down under the streets in the lower layer they call Underground Atlanta. There I wondered for the first time just how far down you could go before you hit that ornery Georgia clay.

But now I wasn't so sure I really wanted to know. When I sat up slowly and looked around, I could see for what seemed like miles, and there was no clay in sight. Not even a streak of red. Just rough, gray asphalt stretching out to every horizon, with a bit of a slope. It was broken by more potholes than I could count and a single huge crack, about a yard wide, running forever in both directions, parallel to the slope. The air was chilly and damp.

No gangs anywhere, thank goodness.

Down the Great Crack gurgled a dingy stream, with an occasional ripple washing over the edge to the nearby spot where I'd fallen. A bit of relief: When I'd first come to, I'd thought the pool I was lying in was my own blood. But I could see now it was a pothole full of that dirty water.

No blood? But I remembered hitting head first, or thought I did, and that came at the end of a long, long fall. This was pavement, merciless pavement, that gravestone of flattened squirrels and leaping suicides and drunk drivers' prey. One time when I was little, Daddy got mad and pushed me off my bike onto the street; it broke both my arms when I fell just a few feet. So I *had* to have at least a few broken bones now, a bruise, a scrape, something.

No. No hurts, no pain. Just a sudden wave of fear that turned my stomach upside down and my knees to jelly so I had to sit down fast to keep from falling again. I put my head between my knees.

"You coward," I said aloud. "You're even scared of *not* being hurt."

Just how did I get here? Kidnapped and abandoned? In any case, not robbed; I still had my wallet and Daddy's shoes, though my Timex was gone. What had happened?

When I felt more strength, but no less terror, I dared to look straight up.

Nothing there. Not even sky. Gray, but no clouds, no shades of the color, no sense even of depth. Like a concrete ceiling just a few feet above my head, yet not concrete at all. Just gray emptiness, but a thick, heavy emptiness, weighed down by — if nothing else — its own vast expanse as far as I could see in all directions. Like an everlasting, low ceiling with nothing to support it. And no sign of the stairs or the shaft or even the door I might have come through to get here. Who built this place? The structural engineers at Tech would be in shock to see it.

Was I in shock? Even without the fall, this place was weird enough to make frozen ants crawl up your spine. I was numb, and I shook.

Tom, I told myself, you're either dreaming or hallucinating. Or maybe your vision's just blurred from the fall. After all, wherever you look — up, down, out — it's all gray. Even your clothes look gray, your skin is gray. It's your vision, boy. Your rods and cones got jumbled, and your retinas got disconnected from the color screen.

Still, I wasn't convinced. No telling how long I sat there, arguing with myself over one guess after another. Where was I?

You're no dummy, Thomas. Think. Your brain may be fuzzy just now from the fall, but if you could get a doctoral dissertation past that ornery faculty committee, you can figure your way through anything.

What would Daddy do?

He'd pull out a bottle to guzzle his fear away. But once he drank his courage up, he'd take his gun and go looking for a clue to what in hellfire was going on.

That wasn't much help. No booze here, no gun. And looking for anything in this endless gray would be like looking through the dingy water for a dingy rag at the bottom of the sink after washing Sunday dishes — in a sink the size of Texas.

Even so, there was nothing else to do but look around. It was crazy, I knew; it made no sense. But it made even less sense to sit, numb and dumb, as if I were waiting for the next bus to the Twilight Zone. So with no gun and no drink to toast the journey as Daddy would have done, I set out.

There was only one real landmark to explore, so I started in the obvious place — along the crack in the asphalt.

Down in the crack, the murky water flowed along a bed of crumbled pavement. The pebbles it made were rounded, as if the water had worn off the edges with long years of friction.

I had to make a choice: Would I walk upstream to look for the source or follow the flow down to an end — a lake, maybe, or even a waterfall? I didn't feel much like climbing, even on such a little slope. So I took the low road.

The crack was a straight, clean break, not wrinkled slowly by two pressures butting heads over time, but as if it was suddenly snapped open by an earthquake. I walked alongside it for what must have been hours, feeling like a hitchhiker on a deserted road to nowhere. The landscape never changed. But the farther I followed the stream, the darker the water grew, and its bed narrowed.

At last something different, something worth checking out: In the distance I could see a round shape down in the creek bed, and beyond it the water wasn't flowing. Maybe a sinkhole?

It was a hole, all right, but not a natural one. Across it was a manhole cover. I had to cup my hands around small sections of the surface to reroute the water so I could see better what was there.

The metal was all corroded in some places and needed replacing. An odd pattern ran around the rim, like iron chicken scratch — not like any I'd ever seen in Atlanta, though I was no connoisseur of manhole covers. Six holes in the metal let the dirty water fall through into — a sewer?

There was writing in the middle. Maybe it would tell me some manufacturer's name, or at least the government agency responsible for creating this cosmic parking lot. I looked close; the words were in several languages. The last was English:

ABANDON ALL HOPE, YOU WHO ENTER HERE.

What a sense of humor they had, those guys who had put a drain hole in this asphalt Mississippi! And well-read too. The words were from the *Inferno*, that famous tour of hell written by the Italian poet Dante in the fourteenth century — required reading in just about every Freshman Lit course. They'd taken the inscription from the gates of his imaginary hell and put them on a manhole cover.

I looked closer. It was written in Hebrew, Greek and Latin too. All the other tongues were rusted away. Bizarre. If I'd discovered it ten years before, I would have written my doctoral dissertation on it.

Well, I thought, a Ph.D. in historical theology is at last coming in handy for something more than a low-paying slot on a seminary faculty.

But what to do next? The Great Crack ran on, but with little promise of yielding further surprises, educated or otherwise. A sewer hole wasn't my idea of an adventure, but surely it had to lead somewhere, and eventually to someone.

Or some*thing*. They say gators live in New York's sewers, and rats call them home in Atlanta. Who knows what might be waiting here? Judging from everything else, it was bound to be big and gray. Maybe elephants?

Suddenly I heard a footstep, and a voice spoke from behind me. *"You must not go in there alone."*

17

THREE

I jumped a foot in the air, turning around as I came back down to face the one who spoke. My heart came back down a few seconds later and started clubbing my brain.

She was black as burnt ribs, small-framed, skinny and a little stooped, her eyes wide and steady, her hair white wool pulled straight back into a bun. Judging by her clothes, she had just wandered off the set of the old TV series "Daniel Boone" and forgot to change: brown homespun dress, white cotton apron, red calico scarf.

Her gaze turned calmly from me up to the gray overhead. After a long silence she spoke again, but this time to herself.

"Always they send me a man. Always I ask for a woman, and always they send me a man."

Her voice was flat, with no ripples of anger or malice. She was simply stating a fact, turning it over once in her mind, as if reading the words on both sides of a stray penny before she dropped it into her apron pocket.

She spoke perfect English, but with a slight foreign accent — African maybe?

My turn to speak. "Where am I?"

She kept staring off into space, slowly shaking her head. "He reads the ancient words, and still he asks." She turned to me again at last. "Have you truly no idea where you are?"

"Well, it can't be too far from Atlanta. I remember going down, but this doesn't look like underground. Or above ground either, for that matter. I don't know. I asked you first. Where am I?"

"I have never seen Atlanta. But you are at the gate of hell."

I laughed but didn't mean it. "Beg your pardon, but I thought I heard you say we were at the gate of hell. Come again?"

"You heard correctly. You are at the gate of hell." Her words remained flat, like the tinny taped voice calling out stops on the Atlanta airport subway.

She's crazy. This must be the parking lot of some huge state mental hospital, and she wandered out here from the cafeteria when the orderlies weren't looking. Well, at least I know there's somebody around here who can help me figure out where I am and how I can get back to where I want to be.

Humor the woman for now. She could have a kitchen knife hidden in the folds of her dress. Try a few wisecracks.

"What do you mean I'm at hell's gate? I was just in Atlanta a little while ago, and every Southern boy knows that hell's in Chicago and the Devil's from New York."

No smile. "You are at the gate of hell."

"Well, then, I must have taken a plane. No matter where you're flying to from my part of the country, you have to make connections in Atlanta."

Still no smile, nor a frown, for that matter. Her face was carved ebony, motionless and hard.

They say the worst psychotics can't laugh. I took a few steps back.

Her eyes riveted mine. "I will not harm you, but you will suffer unspeakable harm if you go down that hole alone. I have been sent to be your escort."

"I've never dated a black girl." One last shot to crack her, but still no smile. Great goodness, was that a face or a mask she wore?

Time to talk straight. "How do you even know I want to go down there?" I kicked the manhole cover for emphasis.

"There is nowhere else to go. There is no way out but down. And you most certainly do not want to stay here."

The last statement was no doubt a warning, and the ice chunks came back into my stomach. But I had to bluff.

"Look — no blind dates. I won't go anywhere with anybody I don't know. You can call me Thomas. Who are you?"

"My name is Capopia."

"African name?"

"Yes. From the Ovimbundu tongue of southwest Africa, in the area you call Angola."

"And what do *you* call it?"

"I once called it home. Then I lived in Georgia, at the coast on Talahi, an island near Savannah. You are from — Atlanta?"

"If you know Georgia, you must know Atlanta. It's the capital."

"When I lived in Georgia, Savannah was the only settlement of any size. The rest was pine forest, palmetto hammocks and the camps of the Guale people, from whom the land was stolen."

For a state hospital patient, she sure knew her African geography and American history. Do they let them read in those places? Better humor her again.

"That was a long time ago. You must be awfully old."

"Time stopped for me when I came here. The calendar is meaningless in this place. Here we have only one day — today."

Now she's talking like a sixties poster. All we have is today. I shall not pass this way again. Next thing you know she'll be telling me to bloom where I'm planted.

As it turned out, she called for an immediate transplant.

"We never know," she said, her words still flat, "how long that day will last. It could end any moment. So we must go now, right away. You do not want to be caught here when the day ends."

If the gray was any indication, the sun was already down. What could she possibly be talking about? And what would I do next? The place was spooky enough without trusting my fate to Aunt Jemima's role model, and a loony one at that.

I was about to decline her invitation — or was it a threat? — when suddenly a streak of lightning shot out of nowhere and exploded the creek bed a dozen yards away. Before I could even ask if the day was done, there came another bolt, then another, then dozens all at once like fireworks, blasting more potholes along both sides of the crack and coming our direction.

She pulled the manhole cover aside, and I forgot all about ladies first. Head first, I dove in, with Aunt Jemima right behind.

FOUR

I landed on my face, drenched with dingy water, in a stretch of thick, gray carpet. The pile was rotted and slimy and covered with a mass of crawling things, but at least it gave a little when I hit. Though you've never seen anybody jump up again so fast, still a few of the crawlers hung on.

Worms. They were gray, twisting worms that bit and stuck like leeches. I slapped them off my face and felt a few drops of blood trickle down my chin.

The air was damp and cool as it had been above, but so thick with the smell of decay that it would have been easier to breathe mud. The stench was a cross between the Okefenokee Swamp and the south Atlanta garbage dump. It settled in my lungs, weighing heavy against my stomach from the inside till I thought I'd vomit.

My escort stood nearby, her face unbitten and still motionless. She must have done this before: She'd jumped feet first, landing like a cat, so she only had to shake off a few worms hitching a ride on her homespun dress. Most of the dingy water tumbling down through the hole had missed her; it poured right into an old nickel-plated tub, then overflowed and found its way through the

21

carpet to lower ground.

The air swarmed with the kind of big, black roaches that crawl up the walls, jump off and fly. Two of the pests dive-bombed into her hair. She brushed them off and stepped on them with a loud pop.

"So this is hell?" I said with a smirk. "Where's the fire and brimstone?"

She replied in the same flat tone. "Further down. Here we are only in the vestibule. But do not forget that hell is known for more than its flames: *Their fire is not quenched, their worm dieth not.*"

So this crazy woman knows some Bible along with her history. Sounds like she's memorized all the gory parts. Maybe she's like the psycho killer in that late-night thriller flick I saw last week: He mutilated his victims using horror novels for instruction manuals. Maybe she's just read about Samson's torture, or Herod's slaughter of the innocents.

No time to waste. I've got to find somebody who can tell me where I really am and get this bird back in her cage.

I put my hand across my throat and felt the blood that had made its way there. Keeping her in sight, I looked around. It was too dark to make out much, but the walls looked like cinder block with gray paint flaked off. To the left I saw a hall entrance, lit up by a dim, ice-blue glow.

Without waiting for the crazy woman, I trotted toward the light, squishing worms and swatting roaches as I went. These sure weren't Georgia roaches — they were biters, like the worms. As I knocked a couple more from my neck, I saw a room at the end of the hall, so I ran there to take a look.

The room was hardly bigger than my granddaddy's outhouse and about as bare as the outhouse visitors. Two pieces of furniture filled it: A faded recliner sat upright with its back to me, ripped and rotted. In front of it was a cracked coffee table with a black-and-white TV on top. The screen showed only a test pattern, which was the blue light I'd seen.

I walked around between the table and the chair to see who might be sitting there. To be honest, I half-expected to find my youngest brother. How many nights had I come home from partying to see him in the same place in our living room, numbed into oblivion by watching hours of whatever chicken droppings they shoveled out on the only station back home?

It wasn't my brother. Some other young man about his age sat there, motionless. But somehow they looked alike: the same slack jaw, glazed eyes, spreading middle, eerie blue halo — signs that their only brain waves in business were nearly flat. If he noticed me, he didn't care, or didn't show it.

He was dressed in the collarless, baggy, big-button pajamas worn by mama's boys and old men. I thought he had on house slippers to match until I saw them wriggle. His feet were covered with worms.

A couple of those sickening crawlers had made their way up his leg and were headed for his groin. At the other end roaches nested in the uncombed crannies of his longish hair.

I didn't dare touch him, but I grabbed the chair and shook it. "Hey, boy, don't you know these critters are making a picnic out of you? Are you comatose or something?"

Maybe he was deaf too. No response, except that one of the roaches leaped out of his hair and bit me on the hand. His gray eyes were hogtied by the light of the tube. Each dilated pupil was a black hole opening into God-only-knew what kind of void. I tried to pry off a few of the worms, but they must have put down roots. My gut twisted.

Maybe a change in channels would break the spell. I turned the knob, but all the stations showed the same test pattern, frozen squares in shades of bluish gray. The knob came off in my hand.

To the left of the chair was another small door, this one closed. I couldn't do anything to help this guy, and he gave me the creeps anyway, so I decided to keep exploring.

I pulled hard and got the door open enough to squeeze through, though it creaked in protest. Another room, just like the first. Same chair, table, TV, test pattern, bugs. Same blue-haloed slug watching, though this one was a girl in a long T-shirt with a portrait of a soap star on the front. Worms bored through the star's eyes.

So it *is* a loony bin. Each one has a little cubicle in isolation, and they give them TVs to keep them pacified. Maybe they even drug them to make them tame.

No call letters, channel number or location on the test pattern. But the fact that it's there means it's late at night, wherever I am. Must be a small town — only one station, which signs off at midnight. Maybe I'm still in Georgia after all.

I've got to find somebody in charge. And when I get out of here, I've got to report this place to the health authorities. If these folks weren't crazy when they came here, it's no wonder they are now.

Another door, another room, another zombie. Then another and another. One long row of pajamaed potatoes, black spots for eyes, nuked through and through by Hollywood microwaves, TV dinner for worms and roaches.

I moved faster, but it was no good. No exits, only endless doors between blue-frosted prison cells. I pushed my way into one more, then fell back against the wall.

No way out. All closed up. And I can't stand being all closed up.

The wall pushed back at me, leaned in on me, stifled me. Just like the walls did that night when I was a kid and my brothers locked me in Granddaddy's outhouse without a flashlight, alone with the slimy critters in that smelly, dark hole. I screamed for an hour, but Mama wasn't around, and the men were all drunk in the kitchen.

Ever since then I can hardly go three floors in an elevator.

The ceiling sagged, sank, slithered down the walls toward me. Below the hum of the tube I could hear the worms creep across the moldy carpet, headed for my feet. I held my breath and started to black out.

Suddenly the door creaked open and two strong arms caught me. I opened my eyes. It was the crazy woman.

"Are you at last tired of trying to find the way alone?" Her tone was firm but not hostile. "I told you there is no way out but down."

Strengthening, I straightened up and stepped back from her. I was shaking, but the questions exploded, fueled by fear.

"Look, Jemima — "

"I told you my name is Capopia."

"All right, all right, Capopia, then. Well, come to think of it, you're old enough to be my grandmother, so I shouldn't be calling you by your first name anyway. How about 'Miss C'?"

"I could be your great-grandmother's great-grandmother, child, she said. "I suppose 'Miss C' will do."

"In any case, where am I really? Who are these people? What are they doing here?"

"I told you this is the vestibule of hell."

"And I suppose these are all damned souls?"

"These you see are called the 'neutrals' — those who lived a lukewarm life that was neither hot nor cold, praiseworthy nor damnable. They were not believers, yet they were not blasphemers either."

"Why are they here?"

"They refused to make the important choices of life for good or evil. Instead, they withdrew into their own little worlds or occupied themselves with frivolous things. This outer circle of hell is their fate."

She's still talking weirdness — articulate weirdness, but weirdness all the same. Sounds like some of those old windbags over in the philosophy department at school. Educated crazies are the worst kind, so I'd better keep playing along, at least until I can trick her into telling me the way out.

"So you're saying these neutrals, as you call them, spend eternity in the rotted lobby of hell because they watched too much television?"

She swatted at a roach. "Some of them no doubt spent their lives sedentary as you see them now, lost in endless diversions: television, romance novels, motion pictures, athletic events. But not all. Some simply made all of life a spectator sport, watching idly while others pushed the world toward good or evil."

"They're punished for *not* being criminals?" My voice was rising.

"They were not criminals, but they could have been saints and heroes if they had tried. They could have wiped out a disease, prevented a war, played with the neighbor's children, written a letter to someone lonely. But instead they let others live their lives for them, and all their pains and pleasures were vicarious."

I felt the blood rise to my face. She was preaching now, beginning to sound like one of those self-righteous, high-and-mighty religious fanatics.

"For *that* they deserve hell? Just for being ordinary human beings?"

She shook her head sharply. "No — not ordinary human beings; in fact, hardly human beings at all. The human will was made to act, and when left unused it rusts like any tool until it corrodes into something less than human. This is the final end of such decay."

"But nobody deserves *this!*"

She looked up into the darkness and shook her head slowly, her face at last twisting into a frown. "If he trembles at the vestibule," she said aloud to no one present, "how will he survive the lower levels?"

She turned back to me. "Like all those you will soon meet, these are getting not simply what they *deserve* but what they *are*. And what they *are* in this circle is fit neither for heaven nor for deep hell. Both mercy and justice must scorn what they have made of themselves."

I opened my mouth to make another point, but I caught myself.

Am I as crazy as she is? Why am I arguing with a mental patient? Of all the loony tunes in this place, I had to meet up with the resident theologian. Must have lost her mind in one of those fanatic Bible schools.

You know this isn't hell, Thomas, but it isn't Theology 101 either. Here you are, suffocating in a 3-D version of *Night of the Living Dead*, and you waste your time debating with a psycho over who deserves eternal punishment. You gotta get out of here *now* while you've still got half a brain.

"OK," I said, working hard to control the volume of my voice. "Take me to the person in charge here."

"You will have that chance soon enough. Now, if you are ready to cooperate, I will show you the way out of the vestibule."

At last we're getting somewhere — out. I can play along a little more if she can just get me to where I can see the light of day again. Or even a starlit night would be nice. Even back out in the Cosmic Parking Lot, dodging lightning bolts, would beat suffocating in this hole.

"I'm with you," I said. "Lead on."

She turned and walked, not over to the next door, but to the coffee table. Pushing it aside, she pointed to a small door in the floor underneath it that I'd missed. She opened it slowly, and this time she climbed down first, as if she were backing down a fire escape. I followed, glad not to take the lead, but still not so sure I would like what might be waiting below.

As my head was about to disappear through the hole, I turned to take a look at the neutral sitting there. Worms and roaches swarmed over a hand that held a half-eaten chicken wing.

It was Cousin Bubba.

FIVE

I f she hadn't caught me again I'd have fallen down those stairs. When we got to a small landing a few yards down, I had to sit and put my head between my legs again.

"You are feeling ill?" she asked as she let go of my arm, just a little sympathy in her voice.

"That...that last neutral. It was my cousin."

"You were close to him?"

"No. We used to play together as boys, but in the last few years I'd only seen him when the family got together for funerals."

"You were unaware that he had died?"

I tried to answer but couldn't. Thoughts crisscrossed my mind like hounds and rabbits in a hunt.

After a long silence I looked up. "Yes, I knew he'd died. That's why I didn't expect to see him sitting there."

"You thought he would be in heaven? Or in a lower level of hell?"

"No!" I shouted, standing up. "I thought he would be in the *grave*! I saw them put him there, and I expected him to stay there. He should be rotted by now. Why is his body pickled and propped up in that chair?"

Her eyes narrowed. "His physical body is indeed still in the grave. It will join him once more on the Day when it is summoned."

"Then what's in that chair?"

"What you see is the soul made visible."

"I don't believe in the soul. And even if I did, how can anybody see a soul?"

"Even on earth there are those who see at times what is invisible to others."

"Hallucinations."

"No, not hallucinations, but glimpses of a reality even more substantial than the physical world. Here those realities have been laid bare. Here nothing is invisible, nothing is hidden; all things are eventually exposed."

I pounded my fist on the rail of the landing. "Then why doesn't my cousin's soul, as you call it, look spooky like a ghost? It looks just like his physical body."

"The body mimics the soul more deftly than you would dare to think."

"But how can worms eat on a soul? And if there's fire below, how can it burn a soul?"

"Just as the body can be wounded by physical forces, the soul can be wounded by spiritual forces. Sin and its consequences injure and maim the soul just as surely as fire does the body. Remember — in this place you are gazing on spiritual realities, and if they seem to you as solid as physical ones, that is because they are every bit as substantial as the world you are accustomed to experiencing."

"Bubba's not moving. Is he dead?"

She answered me as if I were a schoolboy. "Yes, Thomas, he's dead."

"All those people in the TV rooms are dead?"

"Of course."

"That's why they're not moving?"

The ebony frown returned. "Still you fail to understand? I myself am dead, yet I am moving. All men and women in hell are dead, but most of them, as you will see, are quite capable of motion, a fact you will learn to regret. The neutrals cannot move because the motions of their wills have been slowly stiffening for a lifetime, and now they have rigor mortis of the soul."

"Are you saying I'm dead too?"

"You are an exception. A few have been brought here before their time of reckoning, each with a need and a mission that can only be fulfilled by a tour of hell. I have been sent to be your tour guide."

"Just who sent you? How do I know he isn't some sadistic mental hospital director who loves worms and blood and is sick enough to make a dummy of my cousin so it would scare me silly?"

She looked down and stared at the stairs. Her patience was frayed but not yet torn. "You are like all the others from your century. Why do you find it impossible to believe in hell or that you could end up in it? Do you really think human behavior has no eternal consequences?"

"The consequences end at the grave."

"They did not end there for your cousin."

We were getting nowhere. "Look. I don't know who's in charge here, but I want to meet him right now."

"Do not be obstinate. The One in charge is the One who sent you here and who sent me to accompany you. Your time to meet will come."

"Oh, yeah? Well, you can tell Him I didn't ask to be sent here, and I didn't ask Him to send you."

"But of course you did. You muttered a plea for help even as you were falling to this place."

The moment when I first fell came back to mind, so vivid a memory that I shook. *God help me*, I'd shouted. But how did she know that?

I was on the defensive now. "I didn't mean it. I'm an agnostic — I don't believe in God. It's just a saying, a habit I picked up from my mama."

"Such pleas are always taken seriously, whatever your intention."

Another long silence as I sat down again. Nothing seemed to fit. I hadn't been hurt when I fell on the asphalt. Bubba had never even had pictures made of himself, let alone a full-size model. And Miss C knew things she had no way of knowing. How could I explain it all? I was shaken but still not convinced she was sane. Maybe a psychic loony?

Miss C sat down next to me and folded her hands on her apron.

"What will it take for you to believe?"

"I don't just want to *see* someone I know is dead. I want someone I know is dead to talk back to me. Then I'll know it's not a dummy."

She thought for a moment. "There are millions here. Perhaps you might recognize someone from a portrait in a history book. But the chances of your seeing personal acquaintances are small. And yet...already you have seen one, and there are no coincidences in hell. Keep your eyes open."

She stood, grabbed the stair rail and began her way down again, with me just a few steps behind her.

The climb down seemed to last for hours, but without my watch I had no way of knowing exactly how long, and the endless gray gave no hint of day or night. I've never been too fond of heights, so I didn't dare to look down, though I doubt I would have seen anything but more gray.

The cool dampness of the vestibule, as Miss C had called it, now gave way to stifling steam. Too hot, it seemed, for the flying roaches, which hadn't followed us down.

What was this place made of? Was I surrounded by masonry? No, it was much too ghostly; currents of the gray swirled and floated around me like a winding sheet. Was it smog? It stank like smog, but it was much more dense, like unset concrete searching for a form.

At last the sound of Miss C's footsteps on the stairs below stopped, and I heard a small splash. A few seconds later I was standing beside her on a cement floor awash in shallow, oil-slicked water and floating garbage. Every direction looked alike to me — still all gray, though darker now. But without a word she set out as if she knew just where she was headed, and I had no choice but to follow.

Ravenous rats partied everywhere on the chunks of garbage, but they stopped and stared with fierce eyes as we waded by. At last we came to the edge of what could only be a sewer, where the concrete came to an abrupt end beside a deep, flowing current of the same nasty water. Waves splashed over the edge and sent dingy wet sheets across the floor. The grayness of the air was thinner here, but still I couldn't see more than a few yards in any direction.

"Now what?" I asked. Would I have to swim in that filth?

"We walk this way along the edge until we reach the landing. You will be able to see more from there."

Landing? A sewer with boats?

I was about to ask her what she meant when I heard for the first time a noise, a loud noise, that wasn't ours. I stopped dead in my tracks. If something bigger than rats was down here, it wouldn't be friendly.

Miss C kept walking, but I called to her. "What was that?"

She stopped but answered without turning around. "You will hear much more the closer we get to the landing. You thought we were alone?" She used the schoolteacher voice again.

We didn't have to wait long before she was proven right. The sounds came from every direction except the water itself: first vague and distant, then close enough to be distinguished as voices and footsteps and what had to be a few brawls. Even before I could make out any words, I could tell that whoever was out there wasn't happy.

The "landing" turned out to be acres of concrete where thousands of people were gathering from every direction out of the fog, which was clearing a bit just as Miss C had said. It was a gigantic tunnel of Babel, a mad rush hour of tongues and skin colors — they were all naked — from every corner of the world, pushing and cussing. You'd have thought they were fighting to get into the world's last heavy-metal concert.

Just in front of us two young men wrangled.

"Look, Tony, I told you we should go for the big stuff, but no, you had to go piddling around with those podunk gas stations — till you found the one with a mechanic who packed a .45."

"You think it was *my* fault? I told you to go in quiet, but you had to play Rambo and walk in shooting."

"Aw, shut up, will ya? And what about the time *you* walked in on that ugly old pit bull..."

Their voices were lost in the roar of a thousand others.

I turned to Miss C. "What are all these people waiting for, anyway?"

"Charon will be here soon."

Charon. The name rang a bell, but only a dull one. Charon?

Miss C saw the question on my face. "You are a seminary instructor in theology. You recognized the inscription on the gate.

Surely you have read Dante?"

My jaw dropped. How could she possibly know what I did for a living?

"Well," I said slowly, scratching my head, "I read the *Inferno* just once — in a college freshman literature course, and even then I never finished it. I remember the words on the gate, all right; they're quoted often enough. But the rest is a blur. At the time, half the language didn't make sense to me anyway."

She shook her head slowly, disgusted by my ignorance. "Charon," she repeated. "The demon boatman who ferries dead souls across the River Acheron into hell. Dante wrote about him."

She knows history and geography. She quotes the Bible. She's read medieval literature and remembers the details. Worst of all, she knows personal things about me I never told her.

What if she really...?

My thoughts were stabbed by the wail of a foghorn. Shoving aside the mists was an oil tanker the size of the Astrodome that trailed black crude as it came.

I looked at Miss C and crossed my arms in disgust. "Don't be silly. You're telling me this is the River Acheron and that tanker is Charon's boat? They sure look bigger than the ones Dante wrote about."

She cocked her head up and stared off into the grayness as if she were tempted to fly away, but her feathers never ruffled.

"Hell has grown since Dante's time," she said, "with new precincts opening up for sins Dante never dared to imagine. The river is fed by the tears and sweat of the world, mixed with all the blood that has ever been spilled. So the tide here still swells — in fact, your own century has often sent it flooding over its banks. Meanwhile, millions more have come to these shores since the fourteenth century. Do you think a tiny rowboat could still hold them all?"

The ship was docking now, and a long gangplank let down. Fights broke out over who would board first. Miss C and I stood back, in no hurry to be swallowed by the grimy iron whale.

An old man appeared at the top of the plank, dressed in black leather and gray-lensed sunglasses, his white hair spiked, his hands tatooed with skulls, his ears pierced with a dozen fish hooks. The crowd jeered then screamed as he swung a lead pipe at arm's length and made his way down, beating back those who were closest by.

"That's Charon?" I asked Miss C, with new skepticism in my voice. "All I see is a wrinkled old punker cracking skulls. That's not how Dante described him."

She shrugged. "Do you think there are no fashions in hell? Many of the fads in your generation were in fact first conceived here. Charon is a demon with many names, and as many costumes. The last time I came through, he was dressed like your own Western outlaw Billy the Kid. I think he is particularly enamored of American rebels; it gives him sordid pleasure to mock them when they come through."

I didn't have a headache, but I should have. I rubbed my temples and pulled my hand flat across my face.

If things get any more bizarre, I'm out of here. Who knows what that crotchety old geezer might do to us? Miss C can take a sewer cruise if she wants, but she'll have to leave me behind. There aren't any windows in that tanker, and nobody's gonna close me up in there with a million naked, screaming sardines.

Without warning, the old man, now halfway down the plank, leaped down to the concrete bank, swinging his pipe and cussing with words I hadn't heard since Daddy's worst drinking days. He screamed at the mob: "Damned souls! Damned, every one of you! You blasphemed the One who made you, and now you'll pay forever. Into the hull!"

The crowd surged up the plank, away from the one-man street gang, and we were caught in the press. It was either go with the flow or be stomped. But as we moved, the herd closed in on me, sweating souls stuffed around me on every side, and I couldn't breathe.

My turn to scream now, louder than anybody around. It caught the old man's attention, and he lunged toward me, the crowd parting like the Red Sea as he came.

"You!" he croaked. "Outa here! The rest are dead and headed for doom. You ain't dead yet — you got clothes on! Wait your damned turn!" He paused and grinned wickedly, his front teeth missing. "I promise to make it worth your wait."

I didn't plan to give him time to change his mind. That was a close one. I hadn't been so relieved since the day the draft board let me go.

Then Miss C opened her big mouth.

33

"No, Charon. He will come aboard with the rest of us. Make room."

"It's *you* again," said the punker, facing Miss C with a smirk. "How did you get up here? This better be your last time, you old broad."

"It may well be, but that is not mine to decide. Now let us on board."

"But he's still alive!" The old boy's bellow had withered to a whine.

Miss C straightened herself and looked him in the eye with a gaze that should have bored holes in his shades. "He must pass over the river. *So it is willed where what is willed must be.*"

The boatman threw his pipe down, fuming. But he didn't argue anymore. Something about Miss C's last words carried more weight than the tanker itself.

I glared at her. "Now I *know* you're crazy. Nobody in their right mind would insist on going with *him* in *there.*"

"You have a destiny, as do I, Thomas, and we must not flee it. Come with me now."

Was that a flicker of compassion in her eyes? She took my arm. "I know you do not like closed places. We will find a spot on the deck, in the open; he cannot stop us from riding there."

What could I say? She held all the cards. I walked up the plank with her tugging on my arm.

As we walked I searched the crowd for a familiar face. All I saw was a stormy sea of strangers. We made our way up a narrow stair to the top and stood on the far side of the deck, toward the water. Soon the tanker left the dock.

In seconds we couldn't see much beyond our noses. But the gray couldn't hide the voices that erupted from below deck, and from the receding shore where yet another mob was already gathering. Screams and wails, groans and weeping, curses and obscenities collided and echoed in the hull. I shook.

I'd never been on a battlefield — college kept me out of Vietnam — but I knew this was how a battlefield must sound after the battle, when at last the metal has grown hoarse and the noise of flesh is all that lingers. No, I'd never been on a battlefield, but I'd seen them in nightmares, and my high school buddies had written me about them from the steaming jungles, letters I'd read between ethics class and lunch.

And here I was again, dodging it all, safe on the deck while the others were caged and stifled....

A sharp slap on the back sent my thoughts scampering, along with a grunt and a belch that hung foul in the air just over my shoulder.

"Well," drawled a voice I'd have known even in hell, "if it ain't little Tommy Travis."

SIX

Y ou got the same baby face you always had, you little runt, and the same baby fat too. Even with the beard and bald head you look as sweet as you always did. But I sure didn't expect to see you here. I figured all mama's boys go to heaven."

Coach Schweiss. King of the Killman High football field. Terror of the freshman class. All through high school he'd tormented me every day in P.E. because I wanted to read instead of wrestle.

My brother told me he'd been shot in the head and killed just the day before I got lost.

Coach wiped his nose on his arm. "Now, tell me, Bully Bait, how'd you get such special treatment out here on deck? Were those mean boys picking on you again, or did your mama write you one of her little notes to excuse you from playing?" He guffawed and spit on the deck.

No doubt about it. It really was Coach Schweiss, and he was saying stuff nobody else could say in the way he could say it. Here was somebody I knew talking to me, not like that Bubbadoll in the chair upstairs. But was he really dead? I had to ask one more question.

After all these years, Coach still could make me feel stupid just for opening my mouth. But I had to know, so I took a deep breath and got it out. "Just how'd *you* get here, Coach?"

He slapped me on the back again. "You know, boy, I always reckoned that if this place was real, I'd end up here someday. But I just didn't expect to get here so soon. Happened one evening after tryouts. I was out with the boys downtown, and somebody came up behind me and filled my skull with lead. Never even knew who it was. Sent me straight to hell, and I never even got to pick a first string this year."

Just then Charon showed up on deck, swinging his pipe. "You! Pot belly with the red neck! Down inside! *Now!*" For the first time in my life I saw Coach jump when somebody else said jump. As he started below deck, Charon kicked him in the rear, and he went tumbling, cussing the whole way down.

Charon sneered and turned to us, fingering a fish-hook earring. "He didn't tell you the whole story. He was buying crack for his boys when it happened. Tried to cheat a dealer."

Then the old punker went below too, and my head began to swim. I sat down fast in an oil slick on the deck. No doubt about it now. Somebody must have been listening to what I'd told Miss C and given me the proof I'd asked for.

That was Coach. He was dead. This is hell. I'm up the stinking creek.

The brass-knuckled reality punched me in the gut, and forty-two years of sin vomited up from my memory into my mind.

I saw myself as a freckle-faced boy, lying to my mama and cussing my daddy behind his back. I saw the Zero candy bars we shoplifted, more times than I can count, from the corner soda shop run by an old man too nearsighted to see us and too slow to catch us when he did. I remembered the peep hole into the ladies' rest room at the neighborhood gas station. The rotten eggs we threw at the school buses headed across the tracks to the black schools.

I saw my teenage years, those miserable, God-forsaken, pimple-faced days when I stopped believing this place even existed and started living accordingly. I saw the girlie books I stole from Daddy's hoard down in the crack of his easy chair, between the arm and the seat springs. The booze I guzzled on those camping trips with my buddies — more lies to Mama, denying it all. The joints. The wild parties. The back-seat sex.

Then, as if the sins of the heart and the flesh weren't enough, I'd heaped up sins of the mind in the years that followed. I saw the late-night bull sessions in the college dorm, talking my roommates out of their childhood faith, wrecking their neat little arguments memorized in Sunday school — not because I wanted to help them find truth, but because I wanted to feel smarter than they were. I remembered how I quoted Chairman Mao, even while the thugs of the Cultural Revolution were running wild, even while my buddies were dying in the jungle, because the snobs I called friends would have dumped me if I'd dared to step on their political toes.

I saw the students in my seminary courses who dropped out and went to business school after I played with their minds and gutted their convictions. And the ones who went on to be preachers anyway, though they didn't know why, making converts who were twice as much the sons of hell as they were.

A son of hell. That's what I am. And now I'm coming home. When this grimy tin tub docks, Mao himself will probably be waiting for me with a re-education committee.

Miss C hadn't said a word the whole time we were on deck. Now she spoke, an edge of sternness in her voice. Once again she'd mistaken my long silence for grief. "You pity that acquaintance from your youth who did so much evil? You think he does not belong here?"

"No." I shook my head abruptly, glad to have my thoughts sidetracked, if only for a moment. "No pity. If anybody belongs here, *he* does. A classic sadist. He'll probably even like it here. I wouldn't be surprised if he ends up bringing half his team down with him and being proud of it."

I pulled myself up by the deck rail, still a little light-headed. "I wish I could be the one to pass judgment on the old bear. I'd make him do push-ups till doomsday."

Miss C frowned. "Soon enough he will be begging for a sentence so light. But only One can pass judgment, and that One's executor we will soon meet."

My heart crashed to my toes. "So soon? We're headed for the judge right away?"

"First we must pass through the circle where I and those like me must dwell. Remember your Dante."

It had been years since that college course, and I couldn't remember much. What I did remember made me shiver: fire and ice, demons and monsters, the world's worst nightmares sketched in the most charming of medieval poetry. The story scared me so much I never finished it.

Maybe Dante exaggerated, I told myself, to give his readers more thrills and chills. Maybe it was just a bad dream he had — maybe *this* is just a bad dream *I'm* having. But the steel of this rail feels as cold and hard as any I've ever clutched before.

Maybe if I try to remember all the good things I've ever done, I can build a case for my defense.

I had lots of questions for Miss C, but the ship's horn announced that we had reached the other shore.

In fact, it really was a shore, and not another concrete landing. The mob on board busted out of the hull, down the plank and along the water's edge out of sight — which didn't take long, because the air had grown dark now, as if it were finally night, but without any moon or stars to break the blackness. We could see only a few yards beyond our noses.

When the ship had emptied out, we took our turn down the plank. It felt good to step out on hard ground; even if it was rocky and uneven, it was the first honest dirt I'd seen in this place.

Once again Miss C seemed to know right where she was going, though she headed straight out into the dark. She was moving as fast as a New York jaywalker, and I could barely keep up.

"I want to ask you a thing or two," I said, panting beside her.

She didn't even break stride. "Save your breath for now. When we have arrived, there will be time for questions, though perhaps not for answers."

"Well, one thing I can't wait to ask. When do we eat?"

"Never. You should have noticed by now: As long as you are here, you will have no need for food and feel no hunger pangs. Nor will you need to sleep."

She was right. By now I should have been starving, yet I wasn't. But when had that ever stopped me from chowing down before?

Suddenly Miss C stopped and thrust her hand out for me to do the same. I felt on my face a strong, warm wind, as if it were blowing up from the ground, but as I strained to look I realized that ahead of us there was no ground. We were on the edge of a steep cliff that dropped into pitch darkness.

Without a word Miss C turned backward and started the climb down, so quick and calm you'd think she did it for a living.

"Wait a minute!" I said, grabbing the long apron strings that trailed her. "We're not going down *there*. Not in the dark."

She pulled the strings from my hand. "If you think to wait till the light comes, you will wait forever. There is no other way but down through the darkness."

"I don't like heights."

"You cannot see the heights; in fact, you cannot see more than an arm's length below you. But if you like you may take my hand as we go down." She held it out. "The way is treacherous."

"No thanks." If I had to do it, I'd do it myself, without any help from a woman. I started down beside her, thinking I'd have rather been on Peachtree Street at midnight than where I was right then. "I'll make it. Just go slow, all right? You know where you're going, and I don't."

She nodded. "Come after me," she said, "and step where I have stepped." Then down we went.

The rock was brittle, the path fickle. I followed the placement of her hands and feet as carefully as I could, but often the place where she'd held on crumbled when I tried it. I slipped what seemed like every few yards, though I couldn't tell exactly in the dark how much ground we were actually covering. Each time I slipped, I knew rocks and dust were flying in her face — the wind even blew them back up into my own eyes. But she never complained.

We'd just gotten to a small ledge and paused there so I could rest — she never seemed to need rest — when the rocks began to shudder. In seconds it was a full-scale earthquake that left us crouching on the ledge, hanging on to the lip of a crevice in the cliff wall. Boulders spilled from the rock just above us, bouncing and thundering as they went. Then it was over as fast as it had started.

I sat down, too scared to move. "Does that happen often?"

"Now more frequently than it once did."

"What could possibly shake hell like that?"

"Do you remember the lightning bolts outside the gate?"

"If by gate you mean the manhole cover, yes — how could I

forget?"

"They strike from earth. Every time they strike the gate, the entire abyss quakes."

"Who on earth has that kind of power?"

"Few are those on the earth who worship the Creator, and fewer still who realize the power unleashed by their worship. But when they do, this is the result. Their praises batter the gate and loosen every nut and bolt in hell."

"Is that what caused the big crack down the asphalt?"

"That was caused by the first and greatest quake, I am told, though it was long before I came here."

"Was it caused the same way?"

"It happened when the Harrower made His way down through every level of hell to the very bottom, and there demanded the keys. When He took them, the entire abyss cracked open, and those He came to rescue climbed out of the crack with Him. No others could escape."

I grimaced. She was talking like a fairy tale. A *Harrower* plundered this place? Commando raids in hell?

OK, so the last few hours — or has it been days? — have convinced me I'm in the real hell, or at least in some cosmic horror show that fits the bill well enough to deserve the name. But whose hell is it? Is it a Jewish hell, a Hindu hell, a Muslim hell, a Christian hell, a Buddhist hell? Who's in charge here, Zeus or Moses or Muhammed or Krishna or somebody I've never even heard of?

"Who are you talking about?" I demanded. "What did this Harrower look like? What is his name?"

At last she lost patience with me. "Must I describe in bitter detail the nail holes in His hands and feet? You are a seminary professor, and you do not know the Name?"

I looked down, my cheeks seared by the fire in her eyes. Suddenly the ancient words came back to me from Sunday school, though they hadn't crossed my mind for years: *He was crucified, dead and buried. He descended into hell. On the third day He rose again from the dead.*

I leaned my head back against the rock behind me and spoke slowly. "Then the old creeds are true? The legends about..." I tried to say the word, but no sound came out.

"Do not even try to speak the Name. Down here none can say

41

it aloud. No matter how hard you try, you will find that it only comes out as silence. But, yes, as the Scriptures say, *He went and preached unto the spirits in prison."*

She stood to end the conversation, brushed off her dress and began moving down the cliff wall again. I followed, slipping and sliding more than ever because my mind wasn't paying much attention to where I put my feet. The earthquake hadn't rattled my brains nearly as badly as Miss C had.

I might have had a chance in a New Age Hades. After all, a design-your-own religion just might offer a cafeteria-style hell: I'll take a few stern, consciousness-raising lectures and three million years of self-purging meditation, thank you, but please hold the fire and frost.

Even a Hindu hell might stomp me into a possum's body and let me start the climb up all over again through a thousand reincarnations. But a Christian hell? No second chances. No mercy. Only justice, plain and simple. And I knew how much I had to answer for.

This time Miss C seemed to know my thoughts. "You must not despair. There is always hope until death for those who repent, and you are not yet dead. But you are in danger."

I was tired of the way she kept invading my head. "How did you know what I was thinking? In fact, how do you know so much about me in general? Where do you get your information?"

"I told you I was appointed to your case. I was told your story. How else could I have helped you?"

If my hands hadn't been gripping rock, I would have grabbed her by the shoulders. "Look, Miss C, you know so much about me; isn't it time I found out a little more about you? Put yourself in my place. Here I am, with my life in your hands at every turn, traveling with you through a forsaken heap of ruins I have no choice now but to conclude is really hell, even though up till now I didn't even *believe* in hell — "

"You did as a child," she interrupted, though not rudely. "Who convinced you otherwise?"

I sighed. "That could take a long time to talk about. But in the meantime I want to get acquainted with this mystery woman who knows Dante but not Atlanta, who quotes the Bible but lives among the damned. Just who — "

She broke in again. "There are many down here who have

memorized the Scriptures. Knowledge was not enough to save them."

I rubbed my eyes wearily and shook my head. "The point is this: You've read my files, yet I can't even begin to figure you out. Who are you really?"

For a moment she traced her finger silently in the dust on the rock, though it was too dark to see what, if anything, she had scrawled. "I suppose," she said at last, "it is only fair. But we must keep descending. Ask your questions as we go, and I will do my best to answer. I might as well. Sooner or later there are no secrets here anyway."

The rocks were dustier than ever as we climbed down, and my mouth filled with dust whenever I opened it, but this was my chance. "You said you came from Africa to coastal Georgia. When?"

"It was the year 1750 on the European calendar."

"That was two and a half centuries before I came to this place. You don't age here?"

"Only the living age."

"Why did you come to America?"

"Why did most Africans of my generation come? I was enslaved."

"Judging from your speech and knowledge, you must have been an educated slave."

"Educated? I was the nanny for a young boy in a wealthy family, and when I could I listened in on the lessons of his private tutor. The Europeans taught us only what it served their purposes for us to know. If we tried to learn anything else, they whipped us."

I winced and was glad she couldn't see my face too clearly. It was getting touchy now: The Travises had lived on the coast in those years, and they'd been slaveholders. What if she knew that too? I wasn't about to chase the topic any further just now.

"When did you die?"

"In 1780."

"But a while ago you talked about television, movies, spectator sports. You knew that my century is one of the bloodiest in history. And your English grammar is modern. How do you know all that if you came here in 1780?"

"The dead can also learn. I have met many others from the

years between my lifetime and yours, and I have asked many questions."

"Then what about the details of my personal life you seem to know so well? Did you talk with others who knew me before they came here?"

Another long pause. "I was told about you when I received the mission to escort you. That is how it always is when I must accompany someone."

"Who gave you the information?"

"A messenger from the outside." She laughed gently — the first laughter I'd heard from her. "It was the kind of messenger, in fact, that you probably stopped believing in at the same time you gave up the hope of heaven and the dread of hell."

"So we're talking wings and halos and white robes, right?"

Her tone hardened. "We are talking about blinding light and burning voice. I would not mock them if I were you. I think those are enough questions for now."

I blew it. She was peeved, and though I wasn't finished interviewing by any means, she'd closed up tight. The rest of the way down we climbed in silence.

As we neared the bottom of the cliff, I noticed that the wind was softer now, more like an evening breeze, and it moaned as it blew like a flock of mourning doves. I thought of how the sea breeze sounds that way when a gust combs the Georgia pines; could there be trees in this place?

There were trees. Their branches brushed us as we climbed down the last few yards, fragrant evergreen needles that pricked and delighted and puzzled me all at once. Evergreens in hell? And that sure felt like real grass under my feet.

I was beginning to relax a bit. Maybe things were better than I thought.

But I froze in my tracks when I saw them.

Flames in the distance. Hundreds of fires, scattered out like demon eyes on the black horizon.

My breath stopped and hung onto the walls of my windpipe. No time to figure out what I would say in my own defense, and no place to run.

Miss C patted me on the hand. "Relax, Thomas. Those are campfires. Come on."

I went with her, not so sure she was right. But as we got closer

I could see she knew what she was talking about. What a relief. People were huddling in circles around the flames, not roasting on spits above them.

We walked toward the nearest group, which was deep in conversation. I looked over at Miss C and opened my mouth to ask what it was all about. But the sight of her face in the faint firelight stopped me. She was weeping.

SEVEN

When the folks standing in the nearest circle saw us, they stopped talking and stared. Unlike the doomed souls waiting for the tanker, these people were clothed, though no two seemed to wear clothes from the same period and culture. I saw flowing desert robes and scant jungle loincloths, Arctic furs and embroidered kimonos.

Most of all there were children — crowds of children of every size, playing and running from campfire to campfire through the dark spaces. I was surprised that no one seemed to be supervising them. Who knows what might grab you in the shadows of a place like this.

By the time we reached the camp Miss C's face was dry again, but the last of the hardness had washed away. I stood a stone's throw back from the fire and watched as she approached the people there with a question in a language I couldn't understand. Ovimbundu, I guessed.

One of the men, black and bony, kept gazing at the fire but muttered a few words. He handed her some small object on a chain, which she slipped over her neck and tucked inside her collar. Then he pointed beyond the flames to a young woman sitting on the ground some distance away in the shadows. With a token bow of her head Miss C turned in a hurry and walked over to her. I followed at a distance.

The woman sat motionless but smiling, her eyes closed, her hands folded, her legs in the disciplined pose of Eastern-style meditation. She was wrapped in a sari. Miss C paused a minute, reluctant to interrupt, but at last she lost patience and tapped the woman on the shoulder.

The woman looked up at her face, squinting in the feeble light, then leaped up to embrace her. They talked in a rapid fire of words in yet another language I didn't know, and soon they motioned to me to join them as they started out walking into the darkness.

"This is Thomas," said Miss C, pointing to me as I caught up with them. "This is Lakshmi, my dear friend," she said to me. "Lakshmi will show us the way to the campfire we are seeking."

"Are we looking for someone in particular?" I asked.

"Yes," said Miss C. "My sister."

"You have a sister here?"

"A sister, perhaps a mother and stepmother as well, though I have never found them in all these multitudes."

"Did you have children?"

"A son and a daughter."

"What of them? And what of their father?"

She stopped and turned to face me; I could see the pain simmering in her eyes.

"I know nothing of the fate of my daughter's father. But my son's father, I can assure you, has no place here."

I was sorry I'd asked, but there was no stopping her now.

"He was the first white man who claimed to own me. A married man, a leader in the church — and he raped me one cursed summer night."

"I'm...I'm sorry." I looked at my feet, and Lakshmi looked away. I should have left it at that, but I didn't. "And how did your child die?"

"The night he was born, his father came down to the slave cabin to see what he looked like. When he saw the child resembled him so strikingly, he feared his wife's wrath. So he threw my baby to the alligators."

My eyes were boiling. Please, I thought, please don't let it have been any of my kin.

We walked again, more slowly now. I wanted to ask her about the object the old man had given her, but this wasn't the time. I could have reached out and touched the solid weight of grief in the space between us.

Lakshmi knew exactly where she was going, though all the dark landscape looked the same to me. Maybe she navigated by the constellation of distant campfires, but none of them stood out. In this darkness distance was as impossible to judge as time, so I had no idea how far we were walking. But at least the ground was level; there was no climb involved.

Much later, when I was growing tired fast, I broke the silence, hoping conversation would slow our pace.

"I saw the man give you something, Miss C. Does it have to do with your sister?"

She didn't slow down. "With my sister, yes; with you, no."

She thought I was prying, and I guess I was. At that point I was desperate to know anything that might help me make sense of the grim riddle I'd fallen into. I changed the subject, though still fishing for clues.

"Are we still in hell? This place is so different from what I've seen till now — I mean, there are trees here instead of asphalt. And I haven't seen a single roach or rat yet."

"No," said Miss C, the edge in her voice dulling. "You will see none of those scavengers here. This is still hell, the first circle of hell, but it is only a place of abandonment, not of punishment. We exist here with no physical pain; the fire and ice from regions below never reach us on this level. But we do know the pain inside of eternal separation from the One who made us."

"You mean to say that this is what the ancients called Sheol?"

"Some have called it Sheol; others named it Limbo, the 'hem' of hell. By whatever name, it is the abode of those who never had a chance to hear the Name, and yet loved truth, walking faithfully in the light they had."

"But you're here, and you obviously have a church background. You know more theology than most of my students."

"No. That came later, after I arrived here. On earth I was an animist, as were all my people. We bribed the spirits to do our bidding with shrines and sacrifices. We wore their favorite colors

48

and ate their honored foods."

"You believed the spirits created you?"

"We knew of a Creator, a high God above all the spirits, but we were taught that this God was distant and had no interest in us. Meanwhile, the spirits were near at hand, stalking our villages, controlling our lives, so we trafficked with them instead."

"Then how do you know Western theology?"

"After I came to this place I learned about the Harrower from those who had been here when He appeared. The rest of what I know was filled in by your theological colleagues in the regions below. There is, you should know, an abundance of them there."

Her last remark made me shudder. "But you had to have learned about European religion in America. Didn't the family that owned — I mean, that held you captive — teach you from the Bible? There were slave churches in Savannah."

"The churches came later. But when I was there, no slaveholder was eager to convert a slave. Too dangerous, the whites thought, to tell us stories like the exodus of the Hebrew slaves from Egypt, or the rich man and the beggar Lazarus, who traded places when they died. So they kept us away from their preachers, who were few and far between anyway, and they never answered our questions about their religion. In time, when we saw the depths of their selfishness and cruelty, we concluded that their religion was not worth knowing in any case."

"But now?"

"Now I know the truth of what they believed, or said they believed. Yet now it is too late."

"But how can that be fair? How can those who never had a chance to believe be damned for it? If heaven is just, to say nothing of merciful, don't you think you'll be allowed to go there someday? Hasn't anybody from this circle ever made it out before?"

This time Lakshmi answered. "I lived in India three thousand years before your time and came here when I was still young. I witnessed what happened on the day of the Great Earthquake. Nearly an entire nation escaped from this circle: Abraham, Isaac, Jacob, their people. I saw them go with my own eyes. But those of us left behind had to conclude they were a special case, and we despaired."

"Hasn't anybody left since then?"

"Some of the more famous in our circle seem to have disappeared, and a number of unknowns as well. For a while now no one has seen many of the Greeks — Socrates, Plato and Aristotle all vanished about the same time, though the Cynics are still here. Now I hear that Gautama, Confucius and Lao-tzu are missing as well."

"You think they went to heaven?"

"It is difficult to say. All those well-known men were solitaries, constantly brooding over what they had discovered here, pondering an ultimate reality radically different from what they had expected to encounter. Perhaps they have simply moved to the yet-unfilled regions, on the other side of the abyss, so they can be alone."

"The Harrower, as you call Him, came once. What if He should come back for more of you?"

Lakshmi brightened. "Some now say He will. Even on earth many have declared that we who never had a chance before may be saved in the end if we look to Him — even in this place. So a few now dare at last to hope in Him, even to pray to Him, though we cannot speak His name aloud."

"You are one of those who hope?"

She stopped abruptly. "Yes. I saw His face the day He came, and it was a portrait of compassion. Such a face could not turn away forever from those who fell in love with it."

I turned to Miss C. "And what about you?"

She bit her lip and shook her head. "I am not persuaded. If we had been chosen from before the foundations of the world, why would we have been born in a land and time that knew nothing of the Name? Why have we languished here so long, forgotten in the shadow of hell? I long to be rescued and to meet my Creator face-to-face. Yet I fear I must live out eternity with a barren longing that never gives birth to hope."

"I still say it's not fair."

"Perhaps, Thomas, you should know the meaning of my name," she said. "In my culture the demons often whispered to mothers about the future as they named their children, so the names were prophecies. Capopia is best translated into English: 'I do not dispute God.' Nor will I dispute you in a matter we cannot resolve." The conversation was over.

In any case, we'd finally reached the camp we were looking for.

Children there gathered around us to examine our clothing, and two young men near the fire stepped back to share a place to be warmed, though to me the night wasn't at all chilly. Miss C searched each face in the firelight, her wide brown eyes darting through the crowd. But the search was all in vain. Her sister was not there.

"This was the last place I saw her," said Lakshmi. "She was alone and seemed troubled. When I left to return to our own fire, she stood gazing into the flames, as if she could see beyond them to something that haunted her."

"Perhaps she is now looking for me," said Miss C. "I had to leave quickly this time, before I could even say good-bye."

I tried to be helpful. "Could she be on an upper level? Are others allowed to travel back and forth as you do?"

Miss C nodded, but she looked uneasy. "Only the escorts have that privilege, and we do not have it forever. Even so, my sister is also an escort; she is probably accompanying someone even now."

"In that case she's bound to come back here when she's finished, right? So all we have to do is wait." I wouldn't mind at all, I thought, if she decides to stay here a while; I like it better than anything I've seen yet.

"She may come back, and she may not. Not everyone does."

"You mean," I said, "the escorts could end up staying in the lower levels — in the fire or the ice?"

"Yes. I mean precisely that."

The air was beginning to feel chilly after all. "And what about the people they escort?"

"The same. Even you and I have no promise of finishing our journey."

I wasn't ready to spit out the taste of hope she'd given me before, even if she wasn't sounding so sure of herself now.

"Look," I said. "You probably know the shadows in my past almost as well as I do, considering how much you've been told about me. But like you said, I'm not dead yet. You told me we were on a mission, and we have a destiny, and you were sent to help me."

Miss C nodded slowly. "Yes, I was sent to help you, and I will do all that I can. But there are many factors we cannot control."

I didn't like the sound of this. "Wait, now," I said, "I saw how old Charon gave in when you said those last words to him; I heard the authority in your voice. Can't you just say that to the judge when we get there? Don't at least the escorts have guaranteed passage?"

She looked to the ground. "In hell the only guarantee is justice. We will be especially vulnerable in those circles where we ourselves are guilty of the sin being punished."

It was the first time I'd heard her talk outright about *punishment*, and I didn't like the sound of it. In the seminary where I taught, you couldn't even use the word "punishment" without their calling you a Neanderthal; criminal prisons, they said, were for *rehab*. This was beginning to sound like a horror movie, and here I was in the middle of the plot.

"Why didn't you tell me all this before?" I asked.

Miss C looked me straight in the eye. "I said you were in danger. If I had said any more, would you have come? And yet you must come. There is no other way out."

I took a deep breath and let it out slowly. I needed time to think; maybe I could delay our journey just a bit. "Let Lakshmi and me help you hunt for your sister first. We could start here around the campfires. How many are there?"

She shook her head. "Thousands, perhaps millions. That would never work. She is not beside the fire where we usually meet, nor is she here, where Lakshmi last saw her. So we must go on our way and trust her to her destiny. I have had to do so before. If it is meant for her to return, she will. If not, then what Dante said of us in this circle will be doubly true for me: 'They live desiring, but without hope.' "

I tried one more time. "Maybe she's escaped altogether with the others who are missing. We could ask around."

Miss C smiled weakly and shook her head. "Thomas, you are amazingly optimistic in these matters to have been so recently a confirmed agnostic."

Optimistic? No — terrified. But sometimes the worst fears give birth to a desperate hope. If her sister didn't make it, would we?

"I must return now," said Lakshmi. She gave Miss C a kiss on the cheek and bowed deeply to me. "I believe I will see you again." Her words were at least a small comfort to me, if not to my companion. We thanked her, and she headed back the way we'd come.

I had one last question for Miss C before we set out again ourselves. "By the way," I said. "What's your sister's name?"

"She is named Apangela. It is what the Ovimbundu people call a proverb name, from the old saying, '*Wa pangela ka mali ungende.*' "

"What does that mean in English?"

Her eyes were wet again. "The name was often given to newborns not expected to live. It means literally, 'One who intends not to finish her journey.' "

EIGHT

We had just reached the cliffs again, turning a sharp left around the base of one that jutted out beyond the rest, when I saw looming in front of us the massive silhouette of a building, stark black against an ember-red horizon. It was the first human-made structure I'd seen in Sheol, so it took me by surprise.

I tugged on Miss C's sleeve and pointed to it. "That building — it's the size of a whole city. Is it some kind of fortress?"

"I suppose 'temple' would be a better word for it," she said. "It was built long ago, before the Great Earthquake destroyed it. Those of every religion came together to erect it. I think they hoped somehow to keep heightening it until they could reach the upper vault and escape. But hardly anyone ever comes here now."

"So why are *we* coming here?"

"It is a required part of your tour, according to my instructions."

The architecture was a jumble of styles that made the one building look like an entire city skyline, a tangle of towers and spires, columns and terraces, long, flat roofs and even thatched mounds. I thought of Atlanta. But even the hectic skyline of the Big Peach was no match for this structural riot.

As we came closer I began to pick out the shapes of statues, friezes and other carvings that plastered the outer walls. The material was a porous gray rock mined from the cliffs, once painted but now only flaked with faded colors. It had been sculpted into the stone equivalent of a freshman religion textbook — a random collage that slapped together every god and spirit the world had ever worshipped.

Seven gates we walked through, and seven walls, one inside the other, Chinese puzzle-box style. Much like an open-air stadium, the structure had no overarching ceiling. But the towers erupting upward from the walls blocked most of the surrounding landscape from view, soaring out of sight toward the upper vault.

In one corner was a forest of fancy classical columns, capped with friezes of Zeus and Juno, Apollo and Venus — brazen mixed marriages of Greek and Roman idols. Nearby a chubby Buddha with earlobes that hung to his belly sat smiling, undisturbed, at the bare-fanged Chinese dragon writhing across the courtyard. Above a tapestry of the Hindu Krishna with his goat herds stretched a sparse-lined mural of the African Chineke with his thunderclouds, and the shining sun disk of Ahura Mazda on a delicate Persian mosaic. I knew them all from Religion 101.

In the darkness we stumbled again and again over the rubble: crumbling remains of Australian totems, Druid altars, Mayan hieroglyphs, Shinto shrines, Babylonian zodiacs. The desolate sight gave a new and bitter meaning to the old saying of the Eastern sages: *Men and women seek God down a myriad of roads, but in the end all roads lead to the same destination.*

Yes, I thought, all roads do lead to the same place. And the cosmic dead end is here. How could a God of mercy or even justice allow that?

Anger stirred within me, like a rattler pushing its way up through mud washed into its lair. With each stumbling step I felt it spreading slowly throughout me like venom, numbing as it went.

I stooped down to look closer at what seemed to be a silk-covered scroll among the debris, its rolls penned in Chinese pictographs. As I picked it up I noticed a narrow, dark crevice that slashed across the pavement as far as I could see.

The Great Earthquake had cracked the temple down the middle.

There was no mistaking the center when at last we reached it: a perfect Star of David, several yards across, a six-pointed hole carved in the stone foundation. The crack ran outward from two opposite points of the star.

I sat down on the edge, still holding the scroll and trembling now. Silent and sober, Miss C lowered herself down next to me, deep creases in her brow.

We sat without speaking for some time, my chin in my hands, her hands in her lap. Then I stood and turned around slowly, surveying once more the ruins around me. My lips began to quiver till at last it boiled up out of my heart and burned my eyes: a salty, hot gumbo of grief and rage.

"Do you see this?" I shouted, my voice breaking. "It's the agony of ages, screaming here in shattered prayers of stone. Look at it: endless generations, pleading for survival, for salvation, even for the mercy of annihilation, crying out to a million brawling gods, hoping that at last their words would fly up to heaven and find an answer."

I threw the scroll down on a pile of rocks. "But all along the reality was this: Their prayers fell to the earth with their tears and trickled down through the dust of their ancestors to this wretched place."

Then I wept.

As I wept I remembered bitterly. Haunting images from my youth came back to me — this time not memories of my own sins, but of the twisted 1960s world around me I'd never been able to untangle.

Hideous TV films of skeletal children starving in Ethiopia, their dry-breasted mothers begging heaven for food and water, and dying without an answer.

Buddhist monks in Vietnam setting themselves aflame to protest the obscenity of war, choosing this muted hell I now witnessed over the napalm hell they had already endured.

California gurus and their fresh-faced disciples sitting cross-legged, close-eyed, lost in the vast, empty wilderness of their own souls.

Protestants and Catholics spilling Irish blood on the newspaper headlines. Bombings of Jewish synagogues in France.

So many unanswered questions. So many martyrs whose costly faith in alien gods had shamed me for my own shallowness. So many competing bids to eternal bliss, each beckoning down a different path. And so many who worshipped hatred but called it God.

Under the weight of it all, my Sunday school answers had collapsed. How could anybody say, "I worship the one, true God"?

Even at sixteen I had known too much to believe what my parents had taught me. Better, I thought, to leave all the big questions open, to say of it all, "I don't know."

But here I was at the graveyard of the gods, at the top of a stairway that led down beyond the tombs to screaming answers. Not abstract answers from a seminary classroom, not soft theories or possibilities that could pad the prison cells of my conscience. These were concrete realities, hard, unbending realities — human souls, more solid even than human bodies, who had made the journey long before I did and found their destiny in this place. What I saw, what I had yet to see, refused to indulge my doubts, called me to account, threatened to arrest me and put me on trial.

My mind had stumbled over these ancient stones, and my heart had broken in the fall.

I could no longer say an easy "I don't know" about salvation, about the afterlife, about ultimate reality. Now I knew — not everything, but enough to push me further down, all the way down to the bottom of things. I wanted to know what was at the bottom.

Supposing, of course, that I'd be allowed to get that far. *In hell, the only guarantee is justice.*

My grief was ebbing now, my rage spent. Miss C had listened silently, painfully. Now she spoke in a near-whisper, her eyes scanning the heights of the temple.

"Thomas, when I was enslaved and taken from Africa — on that very first night I lay in shackles down in the belly of the ship, smothered by the stench of seasickness and the wails of children torn from their mothers — I gave up hope in the high God of my father. I concluded in that hour that He cared nothing about us as we writhed in that outpost of hell.

"What is this wretched race we call humanity? I asked, crying bitterly. And I answered myself: *We are a fleeting nightmare in the troubled sleep of God, and when He awakens, He will at last cast us off with the darkness like a sweat-soaked blanket.*

"That night my soul was orphaned, and I knew what it was to be utterly alone. The story of these ruins is my story, Thomas: All we who dwell in Sheol dwell in the orphanage of heaven, built and abandoned in a ghetto of hell."

She stood slowly, with a sigh centuries old, and turned to look me in the eye. "Now we must leave this place and meet our destiny. But before we descend I have one more thing to show you here."

I balked. "I think I've seen just about all I care to see in this place."

Her eyes narrowed. "You have not yet even beheld the fire, and already you wish to close your eyes? What kind of men has your generation hatched?"

I looked away, my cheeks smoldering.

"In the lower regions," she said, turning to walk, "you will see much of the severity of God. The weight of that sight will crush you unless you first glimpse the wickedness of the human heart that has called down upon itself such wrath. Come with me, now, around the edge of this cliff. It will not be far."

In the distance lay a wide, red glow on the horizon, like the sunrise mirrored on a lake, except of course there was no sunrise. There were no campfires around either, but the rosy light bathed everything nearby with a faint luster. There were trees — palms, judging by the silhouettes of their branches — and even fields of flowers, wild and sweet. It reminded me of a south Georgia dawn on the swamp and felt almost like home. But the ragged cliffs, rising starkly on either side of the redness, spoiled the picture.

Before long I could hear the crystal laughter of children, a multitude of children, their voices a sparkling waterfall of innocence. Then in the brightening light I began to make out the lines of their tiny figures, none of them, I guessed, older than five when they'd died.

They played without wrangling or even arguing — many couldn't speak at all — crawling and waddling and a few running or carrying others. There were no adults here. None were needed.

"The Lake of the Innocents," said Miss C with a broad sweep of her arm. "All those who died outside of the covenant before they were old enough to be held accountable for their behavior. They suffer no pain, and though they are outside heaven, they are not aware of the loss. So they are content for now."

"You said you would show me the evil of the human heart. Where's the evil here? They might as well be in Eden."

"Walk with me to the lake side."

The closer we came to the lake, the deeper the color turned, until it became blood-red. The surface was covered with large bubbles, and the water rippled with a regular rhythm, the gentle, double pulse of a heartbeat.

When we reached the water's edge, I saw what the bubbles held.

Babies. Millions of unborn and newborn babies.

"This is the grisly harvest of your century, Thomas. These were murdered by their own parents, the victims of abortion, infanticide and what your people so glibly call 'fetal harvesting.' Here they rest for a season in a womb safe at last from the selfishness of the mothers who rejected them, the fathers who hired killers to take their lives."

As far as I could see to the horizon, the babies floated, wave after gentle wave of countless little bodies, perfectly formed and still.

I had to sit down.

Miss C remained standing. "I have heard of King Herod's slaughter of the innocents. He has his place now in the flames below. But far below him, in torturous pains of conscience Herod has never even dreamed of, lie the mothers and fathers who had their babies poisoned, dismembered, sold for body parts — for the sake of their own convenience or profit.

"Tell me, Thomas: How could you have lived in such a land, where such a crime was protected by law?"

I couldn't speak at all, much less answer her challenge. The damning panorama that stretched out before me had sent a frost up my spine and filled my throat with ice.

"The world," she continued, "has seen nothing like it since the ancient days of infant sacrifice, when children were burned alive to gain favors from the demon Moloch. No wonder that in the Scriptures hell is called 'Gehenna.' It was the name of the valley where Moloch was worshipped with dark fire and innocent blood, where the bones of tiny victims cried out from the dust for justice."

Miss C stood silent for a long moment, then pointed to the far horizon. "Somewhere out there, my baby once slept." Her finger dropped down. "And somewhere below, his father still lies, begging for a mercy that has passed him by forever."

She turned away as her shoulders began to heave, and a wail of raw grief exploded from her lungs.

For the first time I reached out to touch her, and to my surprise she didn't pull away. I put my arm around her and stood in silence till the heat of her sorrow had melted the ice in my throat, and I found my voice at last.

"I'm sorry...so very sorry." The words were lame, but there was nothing else to say.

Some moments later her sobbing had ebbed, and I spoke again in as gentle a voice as I could muster.

"You said they rest here for a season. Do they leave, then?" I asked. "When you claim to have no hope for the inhabitants of this circle, you're speaking only of the adults?"

Her face brightened. "Yes. The messengers come for the children and take them away."

"To heaven?"

"To Him. They say the babies play around His throne."

"Why don't the children go there as soon as they die?"

"They have purposes to accomplish here first. But they are not here long. Even heaven's patience has its limits, and He is eager to hold them."

Something close to joy had dawned on her face. "I was told that when He walked the earth, He once said sternly: *'Let the little children come to Me, and do not hinder them.'* Now even hell has been forced to obey that command."

When I stood and we finally turned to leave, I took a last, long look across the lake. One odd detail about the babies caught my attention: Though all were sucking the thumb of one hand, in typical fetal position, most also had the other hand stretched out, with a single finger pointing downward toward the bottom of the lake.

I asked Miss C about it.

"You will see why," she said gravely, "soon enough."

─────── NINE ───────

Before long we had passed through the darkness to a rocky clearing about the size of an old churchyard. In the middle was what looked like a cellar door, flush with the ground and opening downward. When Miss C unhooked the corroded latch, the door dropped on squealing hinges and slammed against the inside wall of the tunnel it covered. The falling echo of the crash bounced for what sounded like a mile.

The stone steps were narrow and steep, like the ones in the old black-and-white horror movies that led to the dungeons where monsters lurked. This time Miss C climbed down face forward, steadying herself on the slimy stone wall that leaned inward, and she motioned for me to follow. As I did, I was tempted to close my eyes, but I knew that would only make it worse. Soon we were creeping down into a space as dark as the belly of Jonah's whale, and nearly as cramped. Short as I am, my head still scraped the ceiling of the tunnel, nicking my naked scalp again and again.

Please, I thought, let this go fast.

It didn't. The echo of the slamming door hadn't lied; we descended for what had to be at least a mile, one awkward step at a time, turning our feet sideways because they hung halfway off

61

the slippery stone if we pointed them straight ahead. The air was warm, not like the chilly drafts of underground cells, but muggy and musty and foul.

Jonah didn't have it so bad, I thought. This was *worse* than a whale belly. It was more like finding your way through a full-grown brontosaurus gullet.

The thought of light at the end of the tunnel sooner or later kept me from going crazy — until I remembered where we were headed. My heart was already thumping, but now it revved up into overdrive. First we go to Sheol, Miss C had said, then to the judge.

I had no idea who the judge was, but I could guess his temperament by the style of his interior decorator. Till now I'd held on to a dumb little hope that he might be a good ol' boy like the judges back home, and I just might be able to sweet-talk him into letting me by. But I could see it now: This guy wasn't going to be any bleeding heart.

Miss C was more quiet than usual. Was she scared herself? She'd handled Charon in short order, and he was no pushover. Could this fella be that much worse?

At last a faint glimmer below. I stopped. "Before we go out there," I said to Miss C, "I want to know a little more about what I'm up against. Who is this judge?"

When she realized I wasn't moving, she stopped as well. "The judge Dante wrote about was the one ancient mythology called Minos. The Greeks believed he was the legendary lawgiver of Crete, appointed to judge the dead after he himself had died. But he was no man. Like the others who administer justice here, he was a demon."

"But I thought the ancient stories spoke of demons roaming the *earth*."

"Most of them do in fact remain there. They are allowed to test and torment the living until the last Day, when they will all be hurled into the abyss. But in the meantime a few have been confined here with their prince to punish the dead. And you should not be surprised to learn that they take great delight in their task."

I shuddered. "You talk about devils as if you've known them a long time."

"You forget — my people in Africa trafficked in evil spirits as a way of life, a means of survival. I was no stranger to the demons' habits when I arrived here. Nor are they any more ugly or cruel in this place than they were when they used to come haunting our village at night, thirsting for blood."

I turned and surveyed the darkness behind me, which suddenly felt cold. Sheol was looking better all the time, but it was useless even to ask about turning back. I knew what Miss C would say.

Instead I swallowed hard and asked: "What does this Minos look like?"

"Dante described him as a half-man, half-bull monster like the Minotaur of Greek legend. But the office of judge in hell does not long remain with the same demon. They conspire among themselves and overthrow one another; in all my journeys through this place, I have never seen the same one seated in judgment twice. They will probably continue their plottings until the Day when they themselves are judged."

"What other demons have you seen there?"

"I know the names of only a handful I have seen: Lilith, Belial, Anu, Osiris. But the pattern seems to be that they do in fact resemble the evil characters of the world's mythologies, as if the legends in the upper world are themselves based on real encounters with the underworld. There are many, after all, who have come this way before death, though not all have returned."

Her last words turned the temperature down a few more degrees. As she started down the last few steps, I hurried to follow her out of the mouth of the tunnel onto a stone pavement.

There was more light here, bright flashes of it that slashed the air above us like lightning, revealing dark swirls of smoke. But there was no color. In every direction I could see only black and white.

Before us stood the ruins of an immense tower carved out of the same rock through which we had followed the tunnel. It was perched on the edge of what looked to be a stadium the size of a city, its outline made plain in the spasms of brightness. I stared at the eery silhouette, a knot in my stomach. Why did the tower look so familiar to me? Had I seen it before in some nightmare?

We were no longer alone. From the other side of the cliff, hell's newcomers were shoving and shuffling their way forward in a mob, but with a grim silence now. We made our way into the throng and were pushed along through the massive doors of the tower.

Once inside we could hear moans and screams echoing in the great open hall where we found ourselves. As I looked around to find out why, I saw that the back wall of the tower was crumbled away completely, opening up a panoramic view down into the stadium. There was no playing field. Instead, a funnel-shaped hole gaped miles across, its twisted, terraced walls a steel-and-concrete tornado belching smoke. In the far distance below were rings of blazing, white dots, cold fires like sparks of a firecracker frozen in place. In fact, it was a fireworks show of sorts: The light that stabbed the blackness every minute or so came from glowing streaks that shot from somewhere in the tower.

The crowd first moved down through a labyrinth of dark chambers carved in the belly of the rock. Pairs of neon-white eyes stared out from the black recesses of each room; the shadowy figures that bore them appeared to be taking notes. In one room a searing light flooded in from overhead. I squinted and looked up to see the source.

Babies. Thousands of babies, visible through a huge glass ceiling, floating in brilliant light, each with a finger pointed down at a particular man, woman or couple.

"This is the bottom of the Lake of the Innocents," said Miss C grimly. "The child victims spend a brief season there because justice demands that they identify their murderers, though the children themselves are unaware of their role. They are innocently reaching out one last time for the parents who rejected them before they are taken where they will forget — and their parents are taken where they will *never* forget."

Those who were pointed out panicked and tried to run. But they could only push forward through the crowd, so that they got to the front — and the judge — faster than the others.

We went through a number of other chambers till we finally came out again in the great hall of the tower overlooking the abyss. All of a sudden I realized that Miss C wasn't next to me anymore. I searched the contorted faces all around me in panic, desperate to find her. But the human whirlwind around me was rushing toward some commotion at the base of the left wall, where the screams were coming from, and I was trapped in the eye of the storm as it moved. She was gone.

A little distance ahead the crowd was thinning out, but I wasn't sure why. Soon we were almost to the wall. Through the scuffling, doomed souls I caught glimpses of an odd assortment of outdated laboratory equipment: vials and beakers; glass tubing and copper coils; cogs, cranks and levers; ropes, chains and tangled electrical wiring. Again, the uncanny sense that I had seen it all before.

Then I saw him, and I knew why it all looked familiar.

He was seated on what looked more like an electric chair than a judicial bench, his giant frame gangling but rigid. His face was instantly recognizable; it had found its way around the world and into the worst night terrors of generations, including my own. Millions of twentieth-century children had been haunted by those ghastly features: the deathly white skin, sunken cheeks, downward-spiked hair, squared skull, half-closed, murky eyes — and of course the jutting forehead with the brutal scar.

Frankenstein. The demon judge had not bestial horns and cleft hooves, but recycled brains and ill-fitting body parts, stitched together.

You'd think I would have laughed. After years of seeing that face in the silliest of settings — Halloween masks, Saturday morning cartoons, theme parks, even children's dolls — the fright I'd felt the first time I ever saw him should have worn thin. But even as a grown man I'd never completely shaken off the horror of that grisly sight. The monster was my childhood's first, searing encounter with supernatural evil, and in the deepest dungeons of my subconscious he still crouched in chains, awaiting his chance to break out.

Now he was breaking out, and with a vengeance. This was no movie, no mask, no cartoon, no doll. This was the beast itself, in flesh and bolt.

I remembered how the author of the original story, herself a dabbler in the dark arts, once wrote that she'd seen him first in a night vision so vivid it terrified her. Now I knew she'd actually peered beyond the grave that night to this place. Frankenstein wasn't her creation; she'd only been describing a very real demonic personality that clutched at her across the chasm of death.

As I stood now face-to-face with it, my heart was spiked to the floor. My all-time worst nightmare had come true, and I couldn't move or even scream.

One by one the damned were coming before him and confessing their sins, and when they were done, his oversized hands snatched them and tossed them into the abyss. Each time he growled with glee when they ignited in the air, just before they passed out of sight.

And now he was staring at me.

His hooded eyes flashed and burned a hole through mine, piercing all the way through to my brain. He had me. I couldn't look away, and the guilty revelations exploded from my mouth against my will: "Fornication, gluttony, greed, rage, heresy..." I reached the end of the list quickly, and his wire-stitched fingers latched around my throat.

"No!" came a trumpeting voice that hushed the entire hall. "You must not. *So it is willed where what is willed must be.*"

He dropped me like the business end of a cattle prod, and I collapsed on the stone pavement. Miss C was standing over me, her own eyes flashing with the fury of a mama cat shielding one of her brood from a pack of dogs.

The demon was simmering. Unlike his impersonators on film, he was anything but mute. "This is an outrage!" he hissed. "How dare you interrupt the judgment that is mine to enjoy? Who are you, wretch?"

"My name is of no concern to you," she said without flinching. "You can well see that this one has not yet met his appointed time. I have been sent to take him to the very bottom. You cannot interfere."

"I don't take my orders from the likes of you," he said through clenched teeth. "But I will be delighted to shorten your journey by throwing you both down there right now."

Miss C stood her ground, but her hands were shaking behind her back. "Do you not recognize the ancient words of waiver? *So it is willed where what is willed must be.* Perhaps your training for this office has been inadequate. I do not doubt there are those who would welcome grounds for replacing you."

A murmur went up behind us from the base of the far wall. "Yes, yes, indeed!" came one whining voice above the others. "Perhaps we need impeachment proceedings! You may have outlived your competence — if you ever had any!"

I scrambled to my feet to see who was talking, but the demon's answer jerked my attention back in his direction.

"Silence! Of course I know the ancient words. But it is my pleasure to harass them. My orders, after all, are to 'give 'em hell!' " He broke into slobbering laughter, and his buddies in the back joined in. He glared at me. "Now go! And if by some slim chance you should slip through the nether regions, you little weasel, you can be sure I will be waiting most eagerly for you here. Sooner or later your appointed time will come to pass my judgment."

"That is," came the sassy voice from the back of the room, "if you're still in the chair when he comes through!"

I didn't wait to hear the rest of the conversation. The crowd parted and let us through to a side door, where another tunnel, this one without stairs, opened up from the floor. Cramped or not, if it led somewhere else, I was headed down, and this time I took the lead.

When at last I found my voice again some distance into the tunnel, I had a lot more questions for Miss C. "What happened to you? How did we get separated?"

"I must apologize, Thomas," she said, "though it was through no fault of my own. I tried to stay with you, but the crowd squeezed between us and I was pushed backward. We will try to avoid crowds again. I almost lost you, you know."

"But why did he resist you? Didn't he have to let you by?"

She shrugged. "Perhaps he was truly ignorant of his limits; his rivals might have withheld that information intentionally to create a scene like the one we just witnessed. On the other hand, he may well have only been stalling, as he said, to harass us. Perhaps, like many in the upper world, he was flouting the law because he is yet skeptical about the ferociousness of the ultimate consequences of his disobedience. The ways of the demons, after all, are not so different from the ways of our own warped race."

In any case, it was a close call. Whether I'd been up against ignorance, bluff or rebellion, I'd been only seconds away from hurtling down the abyss, the human spark of a hell-bent Roman candle.

By this time I was a few feet ahead of Miss C, so when the tunnel made a sharp left turn, I waited for her to catch up before I rounded it. I didn't plan to lose her again.

"Now I have a question for *you*," she said. "You seemed to have recognized the judge. Was he connected somehow to the myths of your time?"

I told her what I knew of Frankenstein's history as we continued, how we'd been told he was spawned through a scientist's arrogant attempt to usurp heaven by creating life. She wasn't surprised by the story, though she wondered why twentieth-century rationalists toyed with demon tales.

"It's the spiritual pornography of the secular mind," I said. "Whatever's forbidden is attractive. The scientists said that talk about spirits was a no-no, so people flocked to anybody who would tell them about spirits."

Or monsters, for that matter. Politically correct myth-makers had long ago crossed out every reference to the supernatural, but this granddaddy of human-made monsters had found it no trouble to take over where the demons had left off. A high-tech devil, he chased us moderns down the back alleys of our ambition to play God, and we knew he stayed right on our tail because he was the nut-and-bolt shadow of who we were — tragic creatures running from the One who made us, shaking our scarred fists at Him because we thought He'd botched the job.

No wonder Frankenstein was judging us. In his grotesque portrait the damned could see mirrored their own fatal pride and rage.

"What's next?" I asked, though I wasn't at all sure I wanted to know. "I'm having a hard time remembering my Dante."

"The circle appointed for the lascivious," she said. "Those whose lives were ruled by lust."

I stopped in my tracks. "They start with them first thing?" My voice was thin and squeaky. "I haven't got a chance."

"Your generation has packed that particular circle to overflowing, Thomas. Perhaps you will slip through unnoticed," she said, and then added wryly, "unless, of course, all your old friends are there." The end of the tunnel now appeared in the distance, and from it came a low, steady moan that grew louder as we approached.

TEN

There is one important thing about hell you must remember," said Miss C before we exited the tunnel. "Each circle holds the punishment for a different type of sin, and the lower the circle, the more damnable the sin. Those who have been judged may be guilty of many kinds of sin, but they remain on only one level — the level of their *worst* sin."

"So what's the point?"

"If you are guilty of fornication, you will certainly be endangered in the first circle. But you cannot be kept there unless you are innocent of all the sins punished farther down."

That wasn't encouraging. "If I get through the next circle, then, they may just be letting me by so I'll get it worse in a lower level?"

"Yes. I seriously doubt, then, that you will be in much danger in the upper levels."

I snorted. "Thanks a bunch. Was that supposed to be a comfort or an insult?"

"Merely an observation. Now prepare yourself to hold on for dear life."

Outside the exit a furious, hot gale was blowing smoke, cinders and charred debris in an upward arc. The flaming ashes glowed red; color had returned to the landscape now, though it was limited to the hot end of the spectrum.

The tunnel opened out at the top of an exterior wall in what looked like an aging power plant — with a sheer drop thousands of feet into the belching mouths of hundreds of smokestacks. There was precious little to hold onto, just a rusty pipe here, a dangling wire there. But we grabbed what we could and rappelled down the grimy, red bricks, Miss C going first.

To tell the truth, the wind was blasting upward with such power that the only way we couldn't fall was down. As much as I hated heights, that was still not much comfort; one slip and I'd never get back to the wall.

Miss C seemed to be making her way without much trouble. Either she'd done it so many times before that she was a pro, or else sex hadn't been much of a temptation for her. After surviving a vicious rape, I thought, what woman wouldn't look at men with different eyes?

Suddenly I was slammed against the bricks from behind. I held on, but only by a couple of fingers, and someone else was holding onto me by the leg.

I looked down to see a young couple flapping around in the whirlwind, the woman with her long, red nails dug into my left calf, the man with the woman's tangled, black curls wrapped around his fist. They were screaming over the gale, which by now roared like a freight train.

"Help us! Don't let us go! We've been tossing in this blasted hurricane for a century!"

A cloud of cinders blew into my eyes, blinding me. With my eyes closed, I groped for the handhold I'd lost — a rotting window ledge of some sort — but found nothing. Then I felt the woman's nails sliding down to my ankle, and before I could pull my leg up to help, she was gone.

At last I felt slapping against my shoulder what seemed to be a steel cable, and I grabbed for it with my left hand. When I lurched, my right hand slipped away from the building, but I caught the cable just as I was able to open my eyes.

The cable wasn't attached to anything.

I was airborne. The burning whirlwind batted me up a mile and then dropped me, only to hurl me upward again into the darkness. My guts bounced from my ears to my toes and back again, and I was suddenly grateful that I hadn't eaten in so long.

Worse yet, I kept crashing into other out-of-control flyers, getting punched by a foot in the groin or a skull in the jaw. Miss C had been right — it was crowded up here. Some were clumps of several souls, one man with a harem of shrieking women or one woman with a wolfpack of cussing men. A few were flying solo. But most were couples, in all ages and colors, screaming at each other as only infuriated lovers can.

The contorted face of a plump, freckled redhead flew by my ear, followed by a balding, middle-aged man with dark eyes. I only heard a few of her words as they lunged past: "You told me you loved me, you'd never leave me — well, leave me already, you jerk! I can't maneuver with you hanging onto my..."

We were human popcorn in a diabolical air popper as tall as the World Trade Towers. Had I ever till now had any *real* idea of what it meant to be terrified of heights?

The fickle currents had first tossed me far away from the wall where I'd been climbing, but now they were teasing me by sending me back. Just as I came within a few feet of where I'd fallen off, a downward draft sucked me head first, and I plummeted like a bomb only inches from the brick.

Suddenly I was caught up short by a squeeze around the waist that knocked my breath out and nearly snapped my spine in two. Dangling like bait on a hook, I saw what had a hold on me: A twisted piece of angle iron, jutting out from the wall, had snagged my belt as I went by.

Many times I'd cussed that forty-two-inch strip of cowhide for not having enough notches. Now I wanted to kiss it. But I didn't get a chance. The leather was cracked and torn where I'd poked an extra hole in it, and it broke.

I grabbed the angle iron in time, but the belt went flying in two pieces, twisting like a snake into the blackness.

I laughed uncontrollably as it flew, delirious with joy. My pants might not stay up now, but who cared? It was plenty warm, and everybody else streaking by was buck naked.

The muscles in my arms were shot by now, but I managed to work my way back to the bricks and down. What seemed like a lifetime later I was crouching at the base of the wall, where Miss C had held tight onto an abandoned, nondescript piece of machinery and waited for me, though not hopefully.

She kicked open a cracked wooden door, and we pulled ourselves inside, out of the hurricane.

I had to rest, so she waited again, silent as usual. Finally she spoke.

"Thomas," she said, eyeing my unleashed waistline, "do you like food as much as you like sex?"

"Maybe more, though I'd never admit that to anybody else. Why?"

"Because the next circle, you may recall, is for gluttons. We might have a harder time getting to the lower regions than I expected."

She wasn't joking. Had this place been designed especially to wear me down? Why couldn't they give me a break — you know, put something in between fornication and gluttony that didn't involve me, like embezzlement or murder?

Once again she seemed to be reading my thoughts. "You wonder," she said, "why the circles are arranged as they are."

"You guessed it. How about a geography lesson? I don't remember what comes after gluttony, or why — I read the *Inferno* too many years ago. Does hell have an urban planning commission, or does it just spread out like a cancer?"

"I will sketch it for you," she said. With her finger she traced concentric circles in the dust on the concrete floor. "Hell has no planners but needs none; it follows a pattern that emerges from its innermost nature, just as surely as does a cancer cell. As I told you, the circles are arranged in an order that reflects the seriousness of the sin in the souls they confine —"

"Then who ranks the sins?" I interrupted. "I know lots of folks who would put fornicators well below liars, and plenty of others who wouldn't send fornicators here at all. Still others would insist that all sin is the same, so you can't say one sin is any worse than another."

"You are a child of your time, Thomas, and so are they. Centuries before your generation, no such confusion about sin existed, and those who thought the most deeply about it were in substantial agreement. Did you never read Thomas Aquinas?"

"Only a smattering."

"Just what *do* you teach your theology students?"

"Not much that was written before the nineteenth century."

"Then no wonder they are so surprised by hell's architecture. A tragic case of the blind leading the blind."

"Look," I said, my voice rising slightly, "the biblical texts never give details about this place. And they talk about sin as if it's all of one piece."

"All of one piece, yes; but all of one stain, no. Sin is a single wretched rag that wraps the world, but some of it is dirty, and some of it moldy and some of it bloody through and through. Remember the warning of the Gospel parable about the Master's punishments: There are those who are cut asunder, and those who are beaten with many stripes and those who receive only a few. In the judgment, we are told, Sodom and Gomorrah will fare better than others."

I still wasn't convinced, but what could I say? Like our old country preacher used to put it: Somebody with the hard facts of experience is never at the mercy of somebody with a theological argument. I had the argument, but she had the facts, and we were sitting smack dab in the middle of them.

"OK," I said, giving in for the moment. "Just show me your map."

She drew two large circles outside the others. "You know about both the vestibule and Sheol; you have seen them with your own eyes." She pointed to the next ring. "You know that below the judgment seat is circle two, for carnal sinners. Now we go to circle three, for gluttons; circle four, for the hoarders and wasters; and circle five, for the wrathful and sullen."

"Now it's coming back to me. Those four circles, beginning with the carnal, form upper hell."

"Precisely. They punish the sins of incontinence — that is, the sins of weakness. The people there are not guilty primarily of injuring others; they meant no harm to anyone. They acted in response to natural impulses, good in themselves: desires for physical pleasure or comfort. They had normal reactions to the world around them: anger over offenses, sorrow over loss. But they failed to control these natural goods and ended up enslaved to them."

"So their bondage separated them from God?"

"They could serve God or something else, but not both. The inhabitants of upper hell consistently chose something over God; little by little they allowed some created good to matter more to them than God — food, sex, wine, money. They clung to their own little pleasures and possessions, feelings and moods, until they had to let go of what mattered most."

She stood up. "We need to be going. Once we have made it through the next circle, we will speak of other levels and trace the bounds of lower hell. When we do, you will see that the deeper sins of malice — deeds of violence and fraud — corrode the soul more horribly than the sins of weakness."

Her eyes narrowed. "It is true that all sin separates from God; no doubt in the end we can desert Him and flee as far away from Him through petty flattery as through rank adultery. But not all sins are the same in the seriousness of their effects on others and on the soul that commits them. If that were so, earthly courts of justice would be constrained to punish them all the same, and a tax evader would sit in the electric chair alongside the serial killer."

"I guess," I said, "I should take some comfort in knowing that all my worst faults are clustered in the upper circles."

"Are they indeed?" Miss C asked softly, her gaze lowering slowly till it focused on the dust at her feet. "Remember the words of the prophet: *The heart is deceitful above all things, and desperately wicked. Who can know it?* I would not be so sure, Thomas. I would not be so sure."

ELEVEN

The room we'd crawled into to escape the winds was actually a long corridor. Stagnant air was dimly lit by a single, naked light bulb halfway down its length, dangling from the frayed wires of an old ceramic socket. The floor was filthy concrete, with an occasional surviving linoleum tile, faded and caked with dirt in the cracks. The hall stank from garbage scattered in piles, some small enough to walk around, others we had to climb over.

We weren't alone. Rats and roaches burrowed through the garbage, stuffing their little bellies. Spiders hung in the corners where the walls propped up a low, sagging ceiling, and they had no shortage of food: Green flies were everywhere, with enough caught in the webs to invite the neighbors over.

When we opened the door at the end of the corridor, we were soaked by a foul-smelling downpour of sooty sleet and freezing rain the color of dishwater. Always the smart-mouth, I tried to shout "Forgot my umbrella!" to Miss C, but when I did, I got a mouthful of cold muck. There was nothing to do but make a dash across the flooded street where we found ourselves and seek shelter under the awning of one of the tacky little buildings that lined the sidewalk.

We didn't get far. The slippery muck was ankle-deep in some places, and I fell almost as soon as we ran out. There I sat, feeling like a chewed-up straw in a mud-flavored snow cone, until a woman's head stuck up out of the water only inches away from my elbow.

My legs were numb, but that didn't keep me from jumping up so quick I almost knocked Miss C down. She was just as startled as I was, though she knew right away what was going on. The head's shoulders were showing now, and we could both see that a broad pothole had been stuffed with a female torso the size of a washtub.

She looked like the hefty woman who dipped the ice cream at the Tastee-Freeze back home. "She's so fat," Daddy used to whisper between spoons of his butter pecan, "her boyfriend has to hug and then chalk so he'll know when he's made it back around." Of course, Daddy was none too skinny himself.

She swatted at a moldy Twinkie wrapper brushing by her shoulder, wiped some slush off her lips, then pointed a stubby finger not quite in my direction. Her eyes were blank; she'd been blinded by the freezing sludge.

"Watch where you're stepping, fatso!" she shouted. "I'm sitting on the head of a chubby little hot tamale from Tijuana, and there's plenty of room to stuff you down there too! Outta my face!"

We were glad to oblige. But as chilling as the sleet was, we didn't dare to run; already there were other heads and hands popping up out of potholes, grabbing blindly for the garbage that swirled all around them. Most of the faces were puffy, the chins double or triple; but you could also see sunken eyes and bony shoulders attached to needle-pocked arms.

Despite their blindness, they'd gotten to be experts at snaring the trash as it went by. Some were gnawing on bare chicken bones or licking off the rancid smears that clung to crumpled margarine wrappers. Others were shaking old liquor bottles to see if a drop or two was left. A few, with soggy cigarette butts hanging from their lips, demanded that we give them a light. Still others were poking themselves with bent hypos, though all they got was a vein full of dirty water.

About a block down the street we heard screams. Picking our way with care through the half-submerged crowd, we went to find out why. The noise was coming from the other side of a gutted drive-through menu sign.

Once past the sign, we saw a pot-bellied man — no, a pot-bellied demon — with eyes like red-hot charcoals and a complexion like raw hamburger. He was decked out in a ridiculous plastic robe and crown, and he gripped a barbecue fork like a scepter. The souls stuck in potholes nearest him were making all the racket, and no wonder: Every few seconds the demon jabbed one with the fork, guffawing and shouting with a gravelly voice, *"Have it your-r-r-r way! Have it your way — forever!"*

He was having too much gruesome fun to notice us, so we ducked into a building on our side of the street two doors down. We'd passed by the abandoned remains of a liquor store, a tobacco shop and a crackhouse, but this place had been a health club. All the mirrors were shattered, and all the exercise equipment was rusty and falling apart. But in the far corner was a well-tanned, well-sculpted bodybuilder, chained to a weight machine and bench-pressing four hundred pounds.

He heard us come in, though he couldn't see us any more than the others could. The reps went on, furiously, while he spoke. "Who's there? Is it another one of those blubber-guts trying to escape, or have I finally got a buddy who knows what it takes to shine?" His words were broken with grunts and pants.

"Sorry to disappoint you," I said, keeping my distance from those steroid-packed biceps, "but neither one. We're just passing through. Aren't you a little lonely in here?"

"Lonely for what?" he said, still pressing. "I've got all I need right here: a lot of muscle, a little sweat and plenty of iron to pump."

A stiff smile crossed his face. "Actually, I could use a drink, bud. How about if you step out that door and get me a handful of that slush?"

Miss C reached out to stop me, but I had already darted for the door. This guy, I knew, could pack a punch and a half; maybe if we did him a favor, he'd help us get past the Burger Demon.

A mangled soda cup with "The Real Thing" printed on it was floating by the door, so I grabbed it and filled it with the least muddy water I could find — crouching and keeping an eye all the time on that barbecue fork down the street. The slush was still filthy enough to gag me, but when you're thirsty, you're thirsty, and besides, he couldn't see it. I crawled back inside the club door, stood up and took it over to him.

"Thanks, buddy," he said, stopping his reps and reaching out with his left hand as if to take it — but he grabbed my wrist instead.

"Gotcha!" he said with a sneer. His other hand grabbed a fistful of flab around my waist. "I knew it!" he shouted. "You're just another one of those blobs! What are you doing in my space, pig?"

I tried to pull free. No luck — his grip was iron, and he had plenty to hold onto. It hurt, but I put on my best macho voice. "Maybe I should ask *you* that question, bud. These other slobs are getting what they deserve, you know. But what are *you* doing here with the gluttons?"

He relaxed his grip and wiped the sweat off his face. "Beats me. All I ever wanted was an awesome body. I did whatever it took — hours in the gym every day, steroids, the works. I never stuffed myself with junk food like those hogs out there. I was looking like a Greek god, man. Now I end up with all those porkers I hated most. What gives?"

I knew it was coming; Miss C couldn't stay out of a conversation like this. I turned toward her and put my finger across my lips, but it was too late.

"Gluttony takes many forms," she said firmly. "You may crave sugar, alcohol, nicotine — or you may crave muscles, physical beauty, even the adrenaline high of exercise itself. What every form of gluttony has in common is an obsession that revolves around the body and what you do to it."

"But I'm not like those others out there — I should have gotten all the trophies for taking care of myself!"

She shook her head and frowned. "Admit it: You were addicted as much as any wino. You thirsted for the perfect body, and you sacrificed everything else to get it — even life itself. Did the steroids kill you?"

"Shut up!" he shouted and knocked me backward over a bent exercise bike nearby. "Get outta here! It's not fair, no matter what you say! You don't know nothing!"

By then the commotion had blown our cover. Standing in the door was the Burger Demon, twirling his barbecue fork and grinning at us. "Where's the beef? Oh — there, right where I left him."

He slammed the fork against the doorframe. "Get back to pumping iron!" he commanded. "Stop again, and I'll grab the closest behemoth and sit him on your face while you press for the next thousand years." He trotted over to the bodybuilder and began pricking him with the fork on every bulging muscle he could find. "Say it!" he bellowed. "Say it now! Don't ever stop saying it!"

The bodybuilder was clenching his teeth and groaning, but he could only take so much. Finally he obeyed. "No pain, no gain!" he shouted. "No pain, no gain, no pain, no..."

The demon applauded as the words repeated endlessly. "Very good, boy, very good. Keep it up, now, while I take care of yet another *pressing* matter!" He laughed idiotically at the meager joke and turned to us.

Those burning eyes were now focused on my belly. "Surely you don't belong in here," he said. "Out in the street! You coward — thought you could hide from me." He pushed the crown back and whirled his cape. "But I have a special place for chickens like you. Yessir — we do chickens *right!* Aha, aha, aha-ha-ha!"

Miss C sprang toward the back door of the club, just behind the bodybuilder, expecting me to follow. But suddenly the barbecue fork went flying through the air, straight into the fat around my navel. It seared like a branding iron, and the pain felled me. I ripped my shirt off trying to get at the wound, then pulled the fork out and wadded the cloth shreds up for a bandage. The Burger Demon continued to laugh as he watched, amused, and at last walked slowly toward me.

"I was aiming for barbecued ribs," he said, belching loudly. "I won't miss the second time."

He lunged toward me, teeth bared, coming to lock his jaws in my side. I tried to dodge, but I wasn't fast enough. He missed my ribs again but hit me in the middle, getting a mouthful of bloody rags. For a second he choked on them, and I saw my chance: I caught him in the throat with the tines of the barbecue fork, still in my hand, and thrust him backward onto the bodybuilder.

The muscleman wasted no time. He got one massive forearm around the demon's throat, pulled out the fork and started pricking him with it. Then he spit in the choking face and mocked him. "Where's the beef? The beef's got you, suckah, and he ain't letting go!"

I got up, holding my stomach, and stumbled out the door. One of the gluttons had grabbed Miss C's ankle from behind and was demanding that she help him out. I gave the dripping hand a sharp kick, grabbed her by the shoulder and led her running down the sidewalk, as far away from the potholes as possible.

"Just one more block!" she shouted through the thunder of the downpour. I was hobbling, losing lots of blood, dying the slush red as I ran. But finally she pointed to a manhole cover a few feet ahead and motioned to go down. She lifted it, climbed down a few steps on the rusty iron ladder and offered me her hand. I was too unsteady to refuse, and slowly we went down together.

The floor of the underground chamber was only six feet below. When she'd managed to get me down to it, I lay out flat, with my head on a stray brick, while she climbed up again to pull the cover back. By then one last flood of cold ooze had poured down on me, but I didn't care. The next thing I knew was blackness, and the last thing I heard was the sound of the metal scraping into place.

──── T W E L V E ────

Adoor in the darkness opened, and brilliant waves of
light poured in to wash my face. I squinted and stood
up slowly, holding my throbbing middle, then made
my way to the door.

When I looked outside, my jaw nearly dropped to the ground.
As far as I could see there stretched out an emerald, grassy plain,
sparkled with dew and speckled with flowers of every kind and
color I'd ever stooped to smell, and then some. Overhead was a
singing blue sky, all decked out in flecks of cotton fluff.

After all the gray I'd seen, it was like being slapped in the face
with a wet rainbow.

I took a few shy steps out, but I couldn't hold back any longer.
Dropping to my knees and then down on my face, I grabbed
ahold of the green beard of the field and kissed it over and over
again. The dirt and the dew-sweat rubbed all over my face, the
whole earth seemed to wrap around me and I curled up in a ball,
crying.

Suddenly from out of nowhere came a raspy, old voice, once
rich and baritone, a voice that shouted as far back as I could
remember. "Come on, boy," it said, "give it a try. Climb up there

and see what you can see. Don't you worry, son; if you fall, I'll catch you."

I looked around for Daddy, but instead I saw — in the distance just over my left shoulder where I hadn't looked before — a ladder tall as heaven, top in the clouds, standing proud on the plain. There were people all around the base, waiting their turn to climb, while others were already making their way up and down the rungs — some folks going up on one side, some folks coming down on the other.

I stood up and walked toward it, feeling stronger with every grassy step, my head thick with the scent of honeysuckle and jasmine. Folks around the ladder moved out of the way when I got there, so I grabbed the sides of it and started climbing.

Up I went, though it wasn't easy. Every time I looked down my brain would spin, and there were people above me moving too slow, and people below me pushing too fast. I had to compete for a spot to place my hands with folks on the other side coming down, and all the while the voice repeated, "See what you can see! See what you can see!"

At last the cloud was just overhead, dancing and swirling now, close enough to reach up and touch. I did — and the whiteness scalded me like steam. When I jerked my hand back, I lost my balance, and I was done for.

I fell like the mourning dove falls when the shot rings out, and the hunters cheer, and the dogs go baying underfoot. Through the wild, clear blue I fell, and then right on down through the green and into the black, twisting and twitching and crying with all my might, "Catch me! Catch me! *Catch me!*"

Suddenly I opened my eyes, still crying, as Miss C wiped my face with bandages she'd ripped from her apron. "You are quite weak, Thomas," she said, her brow knitted, her jaw tight. "Rest some more while I try to stop the bleeding." Then there was blackness all over again.

We stayed in that space under McGlutton Street for what felt like several days. My body was slowly making more blood, though how it could do that without any food, I wasn't sure. The wound on my belly was beginning to heal, but black and blue spots surrounded it where the bodybuilder had left his mark as well.

Most of the hours we simply passed in conversation, some punctuated with brief earth tremors that sent loose bricks falling around our heads. As we talked I continued to marvel at Miss C's self-education. She must have interrogated every preacher, seminary professor and theologian that ever came through this way — and by her own estimation, their numbers were beyond the counting.

The circle of the gluttons still bothered me, not least of all because people had called me chubby for as long as I could remember. Once, after Miss C and I had been sitting in silence for an hour or more, I blurted out, "So God actually damns people for overeating?"

Miss C looked stern. "The reality is not so simple. Surely all addictions have their roots in some inner brokenness, often

83

caused by a pain someone else first inflicted on the soul. But as the bondage grows, there are small choices made along the way as well, and through such choices it is possible to dig a pit too deep to climb out of alone."

"So you mean that by that point their will is no longer free?"

"Weak and bound, but not utterly bound. Those who wish to struggle can still exert themselves — if nothing else, they can confess their predicament, cry for help and turn toward whatever means of grace may be nearby. If they do, they will not end up here."

A pain shot through my belly. "Then there are gluttons in heaven?"

"Gluttons who took hold of grace while they had the opportunity. Heaven is full of such — not just gluttons, but also fornicators, adulterers, frauds, murderers, some of every kind who would otherwise have ended up here. There was only one difference between the two thieves on the cross, Thomas: One called out for grace and the other scorned it. But the one is now in heaven and the other, down below us."

I let out a long breath. "That's encouraging. Just about every circle in Gehenna probably has some claim on me."

"No one is perfectly righteous," said Miss C. "Justice pulls us all down like gravity to this place. If not for grace, heaven would be empty of our race."

Her words encouraged me, but still I had questions. "Do you think all of those who ended up in this circle really knew what they were doing?"

"They were aware of the little steps they took, though perhaps not of the ultimate destination. But the consequences of such choices are real, whether or not they are fully known. When these people chose to walk away from heaven, this is where their road led: to the place of final separation from God."

She sighed. "As I said before, they have gotten not simply what they deserve, but what they are."

It was making sense, this steel-edged justice, but still it grated on my mind like a cold, dry razor on morning stubble. "So let me guess: The fornicators let themselves drift along on the sweet breeze of erotic desire till they were caught up in a whirlwind of lust. Now they're battered by impulses that took a lifetime to grow into a hurricane, and they're forever out of control."

"You are beginning to understand, Thomas. And the gluttons, still blind slaves of their bellies, scrounge desperately to feed a ravenous appetite that will never be filled, to scratch a furious itch that will never die."

I winced and swore on the spot that I'd never eat another Twinkie, though it didn't count for much — my stomach was so sore even the thought of food hurt. But it was a start.

When I felt strong enough to travel again, we set out through the maze under the streets to find the next stairwell down, to circle four. Finally we located it, and it led us into a small room with a hollow steel door. Suddenly the whole place shook, and we heard a loud *thud!*

I thought we were having another earthquake, but we weren't. The metal of the door continued to vibrate, and through it we could now hear the scrape of heavy machinery mixed with what sounded like the hubbub of crowds at a football game.

Cautiously, we cracked the door and peeked out. We were on the edge of a landfill, scooped out like an amphitheater and lit up with giant floodlamps like a TV studio. Bulldozers circled the rim, and cranes were scattered across the base. In between the machines were hundreds of people running from the rim to the base, carrying garbage in their arms and screaming at one another.

The bulldozers were pushing down into the hole everything from broken antique furniture and obsolete appliances to smashed limousines and splintered yachts. The people up on the rim with them added to the pile their own armloads of tattered furs, designer jeans, CDs and jewelry.

Not to be outdone, the cranes in the pit below were scooping up everything that had just been pushed in and pitching it back up again. The people down in the pit with them gathered up what they could and dashed, cussing and sweating, over the piles of rubbish and up to the rim, where they threw it in the faces of the people there. They didn't have to run down again; the people on the rim shoved them all back over the edge, followed by more wads of trash and the cheers of those on top.

Not far away from us on the rim, overlooking the chaos, was an oversized TV game show set with a plastic wheel that had the numbers 6 and 66 printed alternately along the edge. Next to the wheel stood a colored-light scoreboard announcing "HOARDERS 66, WASTERS 6."

An oily voice shouted over a fuzzy loudspeaker, "Hey, you sorry squanderers, those mean old misers down there look like they're winning!" A thunder of boos erupted from the folks above. "So whatcha gonna do about it? Is it really true that whoever dies with the most toys wins?"

"No!" shrieked the wasters, shaking their hips in a dance, "you gotta party, party, *party!*" Both sides were looking more and more like ants in a hill that some brat had just stirred up with a stick. The wasters went to their task with more frenzy and fury than ever, and the hoarders matched them load for load.

Now the game-show host stepped out from behind the scoreboard. It was a ruddy-faced demon dressed in a fur-trimmed, red suit, black boots and belt, with a fake, stringy white beard that hung loose from his ears. "Ho, ho, ho!" he bellowed into the mike. "By the way, folks — be sure to stop over at the next studio some time and watch the *Greens* go at it against the *Developers!* Ho, ho ho! Now it's time to *spin the wheel!* Hoarders, what will be your new score?"

He gave the wheel a push, and the arrow landed on a 6. The scoreboard lights twinkled; now it read "HOARDERS 6, WASTERS 66."

The contestants jeered or cheered, according to their place on the bottom or the top of the landfill, and the game went on.

"So turned the wheel of fortune in the upper world," said Miss C. "Just when these thought they had it all, all would be lost, through accident, theft, stock-market crash, finally death. Fortune's task was to teach them how easily possessions come and go. But they never learned."

"Well," I said, "no need to waste any more time here. This is one sport that holds little attraction for either of us."

We picked our way through mangled ten-speeds, rusted gas grills and broken stereos to an asphalt path that led down the slope. The landscape was darker than ever, but the floodlamps at the landfill scattered enough light in our direction to keep us on track.

On the roadside lay a box of musty old books, and I stopped to check them out. "Do not even think about it," said Miss C firmly. I didn't argue, but I was sorely tempted.

In the distance we could see the lights of a thousand other

landfills along the perimeter of the abyss, all crawling with heavy equipment and sweating, panting people.

"What a rotten job," I said, waving my hand at the spectacle. "I used to have one like it as a kid — cleaning fingerprints off the plate-glass windows in front of Sonny's Soda Shop. The kids all thought it was *their* job to mess them up again."

"There was at least one major difference," said Miss C. "I am sure the children *enjoyed* getting the windows messy."

I had to grin. "The damned may not be having much fun here, but the devils sure seem to. I don't mean to sound flippant, but those guys crack me up — when they're not trying to get their teeth in me. Punk clothes, Santa suits, 'Have it your-r-r way!' It's gallows humor, I know, but I still have to laugh."

"In hell," she said, "we must take all the laughs we can get." She chuckled gently. "I must admit the joke about the plastic robe and crown was wasted on me, but not the red suit; your generation's Christmas spending is infamous even down here."

"I would have never thought the Devil had a sense of humor."

"It seems the demons take as much pleasure as we do in mocking human foolishness," she said. "For the time being, this is their playground as well as their post. After all, the jesting helps keep their minds off the fate that awaits them when God Himself will get the last laugh."

"Wait, dahling!" A cultured voice from behind us caught us by surprise. "Do wait! Where are you going? And why do you still wear attire — dreadful as it may be?"

We turned around to see a wrinkled old woman, pink and puffy, carrying an armload of diamonds big enough to choke a grizzly bear. She was just as barren of clothes as all the other souls, but flakes of bright-pink polish still clung to her nails, both hand and toe, and her hair had been braided and tied in a ratty knot on top — a pitiful try at hairstyling in hell.

The diamonds had scratched and bruised her bosom, but she held on to them like a mama possum to her brood. "It's simply ghastly here," she whined. "Do you know a way out? I'll gladly pay you for your efforts."

It was rude, but I broke into a belly laugh — till my still-sore middle caught me up short. "Ma'am, it's true we're on our way out, but even as hot as it may get where we're going, I don't think those chunks of ice could do us any good."

She stiffened. "Then I must implore you as a gentleman to give aid to a lady in distress."

All this time she'd been talking to me without even a side glance at Miss C. Whether it was the black skin or the homespun, I don't know, but she was acting as if I were alone — or maybe accompanied by a house servant.

"I'll do what I can, ma'am," I said, still snickering. "My name is Thomas Travis, at your service" — I took a low bow — "and this is Miss Capopia. If you want to escape, you'll have to ask her the way. She has the only map, and it's in her head."

That didn't sit well with the diamond lady. "Very well, then," she said to Miss C, sniffing. "Get on with it. Lead the way." It was obvious she'd had plenty of practice giving orders.

Somebody with a little less grace might have left that pale old prune-face standing there, rocks and all. But Miss C took it all in good humor; her patience, I was finding, grew out of her deep humility. She said simply, "Follow me."

FOURTEEN

W e walked on down the path in a tense and awkward silence. Every once in a while one of the diamonds would drop, and though I didn't want to, I'd pick it up anyway. Maybe some of Miss C's grace was rubbing off on me. Even so, the hairdoed lady would grab the rock from my hand without so much as a thank-you.

Before long we passed a rusty oil well. A cracked pipe running from it dripped black crude on the asphalt, and the drops gathered into a murky, sticky stream that ran downhill. Miss Hairdo complained that it was getting between her pink-flaked toes, but we said nothing.

About a mile farther the path stopped at the edge of a black swamp — or, to tell the truth, an oil dump, because that's where the oil stopped too. It had all collected in a wide, smelly lake, its surface constantly troubled with little waves, as if it were simmering on somebody's stove.

As I fully expected, our new traveling buddy started sniffing and snorting.

"How dare you deceive me!" she said, glaring at Miss C. "I trusted you to get me out of this monstrous place, and now here we are, miles down a dead-end road that leads to...to...a hideous oil spill!"

Miss C stayed calm. "We are not lost," she said. "This is the River of Hate, known in the ancient Greek tongue as the Styx. It is the fifth circle of hell, and we must cross it to get to our next destination."

"You expect me to *swim* in that horrid slime?" asked Miss Hairdo, rolling her eyes.

"We will have transportation soon enough." Miss C was peering intently into the black air, as if to get her bearings. "There."

She pointed off to our left to a spot on the edge of the dump. "There is the tower. See the two lights? And there," she said, pointing across to the far side. "There is the light that answers them. Come now, quickly. He will be there waiting by the time we get to the tower."

She'd made it clear there was no time for questions, so we shelved them and moved out fast. When we reached the base of the tower — a grimy, stone structure with more cracks than windows — a tiny rowboat was pulled up on the shore. Beside it stood a she-demon, holding a dim flashlight in one hand and licking the oil off the other. "Make it snappy!" she said with a black-smeared frown. "I was having dinner when you so rudely interrupted."

"Where is Phlegyas?" asked Miss C.

"He's on, shall we say, a leave of absence," said the she-demon. "The old crank kept insisting on using a torch instead of a flashlight. 'That's the way I've *always* done it,' he said. Till he dropped it in the oil last week, and the whole thing nearly went up in flames. It would have been a pretty sight, don't get me wrong, but you know as well as I do that circle eight, eighth pit, already has exclusive rights on that kind of torment. What's it to you, anyway?"

"I was just curious," said Miss C. "Now let us on board."

"Wait a minute," said the demon. "That one," she said, pointing at me, "still has his pants on. What's he doing down here?"

"That is none of your concern," said Miss C. "He must get across the Styx; so it is willed — "

"Yeah, yeah, I know the rest," said the demon with a snort. "You think I don't know spit, don't you, just because I started last week. I know the formula — shoot, everybody who's read Dante knows the formula. Just get in the boat and shut up."

She looked us over closely as Miss C and I stepped aboard, then shook her head and put her hand out when the other woman tried to board. "Can't get on with those rocks, Miss Judy in the Sky. You're already extra weight — usually two riders is the limit — and those stones will sink this little puppy for sure. Ditch 'em, lady."

The woman clutched her diamonds closer and began to shake.

"Never!" she squealed. "They're mine! I collected them myself! They go where I go!"

I'd lost my patience long before, but I forced myself to sound diplomatic. "Why don't you just leave them here on the shore for now," I said. "If you should come back through this way, you can always pick them up again."

"Oh, no!" gasped the woman. "Those wretched homeless people are wandering around everywhere, and they're sure to steal them." She sniffed. "You simply cannot trust those vagrants, you know — unscrupulous derelicts, every one!"

Miss C spoke sharply now. "If you ever hope to leave, you must give them up. Now or never. Make your choice."

"There *is* no choice," the woman said. "These diamonds are all I have now. I could not bear to leave them. These are my only babies. These are my only friends. They are all I have. All I have..." Then she turned and disappeared into the darkness.

The boat was soon far from shore, the demon's oars making thick, rolling waves in the oil. Her flashlight shone on us weakly, just enough so we could see our faces dimly reflected on the ripples in the shiny, black crude.

I looked at my face long and hard. It was like looking at Daddy. Not because my features resembled his so much — in fact, folks used to say I didn't look much like Daddy or Mama, either one. But Mama always said the likeness was in our ways.

I walked and talked like Daddy, and we did the same things with our faces, like grinning with our noses all crinkled up, and narrowing our eyes to a slit when somebody tried to pull something over on us. Our lips went white when we were mad enough to shake, and when we were ashamed, our heads turned red as a watermelon all the way across the scalp.

Yessir, Mama used to say, forget about the features, and just catch that boy when he's thinking like his daddy and his thoughts are written on his face. You'll see it then, the old man's spit 'n' image, no doubt about it. That boy is his daddy's long-gone childhood, Mama said, dug up and come to life again to haunt him.

But I was the one who got haunted. When I looked in the mirror, Daddy looked back at me; when I scowled, he scowled; when I laughed...well, I don't remember him laughing much; he always said he was too tired to laugh.

Now here he was, floating on the Styx, looking back up at me with eyes hard as flint.

All at once the face leaped up out of the ooze, and two oily, black hands grabbed for my throat. I nearly fell over the other side trying to get away, hollering for help, my heart popping out my ears. The she-demon beat back the attacker with an oar, cussing him in a demon tongue I couldn't understand.

"Now you've gone and done it!" she shouted at me. "Now they'll *all* come up looking for a good brawl!"

Before I could ask who "they" were, thousands of gooey, black figures jumped up out of the slime, swinging and biting and kicking one another like a Saturday night free-for-all at the honkytonk.

"Are you a Hatfield or McCoy?" one man screamed at us, then spit out broken teeth with the crude.

"Blood or Crip?" yelled another a few feet behind him, wiping oil off the scars on his arms. Before I could answer, they turned and looked at each other, shouted obscenities and went back down fighting in the ooze.

I thought we were goners for sure, but Miss C just sat there, quiet as ever. "What's the matter with you?" I shouted, getting in her face. "Can't you see they're gonna pull us in?"

She shook her head. "Just sit down and be still, Thomas. These are the wrathful — they are one another's worst enemies, and thus your best defense: If one gets too far out of the oil, the others pull him back to be beaten all the more. They have no time to cease their quarreling for our sake."

She was right. A few came close to the boat, but they only had their heads out a few seconds before others jerked them back under.

I let out a long, deep breath. "Are they always going at it like that down under there?"

"Of course," said Miss C. "They wage continual war, never

resting, never seeking or even wanting peace. They fed on rage for a lifetime until they came to thrive on it, and they never learned to forgive."

"Even so," said the she-demon, breaking in, "we do have to steer clear of that spot over there where the waves are so big; they make the boat rock. That's where they dump all the hot-headed bosses who come to work cussing every morning and go home spitting nails. They hate it down there — no peons to fire, no rivals to blame and no secretaries to holler at."

As we neared the shallows to avoid the time-clock terrors, I spied a young woman sitting there waist deep, her eyes closed and her head hung low. "One of the sullen," said Miss C in a low voice. "They hold onto their moodiness like a child clings to a favorite blanket. They wrap themselves in silent ill humor and dare the world to come close."

"Leave me alone," the young woman whined. "You get your kicks watching people get abused, huh? Well, just go away. It's not fair, I tell you. I don't belong here. Just because I wrote an honest book about my celebrity mother and told the world what a witch she was and how she mistreated me as a child. Why, she used to *spank* me with a wooden spoon when I was little, and she wouldn't even let me date till I was *sixteen!*"

A head popped up next to her elbow. "Aw, shut up, you little twit!" it said, trying, without luck, to shake the oil out of its curls. "At least *you* didn't have to deal with a ninny of a husband like I did. For thirty years I put up with him, and never once did he do anything right! I should have known what was coming the day we said 'I do': I pulled up the pant leg on his tux, and he was wearing *gray socks* — can you believe it? — *dark gray socks* with a black tux at his own wedding! Never did see him wear the right color socks till the day he died. He used to get up early just so he could read the newspaper before I got to it, and he got it all wrinkled. When he grilled steaks, do you think he could ever get them the right shade of pink inside? Not for love nor money. Why, I still remember the day..."

I started to interrupt, but Miss C stopped me. "They are not interested in conversation; they are only talking to themselves. The sullen do that: They rehearse all the wrongs ever done to them, real or imagined, over and over again. They dwell on their losses and disappointments. Above all, they blame others for their troubles. These two will be sulking here alone in self-pity until the last Day."

In the distance now was a red glow, looming larger as we rowed toward it. "The Seminary of Dis," said Miss C, pointing ahead. "If you are to meet any acquaintances in hell, you will most likely meet them there. I think you had better prepare yourself. It is time, you might say, for a mid-term exam."

FIFTEEN

The seminary, as Miss C called it, looked from the outside more like a fortress than a campus, closed in on itself with a high iron wall that glowed red-hot. Every opening — window, gate and door — was an iron briar patch of heavy bars and massive locks. By the time we reached the front gates the heat was nearly unbearable.

"You said they call it 'Dis'?" I asked.

"Another ancient name the Greeks used for Hades," said Miss C.

I was just about to ask her to refresh my memory about who ended up in this sixth circle when a skinny, sour-faced she-demon appeared at the gate. "What do you want?" she snapped.

"Only passage through," said Miss C.

The demon looked me over. "You know the admissions policy," she said in a thin, nasal voice. "No non-deceased individuals may matriculate."

Miss C spoke more firmly. "We do not plan to enroll, only to tour the campus. *So it is willed where what is willed must be.*"

"My supervisor has instructed me to make no exceptions to policy."

"Then take us to your supervisor," said Miss C. "We have no time for delay."

Just then another demon showed up, this one with a stack of smoldering papers in his left hand and a flaming book in his right. "I am the supervisor," he said to Miss C. "You know the regulations. No non-deceased matriculants, and no tours. Now go back to the Styx or I will call campus security."

"But you *must* let us through," said Miss C. "So it is willed — "

" 'Where what is willed must be,' " said the supervisor, the words greasy with sarcasm. "I have consulted the best critical authorities on that particular text, and they are in agreement that the formula is spurious. At most it represents a psychological construct that — "

"You know full well the true origin of those words!" thundered Miss C, her eyes blazing. "Now move aside!"

The supervisor glared at her for a long moment, then at me. "You may pass through," he said to her, hissing. "But certainly you are aware of the little stipulation that allows us to test the living before they may enter?"

I looked to Miss C, expecting that she would challenge the policy on that point as well. Instead, she nodded. "Proceed now," she said. "I have not prompted him."

The demon turned to me and grinned wickedly. "I will make this short, and we will see quickly whether you are ready to pass through Dis. I will propose a riddle, and you must decipher it correctly."

I swallowed hard. "And if I can't?"

"Then you must turn back, and the Styx awaits you," he said. "You could do worse — much worse. Better the Styx than what lies below."

I looked at Miss C with pleading eyes, but she only looked down at her feet. She must have known this might happen, yet she hadn't warned me. Maybe the "policy" didn't allow her to.

The demon dropped his book and papers, stood erect and folded his hands behind him like a schoolboy about to recite. "Make of this what you can," he said:

"Born a dear offspring, buried a foe;
I drink of the milk, but poison the flow;
I mimic the ancient melody sung

96

With lyrics rewrit in an alien tongue.
Who am I?"

I was clueless. Milk and poison? Alien tongue? What could he be talking about?

I didn't remember much from Dante but enough to be sure that he'd never had to jump through this little hoop. Whatever had happened to him at the sixth circle, things must have changed since then. I searched my mind for a map of his journey.

The vestibule, Sheol and sins of weakness lay in upper hell. Sins of malice went to lower hell. Dis stood between the two, belonging to neither — so what kind of sins brought damned souls here? Think. *Think.* My brain was all revved up, but the clutch was stuck in neutral.

Miss C stood restlessly, her shoe scuffing against the pavement, her lips moving silently. What had she said back in the boat? I might meet some acquaintances here, she'd said. This is some kind of seminary; maybe some of my former professors are here?

But why? They hadn't been evil people, though I had to admit that this place was changing my notion of evil. They were just intellectual types who liked to toy with new ideas and...and to ridicule old ones.

Suddenly I remembered: Dis is the place filled with those who had sinned with their *intellect*. In religious terms, that meant Dis is the circle of the *heretics* — those who turned from God by embracing false ideas about Him. And the fire here is much hotter for people who have also led others astray.

That is, for people like *me*. I thought of all the students whose faith I'd torpedoed, whose lives I'd confused. *I am a heretic*, I thought. The realization chilled me. A heretic...a heretic...

The echoing thought tumbled out of my head and into my mouth before I realized I was speaking. "A heretic," I said. "*I* am a heretic."

"No!" bellowed the demon, pointing his finger at Miss C. "I had him stumped! How did he find the answer? You have tricked me!"

She shook her head. "You know I would never be allowed to pass this way again if I were to break the rule and prompt someone. No, he has figured it out himself — or perhaps he received a word by grace. In either case, mind your instructions: You must

97

let us pass immediately, and you must give us an escort."

I was dumbfounded. The solution of the riddle was *heretic*? I wanted to ask why, but I knew better than to let on that I hadn't known the answer.

The supervisor cussed us, cussed his subordinate, even cussed his own riddle. But he opened the gates, and in we went. Then he ordered the skinny demon to go with us, though I would just as soon have found my own way.

"How dare they make me walk with the likes of you," she said to me in a prim little voice, wrinkling up her nose. "You still carry the stench of the upper world."

Once inside we could hear shrieks and moans coming from every direction. I stayed close to Miss C, feeling the heat, I was sure, much more keenly than she did. Old Sourface stopped and began pointing out buildings. "Our facilities continue to expand. We are proud to note that we have recently added a number of new dorms while expanding the old ones to handle our record-setting enrollment."

The campus was as big as a large city. In fact, I remembered as we began walking again that in Dante, Dis *had* been a city, not a seminary. I asked the demon about it.

She shrugged. "You know how it is with small college towns," she said. "The campus keeps growing and growing till it finally takes over the whole city. We have to put all these heretics *somewhere*."

All the buildings were like the outside wall: red-hot iron with doors and windows barred and bolted. Flames shot out through the bars, making the door and window frames an especially bright red. The ground between the structures was all paved, none too cool itself. And everywhere echoed the sounds of pain.

Sourface pointed to a colossal dorm with too many stories to count. "The second-largest building on campus," she said, with obvious pleasure. "Gnostic Hall. We have inmates — I mean, students — there from every century over the last two thousand years: Marcionites, Manichees, Cathari, Albigensians, Swedenborgians, Christian Scientists. Also a few Pentecostals and charismatics who went off the deep end into weirdness. Best of all, we've had to build a whole new wing just to hold the New Agers. It's amazing how much they all have in common."

"For one thing," I said, "most of them thought hell was only a fable. What do they think now?"

"It depends. The Manichees think they're caught between worlds. The Christian Scientists are still trying to prove that it's all an illusion. Most of the New Agers are convinced they're just being purified for their next incarnation, or maybe being held on another planet by hostile extraterrestrials — though I did hear one say the other day that he hopes Shirley MacLaine spends her next fifty lives as a cockroach."

"That's still a mess of different views," I said. "Don't they ever disagree?"

"Gnostics? Disagree? They couldn't see a logical contradiction if it sat up, barked and bit them on the nose. One says black, the other says white, and they claim they're saying the same thing, only in different colors. You figure it out. Of course, they have other problems to keep them occupied."

She smiled wickedly. "But I understand it's quite a different matter down in circle eight, pit nine."

"Who's there?"

"The schismatics. They can't agree on anything. If the circle of the wrathful and sullen were lower, most of the schismatics would be there instead." She cleared her throat with great authority. "In any case, wherever they might be, the heretics wouldn't be arguing for long. Eventually they all go insane anyway."

Miss C was nodding, sadly. "Reject the greatest truths long enough, and in time even the smallest, everyday realities are lost as well."

We were passing by a flaming sign that said "Materialist Hall," and I was itching to look inside. How many seminary professors had ended up there for teaching their students that the supernatural realm was all a crock? I wasn't brave enough to open the door, but I did take a peek through the bars of a ground-floor window.

Inside, a long corridor held rows and rows of fiery bunk beds, with screaming people strapped down on them in the flames. Demons were busy stuffing something that looked like burning paper down their throats.

"See the guy in the far corner?" said Sourface, looking in over my shoulder. "Rudolf Bultmann."

"Who is that?" asked Miss C.

"A famous German theologian and biblical scholar of my century," I said. "He insisted that all New Testament references to heaven, hell, angels, demons and miracles were myths to be reinterpreted. Demythologizing the Bible, he called it."

As they spoke, several devils waved a burning book under the old man's nose. "Go ahead!" one screamed. "Make my day! Demythologize *me*!"

I couldn't watch for long. We turned away and continued our campus tour as Sourface rattled off the names of buildings.

"Arius-Socinus Hall, for all who deny the Trinity — overflowing these days with Unitarians, Jehovah's Witnesses, Muslims and a surprising number of denominational Protestants.

"Hall of Neo-Pagans and Polytheists — lots of growth there recently: Wiccans, neo-Druids, earth worshippers, to say nothing of all the Mormons and Armstrongites who still think they're on their way to becoming gods."

A few steps further we came to a small monument carved from rough, black stone with the inscription: "Tomb of the Ultimate Concern."

The demon read the confusion on my face. "The death-of-God theologians and the existentialists both wanted a marker here," she said matter-of-factly. "We had to work out a compromise."

Off the main row of structures stood a cluster of small dorms facing one another in a circle. "These," said the demon, "thought their leaders were divine: followers of Ann Lee, Father Divine, Daddy Grace, to name a few. The Moonies are still waiting for their leader to rescue them."

I had seen enough, and I wanted out as soon as possible. But one of the demon's comments had set my curiosity to working overtime.

"You said the Gnostics had the second-largest building. What's the largest?"

She pointed to a towering structure in the distance. "The combined cafeteria and library."

That made about as much sense as penning pigs in a parlor. "You put the dining hall with the reading stacks?"

"Yes, of course. Didn't you just see the materialist souls having breakfast in bed?" I was still in the dark — I'd thought they were being tortured.

"Here comes a delivery devil now," she said. "You!" she shouted to a short, plump demon carrying a tray stacked with flaming books. "Bring that here!"

Sourface pointed to the open book on top of the stack with the byline "Mary Baker Eddy" and read aloud a sample: "Evil has no reality. It is neither person, place nor thing, but is simply a belief, an illusion...."

She laughed a raucous laugh, blew on the flaming volume to make it even hotter and sent the delivery devil on his way. "You see, our library *is* our cafeteria. We have collected here all the heretical works of our dorm residents, and now they must eat their own words — books *flambé*, if you will. The heretics may appear to be enveloped in flames, but in truth the fire is burning from the inside out. As you have seen, we provide room service."

I thought of the last book I'd written myself, full of notions I wouldn't dare claim now. How would it taste? I could just feel it going down: hot as a jalapeño farm in Texas, and twice as dry.

"What is your name?" Sourface asked me curtly.

"Thomas Travis. Historical theology."

"Mmm...the name is familiar," she said. "I think I've seen it in our card catalog. Why don't I check?"

I swallowed hard and looked around, wondering how to change the subject.

SIXTEEN

Just then four demons in smoking academic robes tumbled out of Materialist Hall, gripping one limb apiece of a screaming soul struggling to get away.

"What's the meaning of this?" shouted Sourface over the screams. "Where are you taking him?"

The four devils stopped in place as the man kept wriggling like a worm on a griddle. "He's a transfer," hollered the demon holding the man's left hand. "When he first came, we got him for heresy. But now we know he belongs further down — with the hypocrites."

As the man wrestled with the demons, his face twisted toward me, then froze when our eyes met. It was my old college theology professor, Dr. Perdido. Visiting faculty from Nicaragua. Liberation theologian. Darling of the school's Marxist crowd.

Suddenly he quit the screams and the struggle, speaking now to me in a raspy voice as he hung limp by his arms and legs.

"Tell them, Travis. You knew me; you were one of my best students. Tell them I am no hypocrite, not even a heretic! Even if I were in error — and I still reject that possibility — even then I should not be punished for beliefs sincerely held. I committed no crime; thousands agreed with me! How dare they even speak of heresy in this enlightened age. Down with the thought police! I will *not* give in to censorship, even in hell!"

I remembered his class all too well, and though I shared his guilt, I felt no sympathy. In a way his story was my own — though his had already come to an end. I could see the situation much too clearly now to commiserate.

I looked down to the ground. "You're hardly a stranger to censorship, Dr. Perdido. We both have to admit that I did so well in your class because at the time I shared your Marxist views. And you can't deny that you never allowed any of your students to challenge Marxist dogma in the classroom."

"We had no time for argument," he said with a sniff. "Class time was too short."

I shook my head and looked him in the eye now. "But even when they tried to buck the party line in term papers or exams, you flunked them cold. You used to lower the grade on a colloquy paper if a student happened to refer to God with a masculine pronoun."

"They had to be re-educated," he whined. "It was my *job*."

"It was first-class censorship, Dr. Perdido. It was Political Correctness 101, and *you* were the thought police."

"But I was sincere!" he said, his voice rising again. "I was committed to the truth as I understood it! Who could be blamed for that?"

"That depends on what you mean by sincerity," I said. "If you mean absolute honesty of mind, then you flunked the sincerity test, and so did I. Do you really believe there are no sins of the intellect?"

"Objective inquiry, free from the bonds of dogma, is no sin," he said smugly.

"Your inquiry was neither objective nor free, Dr. Perdido. You didn't arrive at your conclusions in a single moment of pure revelation, nor in a moral vacuum. You came to them slowly, through a long series of choices about what you would permit yourself to believe and what you would refuse to believe. And most of those choices were based on your personal prejudices and ambitions — your hatred for the church and the capitalists, your desire for academic recognition, your pleasure in being trendy."

"That's a lie!" he said. "I weighed all the evidence carefully."

103

"You weighted the evidence according to your private agenda. The Bible prooftexts you cited to call for armed revolution lay right next to eyewitness reports of supernatural miracles. Yet you exaggerated the one and rejected the other, just as I did. You denied the reality of spiritual forces and preached cold economic machinery in their place."

"But religion *is* merely the opiate of the people."

"That's what you really believed all along, wasn't it? Though you never stated it publicly — it would have cost you too much. Instead you sugar-coated your politics with religious language so the people would swallow it and their consciences would be drugged while they fell in line with your ambitions. Admit it, Dr. Perdido: All along you were fishing for a high-level post in the new government after the revolution."

"Lies! All lies!" He was shouting again. "My people were oppressed. Surely they needed a theology that would inspire them to fight for freedom?"

"Even there you skewed the evidence. By the time you'd developed your theology you knew as well as I did that Marxism just plain didn't work — that it had never brought freedom to any nation that tried it and never could. You knew that the state could never maintain such totalitarian control without feeding a lust for raw power. You knew that the first order of business for every Marxist government had been to silence church leaders and faculty members just like yourself."

I looked down to the pavement again, ashamed. "You knew, Dr. Perdido. I knew. We all knew. We were all self-serving, but we fooled ourselves into thinking we were serving the truth."

"Enough!" said Sourface, clapping her hands twice sharply. "He allowed no debate, and neither do we. By his own words he is convicted of hypocrisy. Get on with the transfer." The demons dragged him off, struggling as before.

"I think," Miss C whispered close to my ear, "you have just passed your mid-term."

We began to walk again, this time less like tourists and more like students late to class, with Sourface setting a hurried pace. If she'd had a watch, you can be sure she'd have kept looking at it. "This is taking entirely too long," she whined to herself. "I have mountains of paperwork to do. Why is the admissions office always so understaffed?"

Then she stopped so fast we nearly ran over her. "Over there — one last building on the required tour," she said, pointing off to the right at a long, narrow dorm with no windows. "Preservation Hall. For conservative heretics."

That one set my head to itching. I turned to Miss C. "That's funny. I thought conservatives were the arch-enemies of everybody else here. Folks who preached a lot of hellfire and never met a new idea they liked."

"An old idea, forgotten long enough, looks like a new idea," said Miss C. "You find here not *all* the conservatives — nor all the liberals, for that matter — but rather a particular kind."

"And what kind is that?"

"The conservatives here were blasphemers of the Holy Spirit. They were an extremely arrogant and close-minded sort who equated a neat little package of dogma with the whole of spiritual reality and ascribed everything else to demons."

"But the conservatives I knew were all so dang sure they were defending 'the faith once for all delivered to the saints.' "

Miss C's face turned stormy. "No doubt many were. But others had simply settled for a cramped and narrow system of belief that was little more than a set of propositions to which they gave mental assent. Their dogma was not the ancient faith as they supposed it to be, but only the proud ghost of it, void of mystery and miracle and disdainful of everything beyond the rational mind that makes us fully human: our wills, our bodies, our imaginations, our emotions, our social relations."

"All those other things were in the Scriptures," I said. "If they talked so much about being Bible-believers, why didn't they see it all there?"

She crossed her arms in disgust. "The extremists you find here were every bit as selective in their use of Scripture as your Marxist professor. They avoided entire realms of scriptural truth and experience that did not fit within the limits of their own puny thoughts and habits."

"You know," I said, "they sound just like the materialists."

"Of course," said Miss C. "They dismissed the supernatural to a domain so distant in space and time that you could hardly tell them from those who dismissed it altogether. Their truncated gospel became a different gospel — a withered way of life the first apostles would not even recognize. A mere form of godliness, its power denied. In reality these never knew God; they knew only a dogma *about* God."

"Some like them claim that their 'correct' knowledge of God, as far as it goes, is enough to save them."

"So did the Gnostics. But they need only read the Scriptures to find it otherwise. Not everyone who says, 'Lord, Lord,' will enter the kingdom. The demons believe what these believed — and they shudder."

"Everybody's got to be in error on some doctrinal issue or another. So at what point exactly does an ultraconservative — or an ultraliberal, for that matter — become a damnable heretic?"

Miss C shrugged. "God alone knows. So much is determined by the hidden motivation and the final direction of the heart."

"But what," I asked, "could motivate these folks to reject their spiritual birthright for such a miserable mess of dogmatic pottage?"

She sighed deeply. "The conservative heretics were like all the others here in Dis: Though they claimed to champion truth, in reality they loved something else more than truth — in this case, the comfort of their own smugness. It was a subtle form of idolatry, but idolatry nonetheless."

That little gem of irony gave me plenty to think about, so we walked for a while in silence. Fancy that: feuding theological cousins — liberals and conservatives — the spit 'n' mirror image of each other, bedded down now side by side in flaming poetic justice. Just like the bodybuilders with the gluttons, the hoarders with the wasters.

If there's a beauty to be found in hell, it's to be found in the symmetry of the place.

Sourface at last led us to a small iron building behind the library-cafeteria and stopped at its door. "Inside here is a passageway down to the next circle," she said. "You're on your own now."

I couldn't bring myself to thank her for the tour, but I responded with a nod and took one last look around. Not far away was a crowd of female souls being herded into yet another dorm.

The last woman in line looked vaguely familiar, and after staring at her a few seconds, I recognized her. She'd spoken once at a professional conference, boasting that she opened all her classroom lectures at an Episcopal seminary with prayer — to the ancient Egyptian goddess Isis.

The Seminary of Dis was making more sense all the time.

Sourface turned to go back the same way we'd come. "After your conversation with Perdido," she said, looking sternly at me, "I may have to check that catalog for your name after all. But not now. I have too much paperwork to do, and it's time for our personnel reviews."

She walked away, muttering to herself. "But how do they expect me to get it all done with these interruptions?"

"Now that *she's* gone," I said to Miss C, "tell me quick: What was that riddle all about?"

She smiled. "So you did not know the answer after all. I suspected as much. The words came to you from outside you as a grace."

"But I still don't understand what it all meant. I can't even remember what the demon said."

"I have heard it many times on this journey," said Miss C. "It runs this way:

> "Born a dear offspring, buried a foe;
> I drink of the milk, but poison the flow;
> I mimic the ancient melody sung
> With lyrics rewrit in an alien tongue.
> Who am I?

"Think a minute, Thomas, and you will see the truth in it. The heretics are those who are born within the church but become her enemy; who drink the milk of her teaching but poison it with error; who use the traditional language of faith but twist the words to mean something quite different."

I shuddered. "In that case it's a miracle I made it through this place — my name *has* to be in that card catalog. If I ever make it home, I'll have some words of my own to eat."

"Then we had better be going quickly," said Miss C, reaching for the door that led down.

But I had one last question before we left. The sight of so many heretics, many damned for believing what I'd once believed, still troubled me.

"I can see," I said, "why Dr. Perdido would be here — or rather, why he belongs farther down with the hypocrites. Despite all his claims to be sincere, he's only arrived at the end of a long road of self-deception. But what about the heretics who truly *are* sincere? Do they come here as well?"

"Ideas have consequences," said Miss C gravely. "Sincere error poisons as surely as willful error: Drink a vial of arsenic, believing it to be medicine, and you will still die. Yet I am unconvinced that any of these could claim full sincerity. At some point, however small, they denied the truth as it presented itself to them. Once they got even that single element wrong, the whole sum was added up in error."

"I'm still not sure what you mean," I said. "Could you give me an example?"

She turned and pointed to one of the blazing dorms in the distance. "The arch-heretic Pelagius is there because he believed and taught that we can find our way to heaven without grace. Yet the truth is that fallen human nature is grievously bent, and it cannot unbend itself unaided. Pelagius could not soar into the presence of God without grace any more than he could fly without wings. In both cases the futile attempt only leads downward to destruction."

"And you don't think he was fully sincere in that belief?"

"How could he have been? Even while he still lived on earth, the evidence of his own daily failings would have been enough to prove that he needed grace to reach moral perfection. But he proudly ignored the simple truth that would have shown his heresy for what it was."

I still wasn't satisfied. "But these all believed in God in one form or another," I said. "Surely that should count for something?"

Miss C frowned. "If the god they served was fundamentally false, then it counted for little. Those who worship a bigoted god and live accordingly will spend eternity, not with the true God, but with the bigots. We become what we worship."

I wanted to say more. But Miss C opened the door in front of us, and a gut-wrenching stench blew out into our faces.

"Blood," she said as she took the lead down the stairs. "You had better brace yourself for what lies ahead."

SEVENTEEN

Daddy used to say I had the head to be a doctor, but not the stomach. As usual, Daddy had me pegged. When I was young, I couldn't stay a New York minute down in the slaughterhouse where he worked.

Blood. If it's anywhere but where it's supposed to be — running through somebody's veins — I can't handle it. Not my own, not anybody else's. Not even a critter's; I have to have my meat well done.

It's not just the sight, you know, but the smell. Nothing in all creation smells like blood, and if you can smell blood, it isn't where it's supposed to be — it's spilled out of somebody's veins. That means somebody is hurting, and when I smell blood, I can smell the hurt, feel the agony shoot up my nose and fill the rest of my body till every bone I have gets a whiff of the pain.

Now here was Miss C, telling me there was blood below — as if I didn't know as soon as that stink reached up and grabbed me. A few steps down, and already I was smelling the pain, not just of one life poured out, but of a whole race slaughtered, all the blood shed from Abel on down through the ages. Somewhere below us it was all gathering together, crying out to heaven from the guts of the earth.

At least, you say, we left the flames behind. Well, fire is a terror, but blood is a horror; the one is a lifeless torturer, but the other is tortured life itself, a liquid corpse, a scarlet scream. What we faced next had bred the two and was more hideous yet: The blood had passed through the fire until it was boiling, a simmering, crimson cauldron just waiting for the ones whose crimes had filled it up.

Welcome to the first stop in lower hell.

Miss C told me that circle seven was the fate of violent offenders. While we climbed down a chain of rusty stairwells, she laid out the map in detail.

The seventh circle was itself divided into three concentric rings. Ring one, the boiling blood, held folks who'd committed violence toward others and their property — murderers, rapists, torturers, mobsters, looters, vandals, arsonists. I could already see it: a grand mix of Iroquois cutthroats, street gang warriors, Aztec priests, KGB agents and a Grand Inquisitor or two.

What a sight, I thought, that would prove to be: all the colorful characters from Nero to Napoleon, from Barabbas to Bonnie and Clyde — though I had to wonder why we call such criminals "colorful," when in the end the only color they know is red.

I thought of the megabucks made on slasher films and other grisly "entertainment." Why do we find goodness so bland and boring? Because we can't understand it? Does full-ripened wickedness fascinate us so deeply because we understand it all too well — because we know that, given a certain soil, the evil seeds in our own hearts could burst into the same crop?

The second ring of the violent, said Miss C, was for those whose violence had been turned on themselves: suicides and those who'd thrown their lives and gifts away in less sudden, though no less tragic, self-injury. Ring three held the doom of those who'd been violent toward God, though I wasn't sure what she meant by that. When I asked, she said simply, "You will see soon enough."

The objections I'd raised earlier about ranking sins seemed empty now. The smoky, lusty whirlwind of the second circle weighed almost nothing next to the dense, clotted evil of this place, already pressing in around us. No longer were we sampling the spoiled fruit of human weakness or folly; here we could taste instead the poison of malice, dark and bitter.

The blood scent soon took on a new pungency, and the odor turned me inside out. I was heaving now with each step down, but since there was nothing in my stomach, the heaves were dry. Doubled over, I gripped Miss C's arm and spit out the only words I could muster: "I can't keep going. Let me sit down."

She shook her head. "We must move through as quickly as possible. Breathe through my scarf and lean on my arm." She pulled out the calico scarf that had been half-stuffed in her dress pocket, pressed it over my nose and pulled me on.

Somehow we made it down to the last step. The smell now bothered me less; maybe I was getting used to it, though I'd never thought that possible. Hell's only guarantee was justice, I knew, yet it seemed to me in that wretched moment that a glimmer of grace just might have gotten through. How else could I survive the stench?

At the foot of the stairs stood a heavy iron door, dried blood-stains on its handle. It took both of us to shove it open, and when we did, a tidal wave of shrieks, curses and moans crashed in on us. Outside, the pavement was littered with heaps of weapons of every description: spiked clubs and grenades, pistols and swords, lances and cannons, blackjacks and bayonets. They formed a bank of sorts for a blood-filled toxic waste dump, stretching out as far as we could see in a bubbling, red moat that circled the abyss.

The noise came from the moat. It was teeming with parboiled sinners.

In some places the blood was only ankle deep; in others it reached to the hips or the shoulders or even the eyebrows of those who thrashed about in it, wailing.

"The worse the crime, the deeper they stand," said Miss C. "The cruel tyrants who bathed whole nations in blood are up to their scalps — Nebuchadnezzar, Attila the Hun, Stalin and the like."

"They aren't tied up or chained," I said. "Why don't they escape to the bank?"

A sudden volley of automatic weapon fire coming our direction answered my question. We hit the ground.

Standing in the distance along the edge of the dump was a motley collection of demons, each outfitted in military array as varied as the piles of weapons around us. Some wore black shirts and swastikas, some medieval armor, some camouflage fatigues, some furs and horned helmets. A few sported only war paint and wicked grins.

Whatever the outfit, each one held a weapon and kept it pointed toward the dump, watching for the first sign of someone trying to escape — or even trying to lift one limb out of the simmering blood. Any suspicious movement was immediately clobbered, shot or speared. A few desperate souls tried, but in the end they only suffered worse.

Three devils in Roman helmets and breastplates hurried toward us, shouting, as we stood up again. As they got closer I could see that their faces were a weird mix of human and wild beast — like the man in the old werewolf movies looked while he was still changing, halfway between man and monster. Their jaws were long and full of canine teeth, their ears pointy, and everywhere they were furry around the edges.

One of the demons toted a spear, one a mace and one a lead-tipped whip. "Make one move," shouted the spear-toter, "and it's out in the bubbles up to your ears!"

I panicked and reached for a club, but Miss C caught me by the elbow. "You are not a violent man, Thomas. You have nothing to fear. They may bluff, but they cannot detain you here. They have their orders. Let me deal with them."

"What are you doing with clothes on?" asked the demon with a whip. "Nobody here wears a uniform except us. And how did you sneak out of the moat without our seeing you?"

"We did not come from the moat," said Miss C, no sign of fear in her voice. "We came from above, and we are headed below. We seek only safe passage."

The devils guffawed, and the one with the spear twirled it. "If you're looking for safety," he said with a smirk, "you came to the wrong circle. Ever wondered what it feels like to be a shishkabob?" They laughed and slapped their thighs.

"Maybe you'd like to be up to your nose next to that pleasant little murderer over there," said the one with a mace, pointing to a man who was gargling the blood at gunpoint. "He forced his victims to drink battery acid before he put a bullet through their brains."

"Or maybe," said the whip demon, chuckling, "that hospitable cannibal next to him who just arrived. Collected recipes for liver pâté from the best restaurants of Europe, then went out on the streets, took in strangers and *had them for dinner*." The others jeered and snickered.

"Yeah," said the spear devil, "I heard he ate a Baptist, a Methodist and a Presbyterian, and the next day he had an *ecumenical movement*!" All three demons were screaming with laughter now, stomping their feet and holding their sides.

Miss C was not at all amused. "You have no claims on us here," she said, louder now to be heard over the noise. "You know you cannot stop us from going to a deeper circle. Take us to the bridge, and we will distract you from your pleasure no longer."

The spear devil eyed her long and hard, irritated that she'd called his bluff. He scratched his chin and looked past her toward the dump, biding his sweet time, hoping to get a rise out of her. She didn't budge.

Suddenly he grabbed Miss C around the waist, held her over his head and ran with her, kicking, to the edge of the dump where only the eyebrows showed. He looked at me over his shoulder as he dangled her above the blood, shouting, "Let's see if she can swim!"

I moved fast. Grabbing a bowie knife lying next to my foot, I charged the devil and took aim at his gut.

"Stop!" bellowed Miss C. "They want to trick you! If you stab him, they have a claim on you! Throw away the knife!"

I froze in my tracks, panting. Slowly I did as she said, but I was shaking all over. My own blood was boiling by now, my fists clenched, my teeth gritted. But that was as far as I could let it go.

They'll get theirs one day, I kept telling myself, shoving down the fury; they'll get theirs.

The devil dropped Miss C on the bank with a rude bump. She grimaced and rubbed herself where she landed, a sure bruise, and looked up in my direction. "Throw away your rage as well," she shouted. "In the end, the desire for vengeance will corrode your soul as surely as the act of murder. Let it go."

The soldier demons failed to hide their disappointment as they turned and began walking back toward the rest of their troop. The one with the spear turned around toward us and walked backward a few steps, cussing in gutter Latin. "We cannot keep you, wretches," he snarled, "but we refuse to help you. Find the bridge and cross it on your own."

Then he turned again and trotted off, barking orders at the other two. They stopped beside two male teenagers in the shallows, a black and a white, who'd managed to ease their agony by standing on one foot while leaning on each other.

"Hey, mister," said the white in a pleading tone, "we're cool now. We cut each other upstairs, you know, but down here we done kissed and made up. Give us some slack, man."

The whip cracked, and the boys fell moaning, face first in the blood. The demons went on.

I ran to help Miss C to her feet. "Are you hurt?"

"No, son, just a little flustered." She got up on her knees and then stood, pulling herself up with my hand. "That was a near-disaster for you, Thomas. But even so I must thank you for your courage on my behalf."

"What else could I have done?" I asked. "Besides, I didn't even stop to think about it. It was more instinct than courage."

"No," she said solemnly. "Self-defense would have been an instinct. That was something more, though just as deeply rooted."

We walked in silence for maybe half an hour among the piles of weapons, staying parallel to the moat but as far away as possible. The shrieks and wimpers unnerved me, but there was nothing I could do.

Suddenly Miss C stopped and turned to look me in the eye. "Thomas," she said in a voice that would have been gentle if it weren't fighting to be heard over the screams, "when we are quite young, we believe without question the words of those we need the most." She paused with a sigh. "Who told you that you were a coward — and when will you stop believing him?"

EIGHTEEN

Just ahead stretched a row of abandoned war tanks, and I was glad to have a reason not to answer Miss C's question. "Is this our bridge?" I asked. "They form a line across the shallow part there, and it looks like they reach all the way to the far side."

"Each time I come through, the bridge is different," said Miss C. "But I think you may be right. That is probably why it is so heavily guarded."

The guard demons were clustered around the first tank in line, which lay just at the edge of the moat. They wore sharp-looking hats and suits like the men in the old gangster movies, and they weren't smiling.

A swaggering devil dressed like Al Capone jerked his head in our direction. "Hey, yous! You wanna use the bridge, you pay. Whattaya got?"

Miss C and I looked at each other in confusion. Pay with what? What could we possibly have that they would want?

"Come on," said Capone. "You know what we're looking for. Weapons. Guns. Knives. Battle axes. Whatever. If it hurts, we want it. Now."

"Look," I said, "we don't carry anything like that. We're not here because we're violent. We're just on our way through."

"Not violent, huh?" said the demon, pointing to my belly. "You didn't pick up that pretty little tattoo playing dolls."

I looked down and winced. My brawl with the Burger Demon and his barbecue fork had left its mark: three pink scars the size of quarters, raised up half an inch like three new nipples. That's how it always looked when my wounds healed over — keloid scarring, the doctors called it.

"Well, that's a whole other story," I said. "I'm telling you, now, we don't have any weapons. What else do you want? Here's my wallet." Somehow that skinny wad of leather had survived in my buttoned-down pants pocket all this way. I tossed it out on a pile of ammo.

Capone spit on it. "Now what in hell do yous think we'd find to do with paper money, boy?" His eyes went to my right hand. "But that gold ring is a different matter. Not much to look at, but I gotta dame who likes trinkets."

It was my Daddy's old wedding band, a slip of yellow gold nearly worn through by the time he'd given it to me on his death-bed.

"Not on your life," I said, covering it with my other hand.

"It's *your* life we're talking about, jerk," said Capone. "Yous can give it to me, or we can cut it off." One of his buddies pulled out a switchblade long enough to slice a watermelon.

"He has us at his mercy," said Miss C. "He cannot detain you, but he can injure you. Nothing you possess is worth the risk. Your father would understand."

Slowly, my eyes burning, I twisted and tugged on the ring — I hadn't taken it off for years, and I was heavier now — until I could slip it off. I tossed it to Capone, and he caught it in midair.

"Need to teach him some manners," he said to Miss C. "Now how about it, colored girl? Yous gotta ticket to buy too."

I was hoping against hope that somewhere in one of her dress pockets was an old dubloon, a silver spoon, something. But she didn't reach for her pockets. After staring at Capone for what seemed like an eternity, she reached around her neck, under her collar, and pulled out the necklace the man in Sheol had given her. I could see it plainly now as she held it out to him: a silver cross on a silver chain, delicate and simple.

The demons stared at it wide-eyed, their jaws dropped open,

and Capone stretched out his hand as if to block the sight of it. "Get outta here!" he roared. "Don't ever come this way again!"

We didn't give them time to change their minds. I helped Miss C climb up the side of the first tank, then went up after her. From there it was a long and risky obstacle course across the dump, stepping from wheel to door to turret and over to the next tank's wheel again, all the while knowing that a single slip could poach us.

Even so, we made it across, all out of breath but safe — for now anyway. On the far side of the dump the pavement sloped gradually down toward the abyss, so this time we didn't have to go underground to reach the next level. In fact, I couldn't quite tell where the first ring ended and the second began; I guess we must have passed the border when we came to the first utility pole.

By then we'd caught our breath, and the slope was so gentle that our walk felt more like a stroll than the hike it had been before. The air around us was a gray twilight, almost cool, with a whisper of a breeze blowing. After being where we'd been, this place could even be called pleasant by comparison, though a sadness lingered there, so thick you could feel it brush by as you walked.

We walked on a vast stretch of pavement like the Cosmic Parking Lot, but black instead of gray. Everywhere stood rotting utility poles — street lights, power poles, telephone posts. They weren't arranged in neat rows but scattered out like giant, wooden weeds growing wild, their frayed wires flapping softly in the breeze. None were perfectly straight or upright; all were cracked and decayed and leaning wearily one way or another. In their tops were busted lamps, cracked insulators, gutted transformers, the rusty remains of what had once been electrical life.

We hadn't said much for a while now. It was such a relief to get away from that simmering chorus of pain in the dump, we just had to savor the near-silence. But I did have some questions, and it seemed better to go ahead and ask them while we weren't busy fleeing demons or fire or both.

I stopped and leaned against a telephone pole that tilted at a sharp angle. From the top of it hung a cable — tarnished copper, coated in crumbling black rubber — that dangled by my ear. I pointed at the flash of silver around Miss C's neck.

"Is that what the man around the campfire gave you?"

"Yes. It belongs to my sister. She left it with instructions to give it to me when I showed up. Perhaps she knew somehow I would need it."

"Why didn't you use it earlier to get the demons off our case? I sure could have used some help back at the health club."

Miss C sat down on the pavement. "I am sorry, Thomas, but I had no idea it would have that effect on them. I fully expected to lose it. Even now I am not certain it would stop them again; I think it simply caught them by surprise."

"Do you know the significance of the symbol?"

She looked at me with pain in her eyes. "Perhaps better than most of those who come here having worn one all their lives."

I looked away. My face smoldered with shame, though her intent had not been to shame me. Had I ever learned from anyone as much as I had learned so quickly from this old woman, a "heathen" slave from what was so glibly dubbed "the Dark Continent"?

How often over the years I'd looked with proud pity at the ghostly TV images of helpless Africans, stretching out bony hands to be saved by the overflow of Western plenty. I'd never known it till now, but somehow those pictures had spilled over onto all the black faces I'd ever seen, a beam in my eye that kept me looking for motes in theirs.

Yet here before me, in the true dark continent, was the reality I had missed, or ignored. In her wide, steady eyes I saw the noble and chastened soul of Africa, strong and serene. Here was a woman looking down the corridor of eternity to the nightmare of judgment at its end — and walking bravely toward it nevertheless, in order to lead me along.

I knelt, reached out and took her hand. "Why?" I whispered, my voice cracking. "Why would someone without hope risk the horrors of deep hell to help me find my way? Why would you do all this if you truly believe that in the end God has abandoned you?"

She gazed into the distance. "God has loved to the point of dying a horrible death of His own so that men and women would not have to languish here for eternity. He stooped from heaven to hell to suffer alone these depths of disgrace and pain. Was ever there love like that? Even if it does not reach to where I am, such love deserves my homage."

"But you could pay homage while remaining safely in the shadows of Sheol," I said. "Why are you enduring so much for a stranger who deserves so little?"

"Though I cannot hope to see God face-to-face, yet I can draw close to Him by wearing His humility and sharing in His sufferings. Even an orphan can take comfort in following the footsteps of a father she will never embrace, wrapping herself in the cloak He has left behind."

"Maybe you'll embrace Him after all; maybe He'll come in the end."

"He already came once, Thomas; but I was born in the wrong time and place."

"Could a love so far-reaching be yet so unfair?"

"Think of it, Thomas. The Jewish nation had no idea for centuries that they might hope for heaven, for an eternal life in the presence of God. They hoped for an earthly messiah and his kingdom, but after death all they had to look forward to was Sheol. Abraham, Moses, David, Isaiah, thousands of others served God faithfully with no promise of eternal reward. As far as they knew, that shadowy land was their everlasting lot — and yet they still gave their lives to God. Our notion of fairness is often only a matter of our expectations."

"But what if those people had known of heaven and yet believed that they'd be banished from it? Do you think they still would have served God?"

"I cannot speak for them. Yet even your apostle Paul once said that he could wish himself accursed if it would mean others would be saved. I remain an orphan, Thomas. But sometimes I get to lead the children home, and when I do, I catch a crumb from the table where I myself can never be seated."

"Don't even the crumbs ever feed your hope?"

"They feed my longing, and because longing is all I have, I am grateful."

I stood up straight and leaned against the telephone pole again. "If I ever escape this place," I said, "then my hope is to see Him one day, face-to-face. This is my promise, Miss C: On that day, I'll beg Him to come back for you."

She looked up at me through a single, shining tear in each eye. "If," she said, her voice trembling, "you ever escape this place."

─────── NINETEEN ───────

The breeze was stiffer now, and occasional gusts would make the twisted, broken crossbeams on the poles bend and groan, and the flapping cables whistle. For the first time I noticed that every pole stood solitary, no two connected by wires — the lines between them had all been severed, black fingers now hanging powerless in the gray air.

"This one circle I *do* remember from Dante," I said to Miss C, waving my hand in an arc toward the horizon. "And if my memory serves me right, Dante called it the *Forest of the Suicides*. But all I see are utility poles, not trees."

"By now you surely must realize that many things have changed here since Dante's day," she said. "Hell is fast petrifying, and the closer the great Day approaches, the less in it that appears to have even the semblance of living things."

"To be honest," I said, "I would have expected hell to be a wild, unearthly place, like an eerie moonscape on fire. But instead it reminds me of places I've been before, all urban: choking smog, cracked asphalt, rusted sewers, rotted buildings. Why does hell look so much like the inner city of the late twentieth century?"

"Perhaps you have answered your own question," said Miss C.

"Hell, after all, is not a natural thing, a part of the handiwork God initially called good. No, it is artificial; the demon and human races have built it with the sin of their own hands. Like even the finest engineering feats in the upper world, hell is doomed to decay. Your corroding cities are even now getting a foretaste of this judgment; they are merely concrete prophecies of the misery here."

The phone cable that had been dangling by my ear caught a gust and slapped against my nose. I grabbed it and gave a yank, hoping to pull it loose and toss it on the ground.

The cable screamed.

I dropped that line as if it were a coiled copperhead, my heart clanging on the bars of my rib cage.

I didn't know what to make of it, but Miss C was cool. I looked at her, then looked at the cable, then looked at her again. Swallowing hard, I finally asked, "What was *that*?"

"You would scream too if someone did that to you," she said, slow and sober and a little sad, I thought.

Then I heard a low moaning, not in the wind this time, but coming right out of the crumbling wood of that telephone pole and from all the poles around. These things were *alive* — or I should say they were dead like everybody else down here, and they were making noise like all the rest.

Now devils and dead souls are one thing, but screaming telephone poles are another. That was stretching the limit, and I was beginning to wonder if this might all be a bad dream after all.

Miss C could tell I was getting rattled. "Thomas," she said, "you must understand: The souls of the suicides are imprisoned within those scarred wooden posts. Jerk on a wire like that, and you might as well be snatching someone's hair out. It feels the same to them."

The fire had been terrible, and the blood, horrible; but this was just plain spooky. Souls trapped in poles, with wires that hurt? Where was the sense in it?

I looked at Miss C with a look that said I needed an explanation. She obliged. "Those who take their own lives declare their independence, in the most final way, from the rest of the world, and from heaven as well. In suicide they sever themselves from love and life, from help and hope; they cut themselves off from the power of grace."

121

"And so their souls are stuck here," I said, "one by one, in solitary confinement in these posts...never to be hooked up to the others?"

"It is a lonely fate of their own choosing. They have said to God, 'My life is mine to do with as I please. Leave me alone.' A fearful demand — but God grants it."

"Can they talk?"

"They have lost the power to communicate, save for screams of pain or moans of grief."

"Can they *move*?" I asked, looking at the ones closest to me and beginning to feel like Dorothy picking apples in Oz. "I mean, I know they're stuck fast down in the pavement, but can they lean over when they want to, or swing their crossbeams and cables?"

"You can relax," she said. "They only move when the wind pushes them. The wood and the wire are their jail cell — their doom is not just to be utterly isolated, but utterly confined as well."

I shuddered all the way to my toes. Like being buried alive in a tight, pine-box coffin, where you can't even budge a finger, and the inside of the lid is pressed so hard against your face you've got splinters in your lips, and it makes your nose itch, but of course you can't scratch it. Ever.

Next to that, Granddaddy's outhouse was a five-star suite.

Just then the distant sound of metal grating on pavement pulled our heads in its direction, way behind me where the poles looked smaller and more crowded because they stood so far away. As the noise grew louder we heard a voice as well, as rough as the asphalt, chanting words somewhere between a whisper and a groan.

I knew the words. My mama used to sing them when she was feeling low. She'd sing about whippoorwills too blue to fly, and leaves dying; losing the will to live, and being so lonesome she could cry....

At last he came into view: A somber-faced demon, all alone, dressed in black like a gravedigger and dragging a pickax behind him as he came. He was looking down all the while he walked toward us and kept up his gravelly chant until he stopped, only a few yards from where we stood.

He looked up at us, his deathly white face not smiling but not frowning either, and said: "Don't get much company in these parts. You must be passing through."

"That we are," I said, glad to see the pickax was the closest thing to a weapon he had. "In fact, we were just moving on."

"That's good," he said, jerking his thumb at Miss C, " 'cause the next hole I'm digging will be right where she's sitting."

I gave her a hand and pulled her up. "By the way," I said to the digger, "you know, there's a tune to go with those words you were saying. Why don't you sing it?"

He furrowed his brow and shook his head as if I were talking nonsense. "This is *hell*, mister," he said. "You'll never hear music in hell. In this place, whatever ain't noise is dead silence."

Come to think of it, he was right. The whole time I'd been here, I'd never heard the first note.

We turned and started on our way.

"This one was as crazy as they come," he said, as if he wasn't ready for us to go *that* soon. We stopped and turned back toward him, not sure what to say.

"I mean," he said, scratching his head, "she starved herself to death, but she was living in Beverly Hills and could have all the food she wanted. Anorexic, they called her."

"Not crazy," said Miss C, "but full of self-hatred. The death wish can hide itself within obsessions of all kinds. I would guess you also have dug holes for alcoholics who died of liver disease and workaholics who died of heart attacks. A slow suicide, but suicide all the same."

"But they're like the gluttons," I protested. "They may not have realized what they were doing."

"Yes," she said, nodding. "And like the gluttons, however chained their wills became, they still had the chance to ask for grace. There are anorexics in heaven as well. But the ones here refused heaven's aid."

I looked out at the thousands of poles surrounding us. "Have you dug the holes for all these?" I asked the digger.

"This whole sector is mine," he said, with obvious pride, rubbing his hands together. "That one over there came down in the big stock market crash — jumped from an office window and redecorated Wall Street."

He pointed to another nearby. "That one lost his job, had a wife and five kids, didn't want to take a handout. Finally reckoned he'd rather lose his life than his pride; put a bullet through his own head, and the dog found him on the kitchen floor."

"What about those two leaning toward each other?" I asked.

"Real-life Romeo and Juliet; just young 'uns," he said. "Worshipped each other and died for puppy love that wasn't love at all. I put 'em close together, but not close enough to touch. We got regulations, you know."

He shrugged and waved his hands out toward the horizon. "Of course, they're coming in like a flood now, and we're gonna have to put 'em closer together anyway so we don't run out of room. Shoot — *some*body up there's doing a good job of talking 'em into killing theirselves."

I bit my lip, thinking of the news stories I'd read about doctors with suicide machines and manuals, supported by the Right to Die Society. "In the upper world now," I said to Miss C, "they're arguing over whether people ought to be allowed to kill themselves when they're so sick they're going to die anyway — or when the pain is just more than they can handle."

"I know their plight well," said Miss C grimly. "I myself died slowly, tortuously, as my bones rotted away — your generation would call it cancer — and that in a day when no medicine known could dull the agony. Perhaps all those of us who must face such a dreadful ordeal are in the end judged more mercifully than we dare hope. But few would even debate the issue if they knew death was no true escape. It is a terrible truth, but truth no less. Pain can be redemptive if it is washed of bitterness; but we must choose to let it refine instead of corrode us."

A truth known too late for all these locked up in poles around me. How different it might have been if they had known that the universe bears a sign downstairs marked NO EXIT.

I looked out at the scattered forest of poles, and they looked different now. I could see in their dark silhouettes the twisted, weary shape of everlasting despair. At first I'd thought this place less woeful than some of the circles above; but could the fires there hurt any worse than the fearsome ache of an eternity alone?

To think of all the empty nights I'd felt so low I'd had to look up to see the bottom, and that dangling little notion would go flapping around in my head for hours without letting up: *Just end it all.* How many times had I stepped right up to the edge of this black asphalt, playing with that notion, tugging on it and slipping it through my fingers, while some demon was digging a hole in the ground, ready to put my name on it?

The digger was breaking through the asphalt now, whispering a new chant about how rainy days and Mondays always got him down. I gripped Miss C's arm. "I want out of this place, right now, and I never want to lay eyes on another street light."

"We will need no street lights where we are traveling next," she said. "In fact, you will long for a shade to cover your eyes — even more, a shirt for your back. And you will count it a grace that you still have your shoes."

I looked down at the tattered scraps of leather clinging to my feet. They were all that was left of what had once been Daddy's favorite loafers — now my favorites, ever since he died. I hated the thought of losing them, but I doubted they could last through another round of action like the ones we'd been through.

I looked at Miss C's shoes, a little envious. They were still in good shape. I guess, as Daddy always said, they don't make things like they used to.

"From the looks of these," I said, holding up a foot, "I may end up barefoot whether I want to or not." I turned to the digger. "How fast can you build up a callus in hell?"

He stopped his chant and looked down at his grimy hands. For the first time he grinned. "I been digging now since Cleopatra's snake sent her down with a kiss," he said, "and I ain't got no callus yet. Tell me, boy: How fast can you run?"

TWENTY

Those utility poles were at last thinning out again. The pavement dropped lower and lower, with steep curbs that formed steps down in an asphalt terrace. The air was still gray, except thicker and brighter now; it even began to hurt my eyes, like a night fog on the road that throws your bright head beams back at you. But I couldn't figure out where the light was coming from.

Soon we came to a wall, too high for me to see its top in the blinding gray. It was a dark, soft metal — lead, as far as I could tell — and the way it curved away from us toward both horizons, I figured it must follow the arc of the abyss. The lead was searing hot.

We walked along it to the left, far enough away not to chance burning ourselves, hunting for a door Miss C was sure would appear somewhere.

"How do you know which way to turn?" I asked as she scanned the wall ahead of us.

"To the left, Thomas. The descent into hell is one long turn to the left."

"Are we in the third ring yet?"

"This is its outer boundary. The realm of those who were violent toward God."

I was puzzled. "Violent toward God? I've seen somebody shake his fist at heaven before and even challenge God to come down and fight like a man. But that's a fight nobody could ever win. How could you whomp up on God?"

"All sin causes Him pain," she said, "and you should not forget there was a day when men not only beat Him but murdered Him as well. Even so, we are dealing with something different here."

"So what sort of divine injury are we talking about?" I asked. Now she'd riled my curiosity.

"Tell me: What two kinds of injury toward human beings were punished in the first ring?"

"Malicious acts either against somebody's person or against their property," I said. "That's why murderers and rapists were boiling next to looters and vandals — though deeper in the blood."

"Yes, of course. And the case is much the same with God. People can injure Him by acts against His Name, which is the closest they can get to His Person — except, as I have heard, in the bread and cup. Or they can do violence to God by committing acts against nature itself, which is His own property and handiwork."

That was more than I could chew on all at once. "So who is it that does violence to God's name?"

"The blasphemer and the atheist. The one profanes it; the other mocks it."

"Are crimes against nature what I think they are?"

"If you mean homosexual acts, yes, as well as a few other sins you may never have recognized as unnatural. In addition, sins against art are punished here."

"Sins against art?" I was taken aback by that one. I'd seen some displays in public galleries that were ugly as sin, but I'd always thought the ones who ought to be whipped for it were the fools who bought the stuff in the first place.

"Art," said Miss C, "imitates God's workmanship in nature. It is born in the creative human spirit that is the image of God's own Spirit of creation. In a sense, then, God is the grandfather of art — so to sin against it is much the same as sinning against nature, and against God Himself."

I thought back to a sculpture I'd seen once visiting the Yale campus: a mess of steel shaped like a missile sitting on the bottom half of an army tank. The top part of the tube was painted red. This work of artistic genius was called "Lipstick Ascending on Caterpillar Treads."

Maybe the notion of "sin against art" made sense after all. I was just about to tell Miss C all about that Ivy League masterpiece when she stopped and pointed ahead. "Look! The door."

It was a skinny lead portal as hot as the wall. Miss C took the handle, using the edge of her dress as a mitten. "The wall leans inward a few feet," she said, still holding it shut. "Stay close to it, in its shadow — it will protect you from at least some of the danger for a little while."

She pushed against the door with her shoulder, and it slowly opened, creaking a protest. Beyond it lay a vast plain of blinding white ash. It smoldered red-hot in some places, blazed white-hot in others and was pocked by hundreds of huge craters. The charred, twisted skeletons of what might once have been cities were strown out in clusters as far as we could see.

Towering above the whole, dazzling like a puffy bolt of lightning suspended in space, was a mushroom cloud.

I froze. *The Bomb.* That caustic ghost that hung over my cold-war childhood, eating away at my confidence that the human race could survive its global death wish. From the deepest cellar of my memory it was here to haunt me, face-to-face: a nuclear Sodom and Gomorrah.

The cloud was snowing fire. Everywhere the air was filled with sticky, burning flakes, glowing cinders that fluttered as they fell in the arid wind that swept the ground. How many radioactive particles danced unseen among those falling sparks?

"Do you know what nuclear radiation can *do* to people?" I asked.

"Unnatural things," said Miss C. "Deformed babies. Hair falling out like withered leaves. Hideous tumors and blood corrupted from flowing life into creeping death. Mortal sickness of every kind. And no wonder — the bomb that causes it all is itself unnatural, wrought by the forced mutation of matter into energy."

"It's not safe here! The wall may keep off most of the cinders, but the radiation can still get us."

"Only if we have touched the sins punished here can we be

128

touched by the sickness," she said. "Are you at risk?"

I didn't answer. I knew I was safe when it came to blasphemy. It had never been my habit to cuss in any style — even when I hadn't feared God, I'd had too much respect for language to cheapen it that way. Foul talk was a habit of dull or lazy minds. Of course, in the theology department we were always telling sacrilegious jokes....

The atheists were here too, she'd said. But before I took that fall, I'd usually insisted I was just an agnostic — you know, I didn't deny the existence of God; I just said we couldn't know for sure whether He was there or not. That didn't count, did it?

Then again, she'd said, there were some sins I wouldn't have thought unnatural that were. And what about the things I'd never done but thought about doing, and might have done if only I'd had the opportunity? *The heart is deceitful above all things*.... I could already feel my hair getting loose.

Miss C offered me her calico scarf for my head, but I insisted she use it instead. A singed bald scalp was bad, but if her thick white hair caught on fire, we'd have big trouble. Shading our eyes with our hands, we started walking, again to the left, close to the wall where the cinders only came in if the wind blew them.

The wind was steady, so I was fast getting little burns all over my torso. My pants more or less shielded my legs, but they were beginning to look like a chain-smoker's coffee table. Miss C had scorch marks everywhere on her scarf and dress. We both were slapping and dancing as we moved, like two kids clogging at the county fair.

I stole a glance out at the ashen wilderness — I couldn't look into the blinding white for more than a second or two. It was then that I first realized something more out there than the fire flakes were moving. So far away I could hardly see them, darting between the charred ruins and rolling around on the white-hot ground, were the damned souls of the third ring.

I don't know just where I'd expected them to be, but somehow I hadn't thought they could be out *there*. Not in that sea of death. Maybe I was hoping we'd pass them sooner or later along the wall, sheltered at least a little from the fire, even if they had to fight for space in the shadow. Maybe I'd hoped there weren't so many blasphemers, atheists and "unnaturals" after all.

But now I knew it was a different story altogether: The more I squinted and got a better look, the more I saw that the plain was crawling — and twisting, running, writhing, jumping — with people.

"How could there be so many?" I asked Miss C, brushing the sparks off, but not fast enough.

"So many flakes?"

"So many souls!"

"You have lived in the twentieth century, and you ask such a question? The numbers were only half these before your generation came along."

I was about to launch into a halfhearted defense of my generation when we nearly stumbled over two souls, a male and a female, totally bald and toothless, who somehow had found their way to the shadow of the wall. Little good it did them: The woman lay flat on her back in the white-hot cinders, only one big toe in the shade of the wall. Her eyes were stretched wide, full of rage and ashes, her clenched fists raised in defiance. Screaming for who knows how long, she'd grown hoarse, and her whole body was fried to cracklings.

The man crouched beside her, scooping up the burning debris and dumping it on his head, then rubbing it all over his scorched body and muttering at the ground. Neither one had any idea the other was present, much less that we too were standing near.

I bent down close to the woman's mouth. My ear was scorched, not from the flakes, but from the profanities she was spouting — words that would make a sailor blush on Saturday night.

The man was a little easier to understand, though his vacant gums had trouble forming the words. He spoke low, not hoarse, only mumbling to himself.

"There are no moral phenomena, only moral interpretations of phenomena.... Kicked by a *stupid horse*.... The great epochs of our lives come when we gain the courage to rebaptize our evil as our best.... Everything absolute belongs in the realm of pathology...."

I'd read all those words somewhere before — a reading assignment for a theology course, I was sure. Did he say "kicked by a horse"? That's how Friedrich Nietzsche died, summer of 1900.

"For still our ancient foe doth seek to work us woe.... The devil has the farthest perspectives for God — that is why he stays so far away from him. The devil, in other words, is the oldest friend of insight...."

Yes, that was Nietzsche all right. Son of a Lutheran pastor. Nineteenth-century German king of the flaming atheists, philosophical granddaddy of the Third Reich. Lost his mind long before he died; spent the last twelve years of his life insane.

"God is dead!" he shouted, grinning now at the mushroom cloud. "God remains dead! And we have killed Him! Dead, dead, *dead!*" Maniacal laughter, then he stared long and hard at the ashes swirling around him. "Gaze long into an abyss, the abyss will gaze back into you...."

As we walked away, he was stuffing handfuls of glowing embers into his mouth.

Miss C shook her head sadly. *"The fool hath said in his heart, 'There is no God.' "*

"You know, the atheists of his day considered him a courageous prophet."

"He was indeed a prophet," she said. "With remarkable clarity he foresaw his own damnable fate."

The flakes were falling in large clumps now, and the wind was blowing them into the shade. We walked faster and soon stopped talking. All our attention was focused on slapping away the sparks. The hem of Miss C's dress caught fire twice, and we had to beat out the flames.

Meanwhile, my shoes and pants were smoking, my eyes were stinging, and my scalp was scorched so badly I had to wonder if the few hairs I'd had left before were now burned away...or had fallen out.

──── TWENTY-ONE ────

Just when I thought there was no place left on my back to get burned, I heard Miss C shout, "There it is!" She was pointing ahead toward a straight canal, maybe ten feet wide, that began at the wall and stretched out across the plain as far as I could see. It was brilliant red, with a sparkling pink mist that hung just over it but spread out no farther.

As we got closer, that old familiar smell hit me, and I knew we were looking at blood. I could see it better now: The red bubbled up thickly at the wall — flowing in, I guessed, from the other side — then meandered on down the concrete trough that cut through the flaming ground.

Miss C broke into a run, shouting, "The mist will protect us — run to the blood!"

I hoofed it to the canal's edge and jumped in feet first, not knowing how deep it might be. Relief: It was only an inch deep and not boiling this time. The mist wasn't heavy, but it doused the fire flakes nonetheless, and I was grateful.

Miss C was standing next to me, looking at the burn holes that peppered her dress.

"Why didn't you tell me about this canal?" I asked, panting.

"I feared that if I told you first we would be walking in blood, you would protest. But I knew that once you had walked a mile in the fiery snow, you would not hesitate to welcome even so grisly a refuge as this. It is the only way we could possibly cross the plain." She had me figured out pretty well by now.

My loafers had stopped smoking, but they were little more than two bloody clumps of leather. I pointed down at them and wrinkled up my nose. "I hate to see them go, but I just might trip myself up on these. Maybe I'd do just as well to get rid of them."

"No," she said with a disturbing firmness. "You will need them for our journey across the ice of Cocytus."

Ice should have sounded good right about then, but the way she said it, I didn't get my hopes up. "Does that come next?" I asked.

"Oh, no. Cocytus is in deepest hell — circle nine. Circle eight comes first, with ten pits — actually they are great concrete trenches — of its own."

I didn't even ask. I didn't want to know.

"I see the sparks have been cruel to you," she said gently, looking over my singed back and shoulders. "I wish you had taken the scarf."

"It's OK now," I said, lying. If the truth were told, my back felt like a tin roof on an August afternoon. "But tell me: Why don't the souls out there come get in the blood too? Somebody must have found out about it by now."

She nodded. "They know about it, but they have their guards, just like those in the boiling blood. If anyone is caught trying to gain even a moment's relief, they must lie down in the embers without moving a muscle and be covered with flakes for a hundred years. Not many have been so brave as to make the attempt."

"I haven't seen any guards yet."

"In this ring they are secret police. They disguise themselves as doomed souls and then infiltrate the crowds. One never knows for sure who is watching; the tactic is most effective."

"Will they try to stop us?" I thought about how it would feel to sunbathe in gamma rays in a barbecue pit for a century, and winced.

"I have never had a problem with them here before, since I am wearing clothes. As long as you have on at least one item of dress, in this ring they assume you are passing through and are on your way down."

My pants still hung loose without a belt and looked like a slaughterhouse rag. But I was mighty proud, as Mama used to say, to have them all the same. Even so, I was wishing that I'd gotten in the habit of wearing socks with my loafers. At least the holes in my socks might not have matched up with the holes that yawned now in my shoes.

We started out down the canal, and soon it passed through a chain of blackened ruins where souls clustered in groaning mobs. I kept to the center of the current and hardly dared to look up. The scene around me was too full of anguish to watch, too full of people I might know too well. My stomach was turning, slow but steady.

A sharp scream pierced the air, louder than all the others, followed by a roar of angry voices cussing. I looked up to see two furious crowds facing each other, fists clenched even as they batted at the sparks.

"You!" shrieked a small woman whose short hair, still hanging on, let me know she'd only recently arrived. "What are *you* doing here with *us*? You ought to be with the murderers!" The souls on her side thundered their approval with jeers.

A tall man with a potbelly, his scruffy beard a sign that he too was new here, poked his finger in her face. "Looky here, Miss Savior of the Wharf Rats, I don't know why I'm here *period* — but I sure don't relish spending eternity with the likes of *you* either. Last time I saw you, you were out there protesting under the hospital room window of a man in critical condition — just because they'd saved his life with a baboon liver! You're just plain *crazy*, you old witch!"

"How dare you!" the woman said, swinging at him, but he ducked and she missed. "Animal life is just as valuable as human life. Why should a baboon die so that a man can live?"

"If you don't know the answer to that question, woman, you belong in a cage yourself." His side of the mob was cheering now, and inching closer to the others. "In case you hadn't noticed, I don't see any animals down here. People got souls; animals ain't. That's just the facts of life."

"Maybe they're all in heaven," said the woman soberly.

"Animals in heaven!" The potbelly's voice boiled with sarcasm. "Where would they put all the *horseflies*?"

She smirked. "A heaven for horseflies and a hell for the likes of you could be conveniently combined."

"Aw, shut up, Snow White. Animals ain't got souls; they're just dirt in motion. You shoot 'em, and that's the end — back to the dirt."

"Is that why you felt justified in killing animals for sport?" said a thin man beside her, one hand on his hip, the other slapping fire. "How could you take pleasure in terrifying helpless little deer while you stalked them and then blew their brains out? You think there was nothing immoral about *that*? Evidently it didn't do *your* little redneck soul any good because here you are!"

The potbelly grabbed the thin man by his neck and lifted him off the ground. "Look, wimp — all I done was a little hunting now and then, and there ain't no law against it. Critters were *made* for me to have fun shooting — that's why God put 'em on this earth. And if I had a gun right now," he said, dropping the man into the cinders, "I'd take just as much pleasure in shooting you."

Miss Short Hair jumped back into the argument. "The Jewish Holocaust was nothing compared to what goes on at chicken slaughterhouses every day. You have no right to hunt, eat meat, ride horses or even kill mosquitoes. All species on the planet are equal."

The potbelly guffawed. "Typhoid's a species too — what have you done to help *those* little critters lately? Why don't you just go stick your head in a hornets' nest and ask 'em if they appreciate all you've done for 'em!"

The mob finally reached flash point, and as we walked on, a deep fried riot was in full swing.

"Violence against nature," I said to Miss C. "I can see it in that hunter who takes some kind of twisted pleasure in hurting living things — who violates the nature of animals by treating them like inanimate dirt. But why are the radical animal rights activists here?"

"You do violence to human nature as well as animal nature when you put them on the same par," said Miss C. "We alone were made in the image of God. Did a baboon ever perform an organ transplant? Of course, we have no right to abuse other species; but to say that the victims of concentration camps are worth no more than chickens is worse than idiocy — it is blasphemy."

We passed on in silence for a while, till one more question popped into my head. "Is it true there aren't any animals here?"

"You saw the rats and worms yourself higher up," said Miss C. "Farther down you will see serpents as well."

My stomach was twisting tighter than ever.

"There used to be vicious hounds in the ring we just left," she went on, "but the sin they punished is uncommon now. So they are confined to a distant corner of the ring with their human prey."

My curiosity was scratched about the hounds, but it sounded too grisly to pursue. "I don't understand. So these are all animals that were somehow *wicked*?"

She frowned. "I am not even sure whether they ever existed in the upper world; they may simply have been created for this place. But even if this is for them an afterlife, it is by no means a punishment; they hunt and devour here with great pleasure. As the woman just said, some might even find it a sort of heaven."

The mushroom cloud loomed even brighter now, and though the mist kept off the fire flakes, I was wishing I had some shades for my eyes, just as Miss C had predicted. Soon we came near a pile of charred wood that looked like the remains of a long wharf. The blackened rib cages of several large boats were scattered around it, half-sunk now in a sea of white ash. Miss C pulled her scarf over her face.

"We must hurry through this place," she said, her eyes darting from side to side. "It is not safe."

I decided to wait until we were safe to ask what the danger was, and I started walking in high gear. Then suddenly the smoldering beams in one of the ship skeletons up ahead of us were pushed outward, and three souls leaped out — white males burnt black all over. They dashed to the canal and jumped in, then turned toward us.

"Good day," said the tallest one in a sinister voice. They stationed themselves across the canal's width to block us, then began scooping up the blood and bathing in it.

"Slave traders," whispered Miss C in my ear. "They have grown even bolder than before."

We kept walking slowly, but the same one who'd spoken stepped up close in front of us and held out a skull-tattooed arm.

"You wouldn't be thinking of leaving us, would you?" he said, smirking at Miss C. "It's been so long, you know, since we had the pleasure of dealing in black flesh, and this seems an opportunity we can't pass up, now, can we?"

He snickered as the other two closed in on us. "She'd bring a pretty penny on the market out there, shoveling ashes, you think? That is, if there's a soul around who's not too busy slapping fire to strike a bargain."

He looked me over now. "And I daresay white skin could bring a premium, mates."

"What are you doing in the canal?" I demanded. "You know what will happen if the police find you here."

"Well, now, I don't see any police — do *you* see any police, boys?"

"Not a one," said the shortest, his eyes flashing. "We know who we are, and we know who you are, since you're wearing clothes," he said to us. "So among the five of us, we reckon, there's no secret police to be found, now, is there?"

He grinned a toothless grin and turned to his bald buddies. "And if there's no police, we can take our ease in the sweet blood and have a little fun besides, eh, boys?"

The grin spread to all three faces like a plague. "Let's teach them a lesson first," said the third man, who was missing an arm. He raised the one fist he had. "Just so they'll never forget how outrageous it is that slaves should walk free while their old masters are confined."

"Hold it right there!" boomed a deep voice from the ruins. "Move an inch, and your carcasses will fry."

Out came a tall male, built like a boxer, singed over much of his body but head-turning handsome even through the burns. He swaggered up to the canal's edge and climbed in, glowering.

"So you thought we weren't watching, you gumbo brains," he said. "Don't you know we have eyes everywhere? You can't escape us — ever. Get out of the canal now."

The slavers froze in their tracks. "We were just playing with them, you know? Just a game, that's all."

"Let's see. That's one century each for harassing these two," said the cop. "How'd you like to snuggle for two hundred years with the Devil's own bed warmer?"

"It's not fair," said the tallest slaver, whining now. "That African there don't even have a soul; she's no more than a black mule to be brought to market. But there she is, walking free, and here we are, decent human beings cast out in a heap of ashes like the sweepings from the hearth."

The policeman scowled. "Add another century for resisting an officer."

All three fell to their knees. "Please," begged the one-arm, "have mercy. We won't do it again. Just let us go. We'll run to the farthest reaches of this blasted plain and never set foot near the canal again. You'll see!"

Slowly the cop turned to each one and looked them in the eye with a gaze that would have turned them to blue ice anywhere else. "I'll let you run this time. But I'm making a note of it. And if we ever find you within a mile of this place, we'll bury you head down for the next thousand years with a flaming ship's mast stuffed down your throat. Got it?"

They got it. Stumbling over one another to get away, they ran for the horizon, screaming curses and knocking the sparks off their heads.

"Come with me," said the policeman, briskly. "You've been here much too long already."

We obeyed without a word and followed him down the canal, hoping he meant to get us out of there as soon as possible. I knew Miss C said she'd never had trouble with the police here, but there's always a first time. How can you trust a devil?

I sneaked a long stare at the guy. Thank goodness the demons made themselves look perfectly human in this ring. I wouldn't relish walking far with one of those dog faces back at the boiling blood, or even the pale face with the pickax. This guy could actually pass for a *GQ* cover that was left too close to the stove, though he looked older than most of the models you see in that rag. I never knew a demon could be so good-looking, even one in disguise.

Odd to say, something about him looked familiar.

"Over there on the left," he said, as cheerful-sounding as a tour guide, "you'll see a large crowd of ring three's most disgusting low-life."

So even the demons had their own system for ranking sin. Who would they think were the worst sinners? I took a guess. "You mean homosexuals?" I asked.

He stopped dead still, his face suddenly stony. "No." The voice was as hard as the face. "Most of those have been banished to the outskirts of the desert by the other groups here. Hell isn't known for its tolerance." He started walking again, but at a stiffer pace, and the cheerfulness had died.

I thought it best to keep talking; maybe I could find out something useful. "My mistake. So who are these souls, then?"

"Userers. You know — loan sharks, greedy bankers, junk-bond kings, those types."

"I remember that Dante said they were here. But I never really understood: Why would they be judged as having committed an act against nature?"

The policeman's face was loosening up again; he seemed amused. "Well, just think about what they're here for: charging exorbitant interest. What were they really doing when they did that? They were sticking two pieces of hard, shiny metal together — money that by its nature is lifeless and sterile — and they were forcing it to reproduce like rabbits. What could be more unnatural than that?"

He had a point, but it was scary to think about. Where did they draw the line? Did little old ladies with 3-percent life savings accounts come here too?

We were falling back into a stroll now, with Miss C trailing a few steps behind, silent in her own thoughts. I was beginning to feel almost safe. Back in the role of tour guide, the cop pointed out clusters of ruins where people whose names I might know were last seen — all once famous for their homosexual behavior: some of Plato's buddies, the Roman emperor Hadrian, Richard the Lion Heart, King Edward II. At times he sounded proud to have them there, though I never would have thought that fame counted for much in hell, especially among the devils.

The last ruins we'd passed were now only a speck in the distance; we could see no one and nothing but endless white ash. The cop slowed down to a saunter and then a stop.

He turned to me, grabbed my arm and barked an order: "Take off your pants."

TWENTY-TWO

I shook my head to try to clear my ears out. "What did you say?"

"I said take your pants off — now."

I looked at Miss C in disbelief, but she was silent. "What does a devil in hell want with my pants?" I asked.

His eyes were steely blue, and they bored through me. "I'm not a devil. I'm human. I just put on that act back there to get rid of those creeps. Take off the pants *now*."

"I had my suspicions," said Miss C, not looking much relieved that he wasn't a demon after all. "But I must admit that was a convincing performance."

"Let's just say I've had lots of practice."

Miss C's voice lowered. "What crime sent you here?"

His mouth turned up in a mock smile. " 'Sodomy,' as they call it, though it's hardly a crime. As I figure it, I got sent here by a straight God who slipped up and made me gay, but doesn't like what He made. He blew it, but I have to pay the price — that's justice for you, huh?"

He turned to me. "Now take off your pants before I have to take them off you myself."

He was badly burned and had to be hurting, but with a build like that he could no doubt overpower me anyway. Still, I tried to stall him.

"Look," I said, stepping back, "this is *hell!* You wouldn't try to make me have *sex* with you in *hell!*"

He threw back his head and laughed, with more than a touch of bitterness. "Don't be silly. You think I want your *body*? You troglodyte — I want your *pants*. Give them to me *quick*, before somebody else comes along. You want them to fry you two for aiding and abetting a criminal?"

I didn't quite follow the logic, but he was sure to know better how things were done here than I did. I looked at Miss C, my eyes a question mark.

"Are you wearing something else underneath?" she asked. I nodded. "Better to do as he says for now, then," she said, frowning. "As long as you are wearing something, you should be safe from the *real* police."

"Now you're getting the picture," said the aging hunk. "If I'm wearing your pants, they won't suspect me either. Look — you owe me one for saving your skins back there. And besides, maybe I could provide you with some other service." The last words he said looking me straight in the eyes, as if Miss C weren't even there.

I was glad just then to be wearing boxer shorts; bikini briefs would have looked even worse on me in hell than they did upstairs. I pulled off my pants — ragged, scorched and blood-spattered as they were — and handed them to the man.

"No belt?" he said, studying my midsection. "The waist will be a little roomy, you know. But I guess it will do."

He slid them on, and though his waist was too small, his hips and thighs fit snug — what I had stuffed there with fat, he filled up with muscle. "We'd better get going now. There really *are* eyes everywhere."

"How is your stomach feeling, Thomas?" asked Miss C as we started out again.

I shrugged. "I'll be all right." But my insides were hurting worse than ever, and I suddenly felt tired, much more tired than a long walk could ever have made me.

"Tell us your name," said Miss C to our new companion when

we had walked a spell.

"Stone Jordan," he said.

Bells went off in my head. *Stone Jordan*. The heartthrob who'd haunted the big screen back in the early sixties?

That's why his face had been somehow familiar. Though he'd never been what you might call a star, he'd played second fiddle to some of the biggest names in teenage movies, and he'd always played the devilishly handsome cad. In those days there wasn't much to do on Saturday afternoons in a town the size of Waycross; but every few weeks a new beach flick came through, and the theater was where you could always find your friends. We'd watched every scene he'd ever done.

Stone had been Pat Boone, James Dean and Clint Eastwood rolled into one. By turns, he could show the clean-cut freshness of the boy next door, the sulky sex appeal of a leather-clad rebel and the take-charge machismo of a cowboy who'd just had ten outlaws for breakfast and was still hungry.

He wasn't that great an actor, which may explain why he never made it big. But the directors kept him coming back to please the female teeny-boppers. He never let them down, either, with his sun-bleached curls and hairy, bronze chest, biceps bulging on the beach and baby blues that made the sky over Ft. Lauderdale look gray by comparison.

I'm red-faced to admit it, but Stone had been a hero of sorts to me. In my early years he was everything I wanted to be, and in later years, everything I was sure I wasn't — strong, smart and good-looking. In my little-boy daydreams he showed up at my door, told Daddy he was taking me home, heaved me into the front seat of his cherry-red, fin-tailed Chevy and let me steer while he worked the gears and pedals. What came after that, I never thought much about, though I did once dream that he took me to Hollywood, where I starred in a film as his kid brother.

So why didn't I recognize him in hell right away? To start with, he was twenty-five years older than he'd been when I'd seen him last. Like so many second fiddles, he dropped out of view after five years on the screen and showed up mostly on TV game shows, which I never watched. To his credit, he'd kept his beach-boy physique, and his eyes could never lose that intense blue. But his face was showing the years.

More than that was the cruel way this place had already deformed him. He told me he'd arrived not long ago, and when we checked our dates, we found he'd left his hospital bed only a few months before I took my fall. But the rippling body that once had sent young hearts in Waycross swooning was now pocked with third-degree burns. The gamma rays had thinned his locks and smoothed his once-fuzzy chest, and the soot had filled every new line on his face.

You can imagine, then, how I felt when he told us who he was. Just what do you say when you meet a childhood hero in hell? "Gee — you look so different in person; maybe it's just the light here. Did you bring the red Chevy with you, Stone?"

But that was only the half of it. What do you say when you find out that the beefy beach idol who stole away every lead man's sweetheart and gave millions of young girls the jitters wouldn't have been interested in any of them after all? That his stud roles were more of an acting feat than I'd ever dreamed?

As it turned out, I said exactly what I would have said if I'd met him when I was ten, which was how old I felt at that moment: I said nothing. I couldn't get a word out. After all these years he still had the power to wow me, and the odd mixture of awe and confusion left me mute.

It was Miss C who kept the conversation going when I got all tongue-tied. "We know now who you are and how you got here, but we do not know where you are going."

Stone flashed his boy-next-door grin. "Why, I'm going with you, of course."

"And do you know where *we're* going?" asked Miss C.

"The word going around in Sodom — that's what we've dubbed our camp out there on the frontier — is that anybody in the canal with clothes on is only passing through, though they don't come often. So I made up my mind I'd hide nearby and wait to see for myself. I was hoping you'd be going up instead of down — but at this point I'll go anywhere just to get out of this God-forsaken place."

Miss C looked somber. "I do not think you understand the seriousness of the journey down. The torments only grow worse."

"But if you're headed that way in spite of the danger, then I have a sneaking suspicion it must be because you know a way out. Is that true?"

"Yes, I know the way out. But the way is not open to everyone.

Thomas, here, is not yet dead, as you and I are, so he has a chance of escape. But with the two of us, it is a different matter."

"I'll take my chances, lady. You don't know what it's like to burn and burn and burn and never have a hope of anything else. So what if they catch me somewhere below? Could it possibly be any worse than it is here?"

She turned toward him as she walked, riveting his eyes with her own. "Yes. Infinitely worse. I have heard some below begging to be thrown up here in the blazing cinders."

"You let me worry about that," said Stone, the macho man taking over his voice now. "In the meantime" — he motioned ahead — "I think we've come, as the Brits say, to the end of the bloody road."

He was right. In the distance we could see the edge of the ashen plain, a sudden precipice that dropped like a plumb line at the rim of the abyss. The blood of the canal flowed over the edge and out of sight.

We walked to within a few yards of the crimson waterfall and looked down: The air below was like black smoke, too dense to peer down more than twenty feet or so. But we could see far enough along the cliff wall itself to tell it was made of concrete, darkened now with thick layers of old bloodstains and stretching out in a massive curve like Hoover Dam. No sound or blood spray surged up from the bottom — it was too far below us.

"I take it you're the navigator," Stone said to Miss C. "So where do we go from here?"

"Straight down," she said.

I'd found my voice by now, and I wasn't too happy about that cliff. "There's no way! How could we possibly get a grip on the concrete?"

"We could always rappel," Stone said to me, grinning, "but only if you've got a rope tucked in those shorts somewhere."

"We will neither climb down nor rappel," said Miss C flatly. "We will fly."

Stone and I looked at each other. Had the gamma rays gotten to her brain? I'd seen a lot of things I'd never thought I'd see in hell, but flying souls — especially a fat one still attached to its body — wasn't one of them.

"Well, now, I plumb forgot my wings," I said to her.

She wasn't paying attention. Kneeling by the edge of the cliff, she pulled out the old, tattered scarf from her pocket. Then she filled the center of it with glowing embers, tied the four corners together tightly and tossed it down into the black oblivion. The bundle burst into flames just as it went out of sight.

"What a time for fireworks," Stone grumbled. "Just how do you expect to get us out of here?"

Miss C was unruffled. "This is the precipice that separates the seventh and eighth circles, which lie a great distance apart. We could never hope to make it down so deep and sheer a cliff unaided. I have just summoned the demon Geryon to take us down."

I scratched my head and tried to remember this part of Dante's journey. What I dimly recalled wasn't encouraging: something about a monster with a man's head, a serpent's body, a bat's wings and a scorpion's tale. Dante and his guide rode the critter, bareback, down into the abyss — not at all my idea of a joy ride. If that's the way we had to go, I wanted a front seat, as close to the man head and as far from the scorpion tail as I could get without sitting on his nose.

"Who is this Geryon?" asked Stone. "I hope he's friendlier than the secret police."

"You will find him friendly enough," said Miss C, "for it is his nature to beguile. You will find him attractive as well — each time I meet him his face takes a different form, but always a handsome one, much like your own."

Stone decided Miss C wasn't so crazy after all.

"But beware of his charm," she added. "Whatever his face, his sting is poison. We are, after all, descending into Malebolge."

The name, I didn't remember. "Malebolge?"

"The sins of malice, punished in lower hell, are of two sorts: those of violence — we have seen their consequences already — and those of fraud. Malebolge, the eighth circle, confines the fraudulent sinners. When people are violent, they are acting like beasts; but when they sin through deceit, they are doing what even the beasts cannot do. Those who defraud others pervert the special gifts of intellect that God has given only to the human and angelic races, and thus they incur a deeper guilt."

She talked like she'd studied under Aquinas himself. What a fine professor of ethics she would have made, I thought. Of course, who'd ever let her teach once they found out she believed in a literal hell?

And who will ever believe *you* went there, I asked myself, if you should live to tell the tale?

"You said there were concrete trenches?" I asked.

"Ten," she said. "One pit for each of the types of fraud punished. They form concentric circles, divided by asphalt pavement in between — each one a concrete ring that runs around the abyss. You will see them as we descend."

"How big are they?" asked Stone.

"Wide enough to hold the wretched multitudes of the ages, and deep enough to keep them from escaping. We could not possibly survive if we had to descend into each one and make our way through."

"Then how do we get across them?"

"Steel and concrete suspension bridges — one over each pit. Even so, some bridges are crumbling, and others are guarded. Where the guards are, we will be in great danger. But at least they will not be disguised this time."

Stone scratched his jaw. "This is beginning to sound like a B-rated thriller."

"Yeah," I said, looking past his left shoulder, "and here come the thrills. We've got company."

TWENTY-THREE

Stone turned around, expecting to see some flying monster with a face like Tom Cruise coming up from the abyss. But I wasn't talking about our flight accommodations. Along the rim there came running toward us a pack of male souls, dodging the fire as they ran.

Stone froze. Secret police? What if one of them could recognize him from before, even with the pants? A body like his stood out in the crowd, burns and all.

He turned back around to scout out the rim running in the other direction. It was full of souls now too, headed this way, though these were female. And still no sign of Geryon.

My heart was sinking fast. "Maybe if we stay in the canal they won't touch us — that is, if they're not police. They know the rules."

"Yes," said Miss C, "but the slave traders also knew the rules. We have no idea what these people intend, nor how desperate they are."

"Where's that Geryon buddy of yours?" asked Stone, getting nervous. "Can he give us protection?"

Miss C never answered. We'd run out of time to talk about it;

they had us surrounded.

They were every age, color and size you could imagine. Some were holding hands, but it wasn't easy to do that and slap sparks at the same time.

Nobody stepped across the edge of the canal. Instead they stood right up against it, fists clenched and swatting at sparks. Maybe they followed the rules after all. Their faces were badly seared, but you could see the scowls and sneers right through the soot.

"Who do you think you are, walking in the canal?" shouted one of the men, short and round and bald — in fact, all of them were bald. This crowd had been around a while.

"We got rights too, you know," said a woman on the other side. "What makes you so special that you can cool your little fannies where we can't? Just 'cause you got clothes on, you think that lets you do anything you want."

"Well," said a tall, skinny man with his arm around the fat one's waist, "we can fix that." He giggled. "Take off their clothes, and they'll be just the same as we are. Then they'll have to get out in the mucking ashes like the rest of us."

He started to throw a kiss to Stone, but he caught a spark between his hand and his lips and had to shake it off.

The closest few on both sides jumped into the canal, laughing. A young woman built like a tank grabbed the right sleeve of Miss C's dress and rubbed it between her fingers. "Nice material, Granny," she said, "but it's out of style. You need to show a little more *skin*."

With a jerk she ripped the sleeve off at the seam and tossed it over onto the cinders. Then she pushed Miss C backwards down into the blood. The crowd roared.

"Now take it off. Take it all off." She grinned and pointed at the fine, white ash. "Then we'll give you some of that hot body powder and see if we can whiten you up a bit."

I struggled to get to Miss C, but by now Stone and I were held fast by four men, one on each of our arms. Somebody behind us called out, "The hunk looks familiar. I *know* I've seen him somewhere. Are you one of *us*, sweet hips? Maybe you're not a passthrough at all." The crowd jeered, but Stone kept his mouth shut.

Next the tall, skinny guy looked me over. Then he reached out to play with the three raised scars on my belly. "Hey — look here," he said. "God gave you three extras, and He put them in the wrong place! But why should I be surprised? He put me in a man's body, and I was a woman all along. Maybe God was tying one on when He made us!"

The crowd was shrieking with laughter now, but I shouted over the racket, "If you were really a woman in a man's body, then why does your soul look male?"

He glared at me and kneed me in the groin. I bent over double, the men pulled us down and the mob surged in, cheering. I felt hands all over me.

Cheers suddenly turned to screams. "Police! It's the stinking police!" The crowd fell back as a dented old helicopter missing half its bolts swooped up from the abyss and hovered in the air over us. Blood and sparks were flying everywhere, and the doomed souls — all except Stone — leaped out of the canal, then off to where they'd come from.

Miss C was the first to jump up. She signaled to the chopper to come down closer, and it did, till it almost touched the ground. "Get in!" she shouted, her voice nearly blown away. "Geryon!"

I stood up, still aching, motioned for her to climb in first and gave her a lift. I went next, backing in with my hand stuck out to help Stone. But the chopper started up.

"Wait!" I shouted, grabbing his right hand in mine. But we kept climbing and then swung out over the cliff. I almost fell out, but I hooked my left elbow around a bar by the door and hung my right shoulder out.

It was only half a grip we had, and slipping. Stone dangled in the black air by one burned hand — five bloody fingers away from the abyss.

"Set it back down on the cliff!" I shouted over the roar of the blades.

"Too late!" said Miss C. "We are dropping now!"

We were dropping like a bull on a bungee cord, but with no hope of a bounce. Everything was darkness below. Stone looked up at me, not with terror, but with resignation in his eyes.

No script this time; he was a tough man after all. I squeezed harder still — if that was possible — and felt my insides flying apart. I was crying.

I can't drop him. Not Stone Jordan. Not in that black hole. If I drop him, the little boy that worshipped him will get swallowed up in the darkness too. I can't let go. I can't let go. I can't...

Rings of dark firelight came into view now. The ground was in sight. "Hold on!" I screamed. "Almost home!"

He pulled hard to lift his left side up so he could get a second hand on mine, but it was a mistake. The jerk tore three of his fingers free, and now he was swinging on only two. He was slipping, and I couldn't stop him.

"Please don't let him fall," I whispered into the blackness. "We're almost there. Please..."

I closed my eyes for what seemed like forever, and then the last two fingers slipped away. He was gone.

Five seconds later we touched down. I tumbled out onto the pavement, screaming his name. "Stone! Where are you? Can you hear me?"

A moan came from a few feet behind the chopper, and I scrambled to find him. He lay there looking stunned and broken.

I was blinking back the tears as I cradled his head in my arms. "Stone — I tried my best to hold onto you, buddy. I never let go. It was the blood that made you slip."

He half-opened his eyes and smiled weakly. "You were a trooper, Tom, and you saved my skin. I guess we're even now."

He closed his eyes again and winced. "Just let me lie here a minute. I didn't really fall so far — maybe ten feet. We were almost down, you know. But I hit my head, and I'm having trouble seeing. Can people go blind in hell?"

I thought of the sightless bodybuilder in the health club, but I didn't have the heart to tell him. "You'll be all right," I said. "Take all the time to rest you want."

I walked back over to the chopper door, where Miss C stood talking to Geryon. I hadn't even laid eyes on him yet, and I wanted to know why he'd taken off too soon, so I stuck my head inside to ask him myself.

Geryon was still seated in the pilot's seat — and she was gorgeous.

She had olive skin, steamy brown eyes and coal-black hair that fell down around her shoulders like shiny little strands of licorice.

My jaw hit the ground, and it took a minute to jack it back up. Geryon?

Miss C laid her hand on my shoulder. "I told you, Thomas —

always a beautiful face, and always a new one."

Geryon smiled like the Cheshire cat, then put on a pout. "I'm so sorry, Thomas. I've never taken more than two on board at a time — one traveler plus an escort. I didn't realize until too late that Stone was with us. Once you're over the cliff, you're committed, you know. He's not hurt, is he?"

"He'll make it," I said. "But you sure scared the fool out of us."

"Don't worry. I'll make certain it doesn't happen again." She winked, and the pout gave way once more to a smile. "I hope I see you around, Thomas. You may even like it here. Personally, I think this is the best circle of all — especially the first pit. You're gonna love it. See ya."

With that she put it in gear. We stepped back, and she went off roaring. I watched her climb, amazed that a devil could be so beautiful. That's when I saw the open window on the pilot's side.

Hanging out of it was a long, curled tail with a barb on the end.

─── TWENTY-FOUR ───

Stone was blind.

We'd thought for sure that a little rest was all he needed to get his eyes working again. So he'd lain there a while with them closed, right where he fell on the cracked pavement, though I propped his head up on my hands to make a sorry pillow of sorts.

But when he opened his eyes again, his sight was gone. He couldn't see even a hand just an inch in front of his face.

Of course, neither Miss C nor I could see much farther. The air in Malebolge looked black as a tar pit and twice as thick. Dim light, some of it flashing, crept over the edge of a few of the pits in the far distance, giving us reference points. But making our way was going to be like chasing lightning bugs through a swamp at midnight.

We sat around and talked for what seemed like hours, hoping for a change in Stone. He seemed to be taking it pretty well, though he was convinced the problem wouldn't last long. I wasn't at all so sure.

Meanwhile, I had problems of my own. The pain in my stomach was coming and going, as if somebody had it in a vise they were twisting open and shut. And the hair on my arms was falling out.

"Tell us more about yourself, Stone," said Miss C. "You have said nothing of your family."

He frowned. "There's nothing much to tell. Grew up in a white, middle-class suburb in Des Moines. My father was so busy chasing the great American dream that he never stopped long enough to get to know me. I'm still not even sure exactly what it was he did for a living — some kind of manager, I think, for a food distributor. Kept people from going hungry, I guess."

"And your mother?" I asked.

"A real-life Mrs. Cleaver — warm, witty, president of the PTA, and she made the best cookies on the block."

"Siblings?" asked Miss C.

"An older sister. She split when I was a teenager, and I haven't seen her since. Lives alone in New York somewhere."

"Are your parents still alive?"

"My mom is, in Des Moines. My father died the year after I made my second movie." He paused. "I didn't go to the funeral. Didn't care to."

Miss C looked down at the ground. "I see." I could hear the compassion in her voice, but Stone missed it.

"Look — I sent all three of them a ticket to the Hollywood premiere of my first flick. Biggest moment of my life. But Mom showed up by herself. My father had some lame excuse about having to attend the boss's birthday party — as if he'd ever attended any of *mine*. So when it was time for his own last little wing-ding, I stayed home."

My eyes were burning. Maybe when Stone was little, he'd dreamed of somebody stealing *him* away in a red Chevy. "Did he ever abuse you?" I asked.

"Not physically, not sexually, maybe emotionally. Neglect would be the better word. By the time he died, I'd finally given up hope that he'd ever show any interest in me at all. Figured I didn't really need him anyway." He tossed a broken chip of asphalt over his shoulder.

"Then what happened?" I asked.

"Soon after that I met the first man who ever really loved me, and we moved in together. The rest, as they say, is history."

"How long did that last?" I asked, my curiosity getting the best of me.

"Six months," he said with half a laugh. "We split up when I found out he was seeing two guys on the side."

Miss C furrowed her brow. "And you call him the first man who ever really loved you?" With Miss C, subtlety was not a virtue.

"Well," said Stone, "it was love, all right, but it just didn't last long. It was passionate while it lasted — so hot it just burned out early, I guess."

"Love never burns out," she said. "No doubt it was something else."

"Look, lady." Stone sat forward, gritting his teeth. "I don't need any sermons from you. I lived my life my way, and you lived yours, so what difference does it make to you?"

She stayed calm. "Right now, a rather large difference, considering our present plight. Do you really think that even the most private of your choices were without their eventual effects on those around you?"

"I didn't ask to come here."

"Did any of the damned? And yet they are here by their own choice. They took the cheap shortcuts to happiness and found only dead ends, but at the end of the road it was too late to turn back."

"So what do you want from me?"

"The decisions of your life are of concern to me because they ultimately brought you across my path and set you down on the road next to me. You are planning to follow my lead, so I feel somewhat responsible for your care — yet I cannot anticipate what lies ahead for us without knowing something of your past. What I do know is that, whatever the choices that brought you here, there are no coincidences in hell. There is a purpose for our meeting."

Stone leaned back on his elbows. "You don't really want to help me escape, do you?"

Miss C threw up her hands. "Would that all could still pay the price to escape! But I have never before helped someone get out who has already died and been judged."

"There's a first time for everything."

"So there is. And a last time as well. Most would say you have already passed the last chance for repentance."

"Who's talking about repentance?" said Stone, shrugging. "I just want out."

Miss C shook her head woefully as she peered into his blank eyes. "Stone, what do you really expect to gain from coming along with us?"

He stiffened. "I just told you — I'm blowing this joint."

"I mean beyond that," Miss C pressed. "Even if you made it out of hell, where would you go? The upper world will not receive you back again; even if you could go there you would be worse than a ghost, at most a pale mist in the graveyard without face or form or even voice."

"I don't want to go back to the upper world. I want to go to heaven."

She sat back, surprised. "You would not be happy there in your present condition."

"So what's new? I've never known a day of happiness in my whole life — that's why I had to settle for a few fleeting moments of pleasure. No, I have just a few questions to ask Mr. God Almighty, and I want to go to heaven to demand some answers."

Miss C spoke more softly now. "Which questions are those, Stone?"

He pulled himself up to a standing position, rubbing himself in the sore places. Then he cocked his empty eyes upward and pointed into the air, as if he were on stage again.

"I want to know," he said, his voice rising, "just how God can talk about choices when I've been attracted to men for as long as I can remember. How can He say a four-year-old who aches for an older man's embrace has *chosen* to be gay? How can He say a love is 'against nature' when it feels so natural to me — and going to bed with a woman would feel so unnatural? What if it's all genetic? What if I really was *born* this way?"

His hand fell to his side. "If so, then *He* made me like this, and now He takes some sick pleasure in watching me burn for it. What kind of God would do that?"

Miss C was silent for a few minutes, and Stone sat back down again.

"Suppose that it *is* inborn," she said. "Children are born all the time with deformities, some of the body, some of the mind. But that does not mean God willed it so. The theologians speak of original sin, of a brokenness that pervades all creation ever since the first human said no to God. We are all born broken, Stone. But the goal of life is to overcome the deformity, not to celebrate it."

"How do you overcome something like *that*?" he asked. "Celibacy would have been the only other option."

"Perhaps," said Miss C. "Or perhaps for you the answer would have been found in healing the brokenness of your relationship with your father."

Stone's face was hard. "Either way, the bottom line is that I'm not to blame. Either God made me this way, or somebody else ruined me — my father, my mother, I don't know. All I know is that I got left paying for the damaged goods."

"I agree," Miss C said slowly, "that a child who longs for a father's love is not sinning in that desire, and that the first sin probably lies with the man who allowed his career obsession to orphan you — "

"And that's the way it is with almost everyone back up there in Sodom," Stone interrupted. "If you were ever there for long yourself, you'd know: The seventh circle of hell has all the orphans."

"Not all of them," said Miss C with an edge in her voice. "The other circles have their share as well. But we chose to fill the emptiness in different ways."

"I needed a man's love, and I went looking for it," said Stone. "Doesn't that make a lot more sense than filling up the hole inside with booze or pills or candy bars?"

"Did sex with other men ever fill up the void?"

A long silence. "No," he said finally. "Not for long. Sooner or later I hated them, and hated myself, just like I'd hated my father. But at least the sex dulled the pain a little."

Miss C reached over to take his hand, but he pulled away. "You could have had genuine male love without sex, Stone," she said, "though my guess is that in Hollywood you would have had to look extremely hard for it. And I realize as well that without your father's example, you had little idea of what you were looking for."

"So why," Stone asked, his voice quivering with anger, "am I to blame?"

"You are responsible, not for your father's sin, but for your grievous reaction to it."

"How else *could* I have reacted? I was a child!"

"The critical choice was the one you made as an adult, not as a child. You chose to go looking for male love and identity — for the father you never knew and the man you had always wanted to be — between the bedsheets."

"But I needed to be loved!"

"Of course you did. We all did. The need you had was by no means a sin, Stone; it was a tragic brokenness. But you went down the wrong road looking to fill it, a road you were warned would bring you here."

"So why did the road have to bring me here?"

"Because in the end you could not find wholeness by having sex with male friends any more than you could have found it in bed with your own father. Your homosexual coupling corroded your soul just as surely as the horror it imitated — the incest of parent and child. In the end, however natural it may have felt to you, it was still a sin against your own *nature*: not just the nature of your body, but the shape of your soul as God intended it to be."

"That's enough!" Stone shouted, and jumped to his feet. "How dare you or anybody else who's never been through it lecture me about right and wrong. I'm not to blame. I'm getting out of here, whatever it takes, and when I see God, I'm gonna call *Him* to account for all my pain!"

He turned his head in my direction. "Thomas!"

"Yes, Stone. I'm right here." I reached up from where I was sitting and touched his tensed forearm lightly.

"I can't find my way alone as long as I can't see. Are you going to help me out, or are you with her?"

I stood up and gripped his shoulder. "I'm going to help you, Stone, but I'm also with her. She's the only one who knows the way. You may not like what she has to say, but you've got to trust her to lead us."

"I'll trust *her*," said Stone, "when hell freezes over."

"Very well," said Miss C dryly. "You can start right now. The lower regions have already iced."

She stood and began making her way through the darkness toward the first pit, some distance away. I had Stone take my right arm, and we followed in silence. His hand was trembling — whether with fear or rage or both, only he knew.

When he tripped in a hole I couldn't have seen, I grabbed him before he fell. "I'm sorry," I said, pulling him closer. "Let's try it this way."

I put my right arm around his waist, wrapped his left arm around my neck and grabbed his free hand with mine. "I won't let you get hurt again," I whispered.

For a brief moment he laid his head against mine, his labored breath blowing warm and damp across my cheek. It was too dark to tell for sure, but I thought I felt a hot tear as well, trickling down my shoulder. I squeezed his sooty shoulder to comfort him. But he straightened up, blinked the moisture from his unseeing eyes and pulled me on.

TWENTY-FIVE

We knew we were getting closer to the first pit when we began to hear, even if only faintly, the crack of whips and the scream of the damned. Stone was jittery. "What's that?" he asked, slowing almost to a stop. "What are they doing? Can you see?"

Miss C spoke for the first time since her heated words with Stone. "This is the pit of the seducers and the panders."

"Panders?" said Stone.

"Those who catered to and exploited the weaknesses of others. They not only sinned, but led others into sin as well."

"You mean like pimps?"

"Until your generation, most of them were pimps. But now the trench runs with the blood of a host of other professions, each twisted in some way to urge or coax men and women to evil. Considering the great variety of temptations, you can imagine how many souls are here, and how many ways they once found to prey on others."

We were at the top of the pit now, and the commotion below us was bloodcurdling. "Tell me what you see!" Stone demanded.

I did my best, though words fell short as I wrestled to describe what I saw. The pit was immense — more like a concrete canyon — and packed with shrieking, moaning souls who pushed along its walls like a wild cattle herd. Traffic moved in two directions as if on opposite sides of a highway: Those closest to us moved toward our right; those on the other side, toward our left.

They weren't dragging their feet, and no wonder. Stationed throughout the mob were the tallest demons I'd seen yet — ten feet or more — wearing ridiculous cowboy hats, bandanas and silver-star badges. They were flogging the souls as they passed by with whips made of steel cables, twenty feet long, white-hot and tipped with barbed hooks big enough to snag a shark. The slow-pokes caught it the worst, but judging from the condition of the backs of the mob, sooner or later everybody got a turn.

The white heat of the whips lit up the scene with a ghastly glow, like neon lightning, revealing more details of the torment than I wanted to see.

"Get along, little dogies! You ain't home yet!" a devil in a black ten-gallon taunted a short Asian man while he lashed him around the throat with searing steel. The man groaned and fell to the ground, but the devil gave the whip a jerk and pulled him back up. "No rest for the weary, gringo! Not any more than those miserable little twelve-year-old prostitutes in your ring ever got from you!"

Next to him, a lanky black man was missing half the meat on his back and arms. "No flesh to sell here, Big Daddy!" shouted a fat devil in a red sombrero with gold brocade. "Get it in gear!"

The demons saw us, but they didn't care. They didn't want to miss any chance to peel off somebody's skin. "Come along to the bridge," said Miss C. "We will pass over this one quickly."

Halfway over the span — a dilapidated steel-and-concrete arch with potholes that went all the way through — we stopped to look down on the roaring chaos. Suddenly a male voice called out above the ruckus: "Stone! Stone Jordan! What are *you* doing up there?"

Stone turned his face blankly down toward the crowd. "Who is it?"

The man was trying to slow down and hide from the cowboys behind a huge woman who blocked the view of several smaller souls. "Schmerz. Harvey Schmerz. Hollywood. Producer, director, sometime screenwriter. Remember me?"

Stone laughed. "I sure do remember you, you old lecher. You were out there pushing for smut on the screen way ahead of your time, when everybody else still thought a deep kiss was the hottest thing America could handle."

"Yeah," said Schmerz, "a real pioneer, what can I tell ya. And for that I get to parade with these darlings through a monster-size Vegematic. It slices, it dices, it florentines...Yow!"

He caught just the tip of a barb on his rump. "Why should *I* be here? The cattlebrains who ate up what we dished out...*they're* the ones who oughta be here. All we had to do was goad their hormones a little bit, and they kept stampeding back for more."

"It looks crowded down there," I said.

"You better believe it. Half of Hollywood's here, you know — a veritable Circus of the Stars. Marilyn, Mae, Lennon, the King; you name 'em, we got 'em."

Stone lost his smile. "Is Rock there too?"

"Never seen him. I would have thought he'd be with you. Could be somewhere lower, I guess. Hope not, for his sake. I've heard stories about the lower levels. Though it ain't no picnic here."

He ducked and missed getting a mouthful of burning steel by an inch.

"It's like being on the guest list for one of Liz's weddings. Rock greats, soap idols, just about every TV writer that's died since the sixties. Most of the MTV talent is too young to have made it here yet, but I'm sure they'll be coming. We even got that megaburger corporation president who put pressure on the big wigs to loosen up prime time."

"The one who bought up all the 'distressed merchandise' of commercial time on the networks?"

"What a racket! He advertised on every steamy new show that came along. If nobody else wanted to sponsor the garbage, he could jump in and get it all dirt cheap."

Schmerz dodged another whip, this one with a nine-barbed tip, and figured his time was running out. "Gotta go, babe. You sure you don't belong here?"

"I kept it clean," yelled Stone. "All my steam was off-screen." Even so, he was looking more jumpy all the time.

The crowd pressed on through the concrete canyon and under the bridge below us like a crazed pack of steers. Devildrovers were looking for their favorites in the herd, picking them out with a bloody *crack!* across the shoulders — and other carefully selected spots.

"Hey, you! The one who made condoms with cartoons on the package so the kiddies would go for 'em. Just how many did you sell, you old varmint?" An oily little man got a shark hook between the legs.

"And there's the bandit who drew the pictures for serial killer trading cards! Bundy, Berkowitz, Manson, Gilmore, all your favorites — collect 'em and swap 'em, kids!" Searing steel cable wrapped around the man's drawing hand and ripped three fingers off.

A scrawny woman held her face in her hands and nearly crouched as she ran, trying to avoid notice. But two whips from devils on either side of her came down at once, one wrapped around each ankle. They jerked her upside down and held her flopping over the herd.

"Who woulda thought so many dudes were loco enough to buy your slimy magazine?" said one of them, a she-demon wearing a broad straw hat and a cone bra. "Ten thousand nerds with a shoe fetish — who woulda thought?"

On and on they went, a cosmic sleaze bag of warped humanity: pimps and prostitutes, gigolos and porno czars, girlie calendar models, gossip tabloid editors — and a slew of mainstream producers, directors, actors, writers and advertisers who'd pushed everything from slasher films to prime-time perversion.

If my stomach hadn't been turning already, it would have started right there. The scene brought back one line from Dante I'd never forgotten — a description of hell that said it all: *That woeful sack, stuffed with all the evil of the universe....*

One more voice sailed over the racket from the seducer lane, this one female. "Capopia! Capopia!"

Miss C froze.

"So you pass by once again to mock us in our agony." The accent sounded like Miss C's, though the voice was young and alluring. "I saw your sister not long ago...*eeeyyyiii!*" A whip sliced across her ribs as she passed under the bridge out of sight.

Miss C was beside herself. "She has seen my sister!" she screamed, waving her hand at the mob. "I must ask her when, and what she knows!" She turned to look at me, wild-eyed. "I will run down the far side of the bridge and along the other edge of the pit until I find her. Stay here, and do not leave under any circumstances!"

I panicked. "We'll go with you! Don't leave us here alone!"

"There is no time!" she shouted over her shoulder and disappeared down the crumbling span into the darkness.

"She's gone," I said to Stone in disbelief. "Just like that. She said we wouldn't get separated again. Now she tells me to wait in the pitch dark alone with God-only-knows what else slithering around out here."

Stone gripped my shoulder. "You're not alone, Tommy. You've got me, even if I still can't see yet. But that'll come. Hey — maybe it's all for the best."

"But she's the only one who knows the way!"

"Who needs her? I may be blind, but you're not, buddy. You can make out the lines of the trenches, then all we have to do is follow each one along the edge till we get to the bridge. Piece o' cake."

"She said to wait here. She's coming back."

Stone's voice lowered. "Yeah, but when? Haven't you noticed? Folks who've been down here a long time lose all concept of time. We could be waiting for centuries. *Centuries*."

"But what about after the tenth bridge? How do we get to the next level? And then what?"

"Hasn't she ever talked about the route you were taking?"

"Not much. But she did say once that to get to the bottom you keep taking left turns. As I remember it now, Dante did too."

"Who's Dante?"

"Never mind. Just somebody from a long time ago who left us with a map of this place that I wish to goodness I could remember."

"It'll come back to you, Tommy. Meanwhile, we keep turning left. Easy enough. We'll find our way."

"But she *said* to wait *here*."

"Look, Tommy" — Stone motioned down toward the pit — "if any of those devils start asking questions, I may be up the creek. I was a part of Hollywood like the rest of them, you know. If we stay here, you might lose me too, and then you'd be *really* alone."

I looked at the solid darkness around me and felt it pressing in. No matter what, I couldn't afford to lose Stone too.

Maybe, I told myself, we can find Miss C. If we just start walking down the bridge and along the edge, we should meet her coming back anyway, right? We couldn't miss her if we stayed alert. No way we could miss her.

Stone took my arm again, squeezed up tight against me and gave me a nudge. I gave in. We walked down the far side of the bridge together, dodging potholes, and made our way out slowly into the blackness.

TWENTY-SIX

The going was slow, with the blind leading the blind. It might have been easier if all the bridges had lined up; we could have crossed one right after the other, making a beeline between pits. But the arches seemed to be staggered in a random pattern. Finding a pit didn't guarantee finding a bridge any time soon after.

My stomach had been hurting off and on — mostly on — and although it was too dark to see even my own body very well, I could feel an odd smoothness on my chest and legs. The hair was gone. Meanwhile, there was still the tiredness, dog tiredness, like I'd never felt before.

Miss C was nowhere to be found. I shouted her name again and again, though I knew it was likely to rile a few demons and bring them our way. But there was only a pitiful echo, and then silence. Where could she possibly be?

The edge of the next pit lay some distance away, a flickering, faint, blue-green line of light marking it out against the blackness. To take my mind off my troubles, I asked Stone to tell me some Hollywood stories, especially about some of the fool characters he'd met there. A few laughs, I decided, would do us both good just now.

He had some good ones to tell. Prissy literary types who dined three meals a day on snails and champagne. Big names from the big screen who threatened to walk off the set if their big egos weren't stroked by getting listed first in the credits. Hunks with toupees and fanny tucks nobody knew about. Aging actresses who claimed only half their age and half of all their face-lifts. Models — both men and women — with breast or chest implants that sagged and balled up until they had to be taken out again.

"It's a crazy world," said Stone. "No end to the stupidity."

"There's an end, all right," I said. "It all ends up right here in hell."

Stone was suddenly sober. He let go of my arm and sat down on the pavement. "Do you really think this is the end? I mean, don't you think these people might finally cry 'uncle' and get a reprieve? If *you* get a chance to escape, why not everybody else?"

I rubbed my eyes, weary from squinting so long to see in the darkness, and sat down next to him. "I don't know, Stone. It makes sense. But how many of these people do you actually see crying 'uncle' — even the ones who've been here a thousand years? Looks to me like the only change they've made is to get worse. Did Schmerz sound to you like he was sorry for being a lecher and talking others into joining him?"

"Sorry?" said Stone. "Who said anything about sorry? When longtime jailbirds get parole, is it because they're sorry or because they'll do whatever it takes to get out? Just look at how many wind up behind bars again."

"That's my point exactly," I said. "If nothing's really changed, then what good would it do to let them out? Sooner or later they'd do it all over again. The rest of the universe needs to be protected from these folks."

Stone scooped up a small heap of asphalt crumbles in his hand and let them fall slowly through his fingers. "They could be confined without all the fire and blood — like in the best penitentiaries, you know."

"You could take away all the fire and blood and leave them alone, and still it would be hell, Stone. Confine them together, and they'd make it hell for each other. Keep them in isolation, and they'd torture themselves for an eternity thinking about all the things they could have done to be somewhere else — even if they never had a pang of conscience. Sometimes I think the fire and blood are mercies that keep their minds off their *real* problems."

Stone frowned. "OK, then, suppose somebody really *is* sorry. Suppose he's not just sorry he ended up in the fire, but sorry he did something that made God mad at him. Shouldn't he get a second chance?"

What could I say? I knew we were talking close to home now.

"I just don't know, Stone. It seems to me that we all had our second chances, our third and fourth and thousandth chances, to be sorry before we ever came here."

"But if we're willing to choose differently after we die, why not?"

"I'm afraid there are plenty of choices we make that we can't unmake, no matter how hard we want to. If we say a hurtful word, we can't call it back. If we kill somebody, we can't bring him back. If we jump off the bridge, we can't fly back up again even if we change our minds in mid-air. In some things, once you're committed, you're committed. Maybe death commits us to all the choices we made before it."

Stone wasn't convinced. "God could extend the time for choosing if He wanted to. He could let us choose even in hell."

"But do we have any evidence that if He extended the deadline, we'd take advantage of it? Look, Stone — He's God. He decides when people die in the first place. Maybe He already knows the point of no return for each of us, and He only lets us die after we've passed that point. Would any of the people here you've met so far want to pay the price to come clean?"

"Maybe *I* would."

A long awkward silence. "There's nothing that would make me any happier, Stone," I said. "I believe it's the only way out."

"Do you think God would let me?"

"I sure can't speak for Him. But it seems to me you could take it up with Him directly."

"Where? When?"

"Here. Now. If you like, I can give you some time alone."

An even longer awkward silence. Then, an eternity later, Stone stood up. "Nah. I'll wait till I get out of here first. Come on, Tommy. We've got places to go."

When I stood up, he threw his arm around my shoulders. "It's you and me now, buddy. I don't think your friend's coming back.

She must have had more important things to do. Went looking for that long-lost sister maybe. But we're gonna make it together anyway. You wait and see."

I hoped he was wrong, but I was beginning to fear he was right. There was nothing to do now but cross my fingers and cross the bridges. I just wished Miss C had told me ahead of time which ones were broken down and which were under guard.

And I wished the gnawing in my stomach would go away....

As it turned out, we could have found the next pit if we'd both been blind; all we had to do was follow our noses. The stench spreading out from it was gut-wrenching — every bit as bad as the boiling blood, but nasty. It made Granddaddy's outhouse smell like an Avon lady's bag by comparison.

Actually, pit number two was just Granddaddy's outhouse built to God's specs for the Mississippi. The stink convinced us we didn't want to get anywhere close to the edge — falling in would have been unthinkable — so we found our way to the bridge first thing. It was slimy with mold.

When I looked down this time, Stone didn't have to ask me what I saw; his nose knew. But this time it would have been a whole lot easier to describe. I could have summed it all up in one word.

Poop.

Human excrement. Rivers of it. Mountains of it. And damned souls wriggling around in it like maggots in a concrete latrine big enough for a whole tribe of King Kongs.

All throughout the pit stood giggling demons, eight to ten feet tall, rolling up round globs of the stuff and pitching it at the people like kids in a snowball fight. In between pitches they snapped their fingers and made sparks that exploded the methane into blue-green flames, keeping the playing field lit.

The manure was caked in the doomed souls' hair and eyelashes, smeared on their faces, running in streams down their fronts.

"Some things," said Stone, "are worse than pain. No way you'd get me in there. I'd commit a worse sin that's punished farther down just to get out of it."

I shook my head, revolted. Who were these people? What horrible sin landed them in such a disgusting fate? And where did all that filth come from? You'd have to save droppings from the whole human race for a lifetime to fill this monster cesspool.

"Hey!" I shouted to a middle-aged white man, his hair slicked straight back with the stuff. "What did you do to wind up *there*?"

He hesitated to speak, but finally spit out one word: "Flattery."

Then I knew where all the manure had come from. When he talked, a gallon of it spewed out of his mouth.

Dante's details about the second pit were coming back to me now. This was the place of the flatterers — those guilty of praising too much from motives of self-interest. In Dante's time there were people who hung around the royalty and the wealthy, kissing up to them just for the favors they could charm out of them. I wondered who would fit the bill in my generation.

"What did you do for a living?" I asked Mr. Slick.

He dodged a poopball. "Salesman. Used car salesman. Most of us in this sector of the trench were either in sales or marketing." The dung dribbled down his chin.

Others were looking up at me now and gurgling. "We were just doing our jobs," said a short woman with cheeks like a chipmunk, spewing brown streams down her neck. "We don't deserve this. All I did was write a few jingles."

"Yeah. That's all," said a stubby little man up to his neck. "Billboards. TV commercials. Magazine ads. They were mucking good too."

"Sure they were," said a devil, popping the chipmunk woman in the right eye with a brown blob. He looked at the other players. "They were so good we remember every one of 'em, don't we, guys?"

"How could we forget?" asked another. He plopped a runny pile on the dome of a bald old white man next to him and rubbed it in. "A little dab'll do ya!"

"Try it, you'll like it!" said a skinny devil as he pushed a young black woman all the way under. "It's the real thing!" Her feet came up kicking, and he sat on them. "Aw...she's fallen, and she can't get up!"

Two devils ganged up on a wiry little old lady, splashing the dung in front of her face till her head was covered. "Just a sprinkle a day keeps the odor away! Get zestfully clean!"

"Stop it!" she screamed, and a bucketful poured out of her mouth. The demons grinned. "It keeps on running, and running, and running..."

"I think I've seen enough," I said to Stone. "The more they talk, the higher it piles up. Let's get out of here before Madison Avenue sends a flood tide over the bridge."

"Wait! Come join us!" shouted one of the devils, tossing a flattened patty at us like a Frisbee and just missing Stone's nose. "Membership has its privileges!"

We escaped down the far side of the bridge just before it was pelted with a shower of filth from half a dozen devils. "And to think I almost ended up acting in TV commercials," said Stone. "But really, Tom, don't you think it's just a little too harsh on those guys? I mean, they were just making a living like the rest of us."

I shrugged. "It was more than just a living they made, and you know it. Besides — it's no small thing to bait a whole nation of folks into wasting their hard-earned money on things they don't need that can't live up to their promises anyway. I never did find a toothpaste that gave my mouth sex appeal, or a sports car that came with three blondes as standard equipment."

"I didn't need either one," said Stone, laughing. He stopped and grabbed me by the shoulders. "Come on, buddy, lighten up. You're beginning to sound like old Miss C."

That was a compliment, though he didn't know it. "I sure wish she were here now," I said. "I don't quite remember what comes next, but I know it only gets worse."

"Who says we have to keep going lower?" asked Stone. "If you're not stuck down in one of the pits, this level isn't so bad. We could always find some snug, dark corner where the demons never wander, and just settle down."

"And what would we *do* for all eternity?" I asked.

"Just fool around — you know, keep ourselves entertained." He grinned. "I've got enough Hollywood tales to last the first hundred years. After that I'm sure we'd think of *some*thing."

I didn't respond. "It's not heaven," he said, "but if we're not careful, we could do worse." He slid his fingers over the burns on my chest. "Fire flakes. Flogging. Filth. Much worse."

I wondered how far away we could get from the pits without falling into the next circle — the frozen one. Stone was right. We didn't *have* to keep going down. This south Georgia boy grew up below the snow line, and I never had taken too kindly to ice.

TWENTY-SEVEN

We wandered through the long miles of ominous darkness toward tiny flickers of light I could just make out far ahead. I knew then what it was like to be an ant creeping across a highway at midnight, hoping the growing, bright pinpoints in the distance were streetlights and not headlights.

Stone tried to hide behind his Clint Eastwood face, but I could read him by now. His mind was like mine: raw with questions that had rubbed and rubbed until they'd left a blister. Nothing was simple, nothing was still. Not till then did I appreciate the daily mercy of sleep, that humble salve that gives the mind a chance to scab before ragged thoughts come to prick again. No one in hell ever sleeps, though they all have nightmares.

Only one thing was for sure. We didn't want to camp anywhere near the second pit; the foul air around it could travel on the breeze. So we decided we'd cross over at least one more bridge before we thought any more about scouting out a place to stay.

The third pit, when we finally reached it, was cluttered with the ruins of countless buildings, scattered out as far I could see — churches, I figured, judging by the steeple on most of their long-forsaken shells. Some had been soaring Gothic cathedrals; some, the onion domes of the Byzantines; others were simple clapboard chapels or old storefront rooms. Flames flickered in isolated spots throughout the debris, casting trembling shadows and making me wonder if this was what the churches of Dresden looked like after the Allied firebombing.

It was a costly rubble. Shards of ancient stained glass lay mixed with chips of altar marble. Twisted golden candlesticks stuck out from smoldering wood-scrap heaps, the charred remains of fancy wooden pulpits. And everywhere were the scarlet shreds of velvet pew pads, mocking the once-comfortably pious souls who now knew no comfort at all.

Down the middle of it all, stretching the length of the trench through ruin after ruin all the way to the horizon, was a rotted red aisle runner. Lined along either side of that were two rows of what looked like tarnished brass collection plates. But the brass circles were actually rims around holes in the cracked floors of stone and wood.

Out of each hole stuck the feet of a doomed soul, bare and tickled by a dancing blue flame.

The scene jolted my memory of Dante. "Simoniacs," I said to Stone. "Those who tried to sell the gifts of God. If I remember it right, Dante saw at least one pope down there with his feet on fire, and a whole mess of bishops and cardinals too. They sold church offices to the highest bidders."

Among the screams that spilled from the holes, we could hear muffled voices, some protesting, others still hawking their wares, their words hissing through gritted teeth.

"...but the *Holy Father* sent me on a mission to sell those indulgences. How could *I* have known that ox-face Luther would get so upset..."

"...Our weekend spiritual enlightenment seminar helps you find inner peace — in ten easy steps for only five hundred dollars..."

"...And now you too can reduce your taxes — by sending fifty dollars for a ministerial ordination certificate to..."

"...Because all I did was promise to double the denominational budget for the clergy retirement fund if their department backed me for moderator of the general assembly. You know, you scratch my back, I scratch yours."

I'll say one thing for hell. There's no discrimination here on the basis of religion.

The legs in one particular hole, next to the smashed skeleton of a television camera, were kicking wildly. A voice from that hole was broadcast above all the others.

"Now if you just make a pledge and send me *five hundred dollars*, you too can know the prosperity of *Gawd* in your life. As you can see, this recent setback has left the ministry with *desperate* financial needs, but if you pray, pay and stay with me, I believe we'll see *miracles* of healing and deliverance. If you give to me, I guarantee that *Gawd* will give to you; it's as simple as that. I have a letter right here from a sister in Paducah who testifies that within *three months* after she paid her pledge to this ministry, *Gawd* instantly delivered her from a spirit of poverty while she was on vacation in Las Vegas...."

Stone chuckled. "No danger for *me* here. Spiritual gifts for sale? Who had them to sell? I never set foot in a church in my whole life. Let's go on before somebody passes the plate." We made our way down the bridge and onto the asphalt again.

Stone talked as if it were all a sitcom, but the scene left me with an odd emptiness and an anger I hadn't counted on. I'd never cared much about the church before. But here I was grieving — that's the only way I could describe it — over its reputation. Or maybe it was over God's reputation.

"Why the fire on their feet?" asked Stone as we inched down the slope. "From what you've told me, each torment is somehow connected with the particular sin — either its natural consequence or some kind of poetic justice...though I have to admit I'm not real wild about some of God's ideas of justice. So what's the connection here?"

"I'm not sure myself," I said. "But it does bring to mind the story of Moses and the burning bush. I know you probably weren't too interested in the Bible, but did you ever see *The Ten Commandments*?"

"Six times. Just about got it memorized."

"Why so many times to see a religious movie?"

"Are you kidding? That was Charlton Heston in the prime of his *machismo*. Heck, I would have watched him if he'd done a Billy Graham movie. I even went to see him in *Planet of the Apes* — but don't tell anybody."

I snickered. "I promise not to tell, buddy. Anyhow, remember in the movie what Moses did when he found out God was appearing to him in the bush?"

"Sure. He took off his shoes."

"You got it. Well, the fire is supposed to be a sign of God's holy presence, and getting barefoot was the ancient way of saying you were walking on holy ground, in a place set aside for God."

"I still don't see the connection."

"As I figure it, simoniacs are about as smart as Moses would have been if he'd walked up to that flaming bush and tried to stomp it out with his bare feet. When you trample on holy things, you get burned."

Stone chewed on that one a minute. "Well," he finally said, "that whole scene answers *one* question I had for God."

"What's that?"

"Why He lets religious frauds get away with it. Looks like they *don't* get away with it."

"And don't forget this is only one kind of religious fraud. Farther on, if I'm remembering it right, there's a pit for false prophets and another for hypocrites. We'll probably find most of the religious types there."

Stone wrinkled up his nose as if we were back at the second pit. "Let's don't stay long where the hypocrites are. If there's one thing I can't stomach, it's a hypocrite. The churches are full of them."

"I thought you said you'd never set foot in a church."

"I haven't. But I've seen enough on the tube to know what goes on in those fancy, chandeliered sanctuaries full of sour-faced choirs singing off key. Or just take a look at the church ads in the Saturday papers: Every preacher who can afford it puts his own slicked-back, middle-aged picture in there. What an ego. Who do they think they are — movie stars?"

I had to laugh. "So you think it would be fine to have big egos and put themselves in the paper if they *were* movie stars — like you."

Stone gave me a mock double slap on the face. "All right, all right, you made your point. But whose mug would *you* rather be greeted by first thing Saturday morning: Rock Hudson or the Rev. Hornblower?"

I laughed again, this time with him, but then the smile slipped off my face. "You haven't gotten over Rock, have you?"

He shook his head slowly. "Rock and about a hundred other good friends I knew who dropped like flies. It was all so senseless, such a waste. How could anybody possibly say AIDS is a plague of divine judgment? Especially when you see the little babies dying. If God did that, I've got some questions I don't think even *He* can answer."

I could tell I had to be careful about what I said. "I don't think anybody would say the HIV babies are being judged, Stone. But I guess it's fair to say that AIDS contracted from promiscuous sex is a judgment in the same sense that dying in a car wreck when you're driving drunk is a judgment. If a self-destructive act goes on long enough, sooner or later the act judges itself by bringing its own ugly consequences. Hell is just the place where all those consequences finally catch up with people."

Stone's face told me he didn't like what he'd heard. The last thing I needed was to have him mad at me, but ever since I'd met Miss C it seemed easier to speak my mind, whatever the consequences. He'd get over it. He had to. He was even more dependent on me right now than I was on him.

We'd walked maybe ten minutes more when I knew I had to ask him another question. It probably wasn't the best time to ask, but I did it anyway. "You never told me why you were in that hospital bed when you died, Stone. Did you die of AIDS?"

His whole body stiffened — I could tell from his grip on my arm and the way his walking changed. When the words finally came out, he was spitting each one through his teeth.

"It was still in the early stages. I hadn't yet wasted away like most of them. But I picked up some rabid little parasite on a vacation in Mexico, and it was all over in a few days. My body couldn't defend itself, and the imbecile doctors who worked in the clinic down there didn't know what they were doing."

Suddenly a pain like an ax hit me inside my gut. I grunted, bent over double and fell to the pavement. Stone panicked, swinging his hands around, unable to see what had happened and afraid that somebody had jumped me in the darkness.

"Tom!" he shouted. "Tom, what's wrong?"

I'd hit my head on the asphalt as well, so I was a sorry mess, groaning and lying there curled up like a worm on a fishing hook. "My stomach...it feels like somebody's cutting it out of me."

Stone went to his knees and searched with his hands till he found me. "What do I do?" he asked. "Can you get appendicitis in hell?"

I finally had to face the question that had been eating at me since long before Miss C took off. "Stone," I said, holding my belly as if it would fall off if I didn't, "what about the radiation sickness in the ring you came from? What does it feel like?"

He sighed. "It's not pretty. All the same symptoms as in the upper world: nausea, fatigue, hair loss. Burns, when you're close to the source, as you well know. Eventually, I suppose, it shuts down your immune system just like AIDS and makes you vulnerable to every infection that comes along. But we wouldn't know about that in our ring — no germ could possibly live in that environment."

The ache was letting up a little. "What about the nausea? Does it get steadily worse? Or does it come and go?"

"It's different with every person down here. With some it never lets up, but it's only mild. Others spend all their time bent double like you are now. Still others seem to get it in spells. Same with the tiredness. But eventually, it seems, everybody's hair falls out. I guess that's the final humiliation."

He sat down next to me, his brow furrowed. "There's one big difference between the sickness here and upstairs. In the upper world, of course, after you get the rays long enough, you finally die. But since we can't die here, we just ache and burn forever."

"How bad do the burns get?"

"Those slavers you saw had most of their skin charred black, and that's about as far as it goes. Somehow the nerves are never burned so badly that the pain stops. But the doomed souls are never totally consumed. It's kind of like it was in that movie: The bush Moses saw burned, but it wasn't burned up."

I'd never seen the connection before, but it made sense. "Maybe," I said, "it's all the same fire."

Stone put his hand over on mine, which was still holding my belly. "I think you've got the sickness, Tom."

"I've been thinking that too for a while now, and not just because of the nausea. My hair's been coming out all over my body, and sometimes I'm so tired I can hardly move. But what about you, Stone? You were there so much longer than I was. Are you sick too?"

"Well, you can see what's happening to my hair and how badly I've been burned. I get the nausea off and on; the fatigue too. But mine is mild compared to others; I've never been bent over like you are right now. When it's that light, after a while you stop thinking about it, I guess — in my ring you're too busy slapping the fire away to think of much else."

I was feeling a little better — good enough to lie out flat, at least, so I did. I let go of my stomach long enough to rub my hands over my face and on the lump in my scalp where I'd hit the pavement. "You know, ever since I was a kid, when we saw the movies about Hiroshima and had air-raid drills at grade school, I've had a secret horror of radiation sickness. Nobody was more relieved than I was when the Cold War finally ended."

"Me too," said Stone. "I'll never forget watching that nuclear holocaust flick *On the Beach*, and the tragic scene when the little girl is blinded by looking right at an A-blast. Now here I am — sick, burned and blind too. I once feared it might happen to me, but I sure didn't think it would happen *this* way."

I shook my head. "Neither did I. In fact, I didn't think the sickness would follow me once I got out of your ring. I figured the danger would be over. But I guess that's the whole point of hell. You can't escape the torment, because you *are* the torment."

Stone nodded, staring blankly into the darkness. "I've never been far from fear my whole life. But the worst of all is to be afraid of yourself. The monster isn't under the bed like it was when you were a kid, or even in the bed beside you. The monster is in you, and you're in the monster. That's the final horror, isn't it?"

I reached over and took Stone's hands. He grabbed me, threw his arms around me and squeezed hard — not the embrace of a lover, but the wild clutch of a terrified child.

──────── TWENTY-EIGHT ────────

Few in hell ever set their thoughts on the future, and for good reason. Most have no chance to think beyond the present miserable moment; their attention is riveted to whatever torment may be tearing at them, so they dodge its claws. Those who do steal a second to ask what lies ahead only hear the question echo back bitterly from the abyss, which is hell's way of whispering, *More of the same, forever.*

Even so, the future had become my obsession now: what would happen to Stone, to Miss C and, of course, to me. Stone was like a wounded butterfly, flitting back and forth between hope and a hard heart; did so wobbly a will as his have any chance of getting out? Maybe he had, after all, the proverbial snowball's chance in hell — which is not so bad when you remember that deep hell is a deep freeze, and the odds of survival for both snow and Stone looked better the lower we went and the closer we got to the exit.

Miss C, for all I knew, could be with her sister, throwing a homecoming party like Sheol had never seen before. Or she could be shouting herself hoarse, calling my name in some miserable pit we hadn't yet spied on. Or...

...Or the slavers could have snatched her while she searched for her kin and left her buried six feet under the ash, unable to scream or even hope for rescue. My stomach was twisting again.

And what about me? Did I have any better chance at escaping than Stone?

By now Miss C's words had become a haunting refrain in my head: *In hell, the only guarantee is justice.* And yet I still hadn't been shut up by the justice I knew I deserved. Little grace notes kept showing up when I needed them most — my belt that snagged me from the winds, Daddy's ring that bought my freedom from the devils, Stone's act that cowed the slavers, Geryon's perfect timing — so now those other words of Miss C's were sounding a counterpoint to the refrain: *There are no coincidences in hell.*

Meanwhile, we were still moving down slope, slowing down when my stomach got worse and stopping when the tiredness was more than I could handle. Stone, by his own admission, was struggling with the same symptoms, though his never seemed as severe as mine. Of course, he could have been covering; I had to keep reminding myself that he was, after all, an actor.

Stone hadn't said any more about settling down, and I was glad to leave the topic alone for now. We still had time — in fact, we had eternity — to think about that, and I kept hoping Miss C might show up after all. As long as we were on the lookout for demons and stayed out of their way, I reckoned we'd be all right.

The fourth pit announced itself some distance off, not with sharp screams of pain, but with the kind of long, low wails children let loose when they cry over a broken toy. By the time we reached the bridge Stone and I were both puzzled by the sound.

We climbed a few yards of the concrete span, this one was shorter than the others because the trench was narrow and shallow — so shallow, in fact, that the heads of the people in it were passing only a few feet below. I looked down to see what was going on there, but it was hard to tell much in the darkness, and there were no flames this time to light the pit. All I could make out were crowds of people slowly walking the length of the trench and weeping while they looked back over their shoulders.

Who were they? Why were they crying and looking backward? Were they scared that somebody or something was following them? I was having trouble remembering this one from Dante; a walk around a cosmic track — even an endless walk — seemed hardly memorable as torments go.

"What do you see?" asked Stone.

"Not much. It's just a bunch of people bawling their eyes out."

"Do you recognize any of them?"

"It's hard to make out any features in this pitch dark. And besides, they're all looking backward, over their shoulders."

Stone was curious. "Look a little closer. Maybe somebody's face will click with you."

I did, craning my neck and squinting at the dark, moving shapes. Still no clue.

One of them must have heard us talking; she stopped right below us and looked up. When she did, I knew why they were wailing.

They weren't looking back over their shoulders after all. No — their heads and their bodies had been disconnected and re-aligned, back to front. They faced toward their own hindsides, and as they walked none of them could see where they were going. I told Stone what I saw.

The woman below us had stopped crying and turned around so her back and her face were both toward us. "Who are you?" she asked hoarsely. "What are you doing up there?"

A man with long blond curls down his front stopped beside her. "What's the matter, Sister Stella?" he said. "Isn't your crystal ball working? Just use your *powers* to tell us who these guys are and why they're here."

"Shut up!" she said. "I never used no crystal ball. I just read tarot cards and people's auras. That stuff don't work here anyway. Leave me alone, you old toadyfrog."

The man pushed his long hair aside to show a pentagram tattooed on his chest. "Talk to me that way again," he hissed, "and I'll put a curse on you."

"That stuff don't work down here neither," said Stella, wiping her nose. "Ain't none of it working here — you can't cast horoscopes, can't read palms, can't hex nobody. Shoot — you can't even see your own navel here, let alone the future."

The long-hair walked on ahead, keeping his eye on her and muttering.

"Dad-blasted warlocks," she said. "They think they and their witch women are better than all us spiritual advisers. At least *we* didn't ask the *Devil* to help us."

"Just who *did* you ask for help?" said Stone.

"Nobody. I could see it all myself, using the cards and stuff. Or I used to." Her face puckered. "*Nothing* works since I got down here...." She started to cry again, the tears flowing down between her shoulder blades.

The wailing was suddenly interrupted by the brassy call of another female voice. "Amon-Ra! Amon-Ra! I am here, O Amon-Ra! Where have you gone? Come inside me, Amon-Ra! I have so many questions to ask of your wisdom."

"Oh, brother," said Stella, stopping the tears again but still sniffling. "It's that freaky channeler from Colorado. She and her Amon-Ra are about to drive me crazy. If she's so sure everybody gets reincarnated, then what's she doing down here trotting through the pit of hell with the rest of us? I wouldn't be surprised if her precious little Amon-Ra isn't out pitchforking some damned soul in a circle lower down right this very minute."

Stone turned toward me, his face saying he wasn't quite believing what he heard. "What *is* this place — hell's freak sideshow?"

By now I didn't have to guess. "This has to be the pit of the false prophets," I said. "The people who turned to supernatural sources other than God to find out about the future. If Dante was right, it's full of sorcerers, astrologers, diviners, fortunetellers, spiritualists, occultists of every stripe."

He wagged his head. "I still can't understand why they're crying like that."

"Sounds to me like they're all lamenting their lost powers," I said. "Powers that never really belonged to them in the first place."

"Hmph," said Stella.

"They once claimed to see what lay ahead," I went on, "but now their claims are stripped away. All they can see is what lies behind, and even that's wrapped in darkness."

I squinted and looked out over the throng in search of faces I might know — not from home but from the history books. Along with the occultists, I figured, was a good measure of religious types who went off the deep end thinking they had a hotline to heaven with an unlisted number. Church history was full of them. Everybody from Thomas Muenzer and Gregory Rasputin to Joseph Smith and Ann Lee — all of them claiming to tell the secrets that God had refused to share with anybody else.

Just then an older black man with white hair flowing from the back of his head down his chest waddled over to stand by Stella. He was mumbling so low we couldn't make out his words. But he looked out over the crowd and suddenly pointed toward it — backward, of course — and began to preach.

"Now listen here to Daddy, children. Never mind about God. I done give God a vacation, and since God is on vacation, you sure don't wanna worry Him. Now if you sin against God, I can save you, but if you sin against me, ain't nothing God can do to save you...." He looked at Stella. "You know, honey," he said, "you looking good to me now...."

"Hmph," said Stella. "You're plumb crazy, Pops."

"Daddy" kept preaching. I guess false prophets don't have to turn to the spirits after all. They can just as easily turn to the ego and the flesh.

"Keep it moving, old man," said a tall, pale woman who bumped into "Daddy." He stood his ground. "Get out of my way, fool!" she shouted and pushed him down. Somebody tripped over him, and before you knew it there was a chain reaction, a punching, kicking pile-up that would have made pro wrestlers proud.

We'd seen more than enough. I took Stone's arm, turned to go — and stopped dead still. Out of the corner of my eye I'd caught a movement in the darkness on the bridge. "Who's there?" I demanded. "Who's on the bridge?" Stone gripped my shoulder and cocked his ear, trying in vain to hear over the din below.

"Thomas," came a female voice from the shadows. "Thomas, is it you?"

A short, slender figure trotted up to me and stopped a foot away. "Thomas," she said again, panting. "Do you remember me?"

It was Lakshmi, the Indian friend of Miss C's I'd met in Sheol.

I was dumbfounded. "How did you get here all the way from Sheol? And how in the world did you ever find us?"

"That will take some time to tell," she said. "Perhaps we should go find a place to sit down away from this terrible commotion. But first, please introduce me to your friend."

"Lakshmi, this is my friend Stone Jordan. Stone, this is Lakshmi, a friend of Miss C's from the first circle."

Lakshmi bowed, but Stone stood there with his hand stuck out in front of him.

"Stone was in an accident," I said to Lakshmi. "He has trouble seeing just now."

"I am terribly sorry," she said to Stone. "I hope you will heal quickly."

"Thank you," said Stone, dropping his hand awkwardly. "I'm pleased to meet you." He took my arm, and we walked down the bridge and far enough away so that the noise couldn't keep us from hearing one another.

Lakshmi waited for us to sit down, then seated herself facing us. I had a closer look at her sari now; it was singed, torn and bloody.

"Lakshmi!" I said, taking the edge of the cloth in my hand. "Have you been hurt?"

She shook her head. "Do not worry — the blood is not mine. But I have had some narrow escapes on my journey."

"You came down the same way we did — through all the circles?"

"Surely you must know by now, Thomas, that there are no shortcuts in hell." She smiled a sad smile, though without bitterness.

"Have...have you become an escort?" I asked.

"I believe I have now been called to that task. But that is why I am here."

"You're going to act as our escort now?"

"Why, of course not. You have Capopia. By the way, Thomas, where is she? I assumed when I did not see her that she is scouting out the path to the next pit."

I looked down at the pavement. "No. I wish I knew where she is, Lakshmi. She's disappeared."

Lakshmi leaped up and stood staring at me, horror-stricken. "Disappeared? But how could that have happened?"

I told her the details. As she listened, she clasped her hands over her mouth as if to hold back a scream, and her face was creased in deep distress.

"Oh, Thomas," she said, close to tears, "you cannot know how serious this is. The demons consider granting safe passage through hell to escorts who journey alone only when they are traveling upward to Sheol, and then only grudgingly. They assume that escorts traveling upward are returning from their commissioned journeys, so they fear being punished should they try to delay the purposes of heaven."

I didn't like the sound of this. "So what happens if an escort travels alone going *down*?"

"Then the demons take their liberties. They conclude that the escort must be attempting an escape, rather than traveling under a commission."

My heart was pounding. "Can't the escort somehow prove that the journey has been commissioned?"

"How could they do that?" she said. "The devils trust no one, and even official papers would be suspect as a forgery. All the escorts have is the spoken formula. Surely you have heard Capopia use it by now: *So it is willed —* "

" *— where what is willed must be,*" I said. "Yes, we had to use it several times." I stood up and took Lakshmi's hand in mine. "Then how did you get down here alone?"

"I was not alone until I came to this circle. I came with another woman from Sheol who has also been called."

"Why *have* you come, Lakshmi?"

By now she was trembling. "This journey is a trial for both the other woman and me — a test to see whether we can endure what must be endured in order to serve as escorts. Capopia also survived such a test before she began her commission."

"How far must the two of you go?"

"Each of us was sent with an urgent message to be delivered. My companion has delivered hers. Now I must deliver mine."

"And who's to receive the message?"

Her lip was quivering. "*You* are, Thomas — and Capopia was to have heard it as well."

I took her by both arms and shook her. "Tell me, Lakshmi, quickly. What's the message?"

Lakshmi broke into tears. "The message was emphatic," she said, sobbing. "Under no circumstances were you and Capopia to be separated, and you were not to trust anyone else. There would be great danger, I was told, if you did."

She pulled away from my grip. "But now...now I fear I am too late."

TWENTY-NINE

I put my head between my hands. "No, Lakshmi. Oh, no. What can we do?"

She wiped her tears with the edge of her sari. "I can do nothing. I have my instructions to return immediately, Thomas, and I dare not neglect them; it would only make matters much worse. The question now is, what can *you* do?"

Stone had been strangely silent through the whole conversation, but now he stood up and turned in Lakshmi's direction.

"I have a question," he said to her. "How did you receive these messages? Who gave them to you?"

Lakshmi looked at him innocently, still sniffling. "Why, I heard them in my mind."

"In your mind?" said Stone, his voice edged with skepticism. "No angel, no demon, no other soul from Sheol gave you your instructions?"

"No. But I am certain of them nonetheless."

Stone's eyes were still empty, but intense. "Just how can you be so sure?"

"I...I have always known certain things that others do not know, ever since I came to Sheol. I have always heard things in

185

my head, and when they were capable of being proven, they always proved true. In fact, I remember telling Thomas that I would see him again."

"She's right, Stone," I said. But he shook his head firmly.

"It'll take more than that to convince me you're not just hearing things," he said. "You may even be hearing things from the wrong source. We just saw plenty of examples of that."

"Lakshmi," I said gently, "Miss C — I mean, Capopia — told me that she received her commissions from messengers. Shouldn't it be the same for you?"

"I cannot speak for Capopia," she said, "but I can tell you with all my heart: This message is from the same One who brought you here, and your destiny hangs on your obedience to what He has said."

I was in a terrible bind. I didn't want to agree with Stone, but I had to. There was no doubt in my mind that Lakshmi's heart was right, but that didn't mean she wasn't being fooled by some devil who knew how to get inside her head. If the fourth pit was any indication, hell's unemployment line was long with spirits of false prophecy, hanging around with a lengthy resume in their hands and looking for a new job.

Lakshmi turned to Stone, her hands clasped together. "You must believe me, Stone. I would not have come so far and endured so much to tell something of which I was not absolutely certain."

Stone turned away toward the darkness. "You said Tom wasn't to trust anyone. Maybe that includes you too."

Lakshmi faced me again, and I looked deep into her eyes. They were pleading now. "It is too late for Capopia to obey. But you must heed my words, Thomas. Find her if you can. And do not trust yourself to —"

"We'll keep that in mind, Lakshmi," said Stone gruffly. "Now I think we'd better be going. Good luck on your journey."

She looked long and hard at Stone. "Before I leave, there is something I must ask you. Those pants you have on — if I recall correctly, they belong to Thomas. How did you come to be wearing them?"

Stone shrugged. "He lent them to me."

"Then you are one of the damned?"

"That remains to be seen."

Her eyes narrowed. "Yes, it does." She took one last long look at me. "Keep your eyes open, Thomas."

As Lakshmi turned to go, I remembered one more question of my own. "Wait," I said. "You never told us how you knew to find me on the bridge of the fourth pit."

She sighed. "I told you already. I heard it in my head." Then she bowed quickly and slipped off into the darkness.

The next hour of walking was passed in uneasy silence. If Stone hadn't had to hang onto my arm, he'd have probably walked alone a few steps ahead of me. His grip was tense and stiff. Every once in a while I'd call Miss C's name out loud into the darkness, and when I did, his fingernails would cut into me even deeper.

At last I broke the silence. "Stone," I said gently, "I know what you're thinking."

He stopped and pushed my arm away. "How could you possibly know what I'm thinking? Are you some kind of self-appointed prophet, too?"

"Stone, I have doubts just as you do about whether Lakshmi knows what she's talking about."

"Good, then. We're agreed. You can just forget she ever showed up."

"But you have to admit she was right about where to find us."

"Coincidence."

"There are no coincidences in hell."

Stone threw his hands up in exasperation. "Gimme a break, Tom! Look — if she really has some special power to know things like that, then why didn't she know Miss C had already split? Tell me that, huh? Or if she knew exactly where to find us, why couldn't she tell us where to find Miss C?"

He had a point. "I don't know, Stone. All I can say is that nobody could know everything. Maybe she can't pick and choose what she knows."

"Well, it seems to me that when it comes to things so vital to fulfilling her commission, as she puts it, you would think she'd know at least that much."

I started pacing, trying to sort it out.

"How do you know she's not being guided by some devil?" Stone demanded. "A demon could easily have known where to find us. This could all be some big trap to lead us down to a place that's ten times worse than where we would have been otherwise. Hasn't everybody said all along that the deeper you go, the worse it gets?"

"For it to be a trap, Miss C would have to be in on it. There's no way *she* could be deceiving me."

"And why are you so sure of that?"

"She's risked too much to help me. You saw what nearly happened to her twice in the seventh circle alone."

Stone pounded his leg and scowled. "Can't you see? Even if you can trust Miss C — and I'm not convinced you can — she could still be a pawn, with Lakshmi or somebody else making the moves."

I stopped pacing and put my hands on my hips. "Stone, I think we're talking about two issues here — the message and the motive. It seems to me that unless you're a prophet yourself, the only way to judge a message from God is by its accuracy. And the only way to judge a prophet is by the prophet's character. So far Lakshmi's given me no reason to doubt either one."

"So you're calling her a prophet now?"

"I'm just talking about possibilities."

"Well, the problem is, we've got to talk about realities, Tom. It's nice to be able to look back later and judge a supposed message from God according to whether it finally turned out to be true or not. But we don't have that luxury. You've got to make some decisions *now*. And everything could depend on what you decide."

"Don't you mean what *we* decide, Stone?"

"I've made my decision. I don't trust either one of your buddies from Sheol. Now it's your choice. And from what Lakshmi said about not trusting anybody else, it looks like you'll have to believe her and dump me, or else forget about her and trust me. You can't do both."

I closed my eyes and rubbed my face. "I don't really think the choice is as clear as you make it out to be, Stone. Maybe she could be right about one thing and wrong about the other. Or maybe when she said not to trust anybody else, she wasn't talking about you. You and I were already friends by the time she came, so maybe the message just meant I wasn't to trust anybody *else* who came along after she gave it to me. It could mean a lot of things."

"You're just grasping at straws, Tom, and you know it. I still think it could all be staged. God — or whoever's really in charge here — doesn't seem to have spared any effort to tailor-make the torments for each soul. Maybe *you're* one of the damned, Tom. Maybe you're a pinball ricocheting around God's infernal little machine, and He wants to see how far you'll bounce before you end up in the hole. And maybe Satan himself is just waiting for you right by that hole at the bottom — ready to chew you up and spit you out."

I couldn't listen to any more; my head was buzzing like a dull mill saw. If Stone was right, then all was lost. If Stone was even *partly* right, then I was still in big trouble. And if Lakshmi was right, I had other problems altogether.

I took a deep breath and let it out slowly. "Stone, I don't know what to make of Lakshmi's message or where it really came from. But the one thing I *do* know is that I can't just run off and leave you here in your condition. No matter what Lakshmi said, I'm staying with you. You can count on that."

Stone let out a deep breath of his own. "Good. Now we're getting somewhere. The next question is what you're going to do about Miss C. Will you go looking for her? If so, having me along is sure to slow you down. And where will you look for her, anyway? Go back up slope, and you might not make it down again, you know."

He was making lots of sense, but I didn't like it.

"Here's my plan," he went on. "Remember how we talked about settling down somewhere? Well, let's pick a place near a safe pit — you know, like the one for the hypocrites or something, where they won't be after us — and then camp out in sight of the bridge. If we chase after her in this darkness, we could be staying half a mile behind her the whole time and never even know it, much less catch up with her. But if we stay put, we make it easier for her to find *us*, and she's sure to cross over the bridge sometime — that is, *if* she's still looking for us."

The plan was reasonable, but those last words grated on me. I *had* to believe she was still looking for us. She was too dedicated to her calling to give up.

But then again, somebody or something could have *stopped* her from looking for us. What if she was being molested by that crowd at the canal? I shuddered. I just had to put that kind of thought out of my mind.

If anybody knew how to get around hell — in *either* direction — it was Miss C. I had little choice but to trust her competence as well as her motives. It was either that or go looking for her in this infernal black hole. If I did, I was sure to get swallowed up, and then we'd *both* be lost.

"Let's go, then," I finally said to Stone. "We should be getting close to the next pit, and we can check it out. If it looks safe, we'll camp near the bridge and wait."

"Great," said Stone, smiling at last. "I hope you remembered to bring your chess game."

"Are you kidding?" I said. "Where I come from, we play checkers, boy. Give me a few asphalt pebbles and a concrete chip to draw some squares, and we'll be in business."

He took my arm and off we went with a chuckle. To be honest, my predicament didn't look any better. But it felt good, at least, to be on speaking terms with Stone again.

Meanwhile, I could hear in my own head what Daddy used to say when I couldn't make up my mind about which way to go — something that happened often enough when I was growing up. "Well, come on, boy," he'd say. "You gotta do *some*thing, even if it's *wrong*."

Daddy would have been proud; I was doing something. But I couldn't get over the feeling that the something was wrong.

THIRTY

Soon we knew the next pit was near because of its strange odor, like the smell of a child's new bathtub toy when it's just come straight out of the package. Stranger still were the sounds: not screams or wails or moans; not any human voices at all. Instead, we could hear a mechanical humming and clunking, like heavy machinery, and a gurgling, bubbling noise.

We were almost to the edge — which was outlined by bright, white light from inside the trench — when I noticed not far away a life-sized male mannequin dressed in a white apron. It seemed to be plastic rather than wood and was posed in a sitting position on the rim, holding what looked like an oversized fondue fork. The molded, curly hair on the head was painted blond, the smile was daubed on in dull red and the skin was pale.

I looked along the rim of the pit and saw that the dummy wasn't alone: More plastic mannequins were stationed at regular intervals, dressed in more aprons. All their faces pointed down toward the middle of the pit.

I followed their gaze to see what was there myself. This concrete gully was much wider and deeper than the last one, lit with sputtering white fluorescent lights and packed to the walls with

191

enough decrepit equipment to outfit every run-down factory in the Rust Belt.

My attention was grabbed right away by a slew of huge vats, boiling with something thick and black. More dummies were posed standing on platforms around them and holding more forks. I realized then that the odd odor was coming from the steam off the vats: It was the smell of molten plastic.

Stone asked what I saw, and I told him.

"This one's as weird as they come. No sign of demons?" he asked.

"No. No doomed souls either. I wonder what's going on here."

"That's funny," said Stone. "Didn't Miss C say some of these bridges would be guarded by devils? But we haven't had any trouble yet."

"I wouldn't speak too soon, buddy. We've still got a few to go."

I looked back at the first dummy and nearly jumped out of my skin.

Its face was turned to look at us now.

"Stone," I said. "We're not alone. One of the dummies just turned its head — or, I mean, somebody turned it — and it's looking at us."

"What?" he said, too loudly.

"Shhh!" I turned to put my hand over his mouth, then looked back at the mannequin. The face was pointed toward the pit again.

I rubbed my eyes. Maybe all this squinting in the dark was finally taking its toll. That's *all* we needed — now one of us wasn't seeing what was there, and the other was seeing what *wasn't* there.

Just then there was a commotion in the vat closest to us, a ripple of movement that wasn't a bubble. Suddenly a head popped up out of the plastic, followed by shoulders and arms. Two eyes opened through the black gunk, and then a mouth that screamed: "I can't take it anymore!"

Instantly the arms of all the dummies around the vat went up. Ten fondue forks rammed into the man's torso. As he shrieked and wriggled, the dummies along the sidelines clapped their plastic hands and cheered. Two of them pulled him out and took him to the pavement on the far side. I couldn't see what happened next, but I didn't want to.

"We're in trouble," I whispered to Stone. "That was no dummy that saw us. It's a demon in dummy disguise. He and his buddies are stewing souls in those pots, and it looks like there's plenty of room for more."

"Is he still looking at us?" asked Stone.

"No. All their attention seems to be on the vats while they wait for some poor sucker to stick his head up. Kind of like spear fishing, I guess."

"Is the bridge guarded?" asked Stone.

I hadn't thought to look yet. When I did, my heart sank: A dozen devil dummies were lined up across the far end like sentries, forks over their shoulders.

"We're trapped," I said. "Got any ideas?

"We could always go back the way we came and wait *there* for Miss C."

"It's too late. Now that we've been spotted, two or three have their sights on us. But they're not making any moves yet."

Suddenly, from the darkness beyond the other side of the pit, a scream rang out. "You can't do this to me!" said the male voice. "I'm a senator of the United States of America!"

The dummies roared with laughter — one of them so hard he fell off the edge into the pit. That, of course, only made the others laugh all the harder.

A tall female mannequin appeared from the shadows with the senator skewered on her fork like a hotdog. "Shut up, you old windbag!" she shouted. "You ought to be glad you kicked the bucket so soon after the banking scandals. If you'd hung around much longer, you might have done something worse — and I don't think you'd like it any better farther down!"

She tossed the old man into the nearest vat, where he howled and tried to keep his head above the boiling plastic. "Show your face again," she shouted, "and we'll dissect you like a frog in biology class. Then it'll be back in the plastic again. You wouldn't like to have that goop bubbling between your liver and your lungs, now would you?"

He moaned and dove under the black ripples.

The she-demon snorted. "He always tried so hard at keeping that plastic smile. Let's see if this is an improvement."

A male demon beside the vat was grinning. "Maybe," he added, "we should boil him in some of those plastic *promises* he made."

"These dummies mean business," said Stone, again too loudly. "So is this a pit especially for senators? I'd expect it to be overflowing by now."

"That may well be the senatorial vat," I said. "But I'm sure there are plenty of others here too. It looks to me like this is the pit where they bring people for committing graft. Dante found them in boiling pitch, but I guess like everything else, they've changed with the times."

"So this place keeps up with all the crooked politicians?"

"Plus anybody else who takes advantage of a position of trust for their own gain. Embezzlers, extortionists, judges who take bribes, policemen on the take — corrupt public figures of every sort."

"Where could they possibly put them all?"

"Those vats stretch out the whole length of the trench, Stone, and each one's the size of a city block."

"Yeah, but think about it: They'd need one the size of Rhode Island just to hold all the crooked 'public servants' from New York."

The dummies around a second vat had grown tired of waiting for their catch, so they started poking around in the black liquid with their forks. "I'd sure like to find Boss Tweed again," said one. "Most fun I've had in centuries. New Yorkers put up such a *fight*!"

"Gotcha, you sneaky little jerk!" shouted a she-demon. She snatched a trim-framed man up from the bubbles, her fork piercing one of his ears.

"Leave me alone!" the dripping soul screamed. "It was my duty as an officer. I was just protecting my men!"

The demon snickered. "But what about your *women*? Did you protect *them* when you covered up all those cases of rape, assault and sexual harassment among your troops?" She dangled him like a worm on a hook and looked at her buddies. "How about some military exercises, boys? Lay him out on the pavement and give him a G.I. cut."

The others cheered. With a toss of the fork the man was on the ground, and half a dozen demons swarmed over him like riled fire ants.

"I can't watch any more of this," I whispered to Stone, looking

194

away. I was gagging.

There were clattering footsteps behind us, and we spun around, though I was still heaving. We were surrounded by mannequins.

"Breaktime's over," said a black one with his fork against my chest. "Back in the bubbles."

"Can't you see we've got clothes on?" said Stone in a macho voice I hadn't heard since he fooled the slavers. "We're on our way down. You know the rules."

"Maybe we do, and maybe we don't," said the devil. "Of course, what does it matter in *this* pit? You damned souls never followed the rules anyway — that's why you're here. So tell us about the rules, fool."

Stone put on his best Clint Eastwood sneer. "So it is willed where...uh, where...you tell them, Tom."

I finally stopped gagging and straightened up. Then I put on *my* best Miss C look of authority. "*So it is willed where what is willed must be.*"

The black demon's jaw twisted in a perverse way — the dummy equivalent, I guess, of a scowl. "You're lying. You belong here. You just overheard somebody else say that."

"This journey has been commissioned," I said, fighting for confidence. "You know you have no choice but to let us through. It could go very badly for you if they found out you were giving us trouble. How would you like to spend eternity chipping souls out of ice downstairs?"

"All right, already," Stone whispered in my ear. "Don't overdo it."

They stood and stared at us with blank plastic eyes as I felt my stomach sinking. I'd just used up a lifetime supply of nerve, and I didn't have any left.

Slowly the black demon dropped his fork from my chest, letting it scratch as it went down. "Get out of here. But remember: If you ever come back this way, you're gonna be fondue cubes."

We scrambled so hard we almost fell into the pit. When we got to the far end of the bridge, the dummy crowd stood their ground and made us push between them, jeering as we did. One of them swung his fork at us, but we both ducked. He hit another one in the neck instead, who promptly returned the favor. As we finally shoved our way through, the two brawlers were going at it, with plastic shivers flying everywhere and the other devils cheering them on.

The pavement there was especially rough; as we ran, we stumbled in potholes every few yards. What had to be at least a mile away, we slowed to a walk, figuring we were far enough to be out of danger. But my stomach had turned inside out, and I felt a sudden exhaustion. "I've got to sit down," I said to Stone. "It'll be safe here."

We plopped down and stretched out on the pavement, hearts pounding, lungs gasping. Stone caught his breath first. "You would have made a fabulous actor, Tom," he said. "I didn't know you had it in you. But don't you think you were pushing our luck a little?"

"Pushing it? Shoot, buddy, I was *shoving* it!" We both laughed a good belly laugh, sorely needed.

Neither of us spoke for a minute, waiting for our chests to stop thumping. When mine settled down, I turned on my side toward Stone. "You know, I didn't know till then that those words Miss C always used with the devils would work for me. Even with that big-time bluff, though, for a while it didn't look like they were going to blink."

He got up on one elbow, facing me. "I think I'd better learn that little formula myself; it just might come in handy. Tell me again what it was you said?"

I repeated it for him till he had it down.

"Stone," I said, scratching my head, "just one question. How did you know to duck when that devil swung at us?"

His face was suddenly straight. "I heard the *whoosh* of the fork coming — couldn't you?"

"No, I couldn't."

He sat up and turned his face down toward the pavement. "Well, they say the loss of one sense always makes the others get sharper to compensate. I guess that must be true after all, huh?"

"I guess."

"Hey, my nose is working better too, so you can imagine what I had to go through back at that cesspool. In fact" — he bent over me, sniffed and grinned — "traveling with you isn't exactly a rose garden experience, bucko."

I swatted at him and chuckled. "You won't have to worry about that when we get to the ice. Something tells me we won't be sweating there."

"Well," he said, "I don't think that'll be anytime soon. It's time to camp out, bud."

"Don't forget," I said, sitting up, "we're supposed to be within calling distance of the next pit so we can keep an eye on the bridge. It can't be too far — we probably ran half the way already. Let's hit the road."

He dragged himself up slowly and walked even slower. As it turned out, pit number six wasn't far at all. Before long I saw an arc of golden light in the distance. When I told him, he stopped. "If you can see it from here, that's good enough. I don't want to go any closer."

"But I can't make out the bridge from here."

"Believe me," he said. "If Miss C comes by this way, you'll see her." He sat down, and I knew that was the end of the matter for him. Maybe he was still thinking about those demons at the last bridge and wanted to avoid another close call.

"OK," I said, "for the time being, anyway. So what do we do now that we're here?"

"Why don't you look for those asphalt pebbles you were talking about, and let's see if we can figure out how a blind man plays checkers."

The pebbles weren't hard to find; I only had to scavenge in a few potholes. But finding something to draw squares on the pavement with was a different matter. I looked around for a concrete chip, but no luck.

"I need something to draw with, Stone — hard enough to dig into the pavement so you can feel the lines with your fingers. I'm going to look around a little to see what I can find. I'll be right back."

He grabbed my arm; his face was so intense it surprised me. "Don't go far, OK? Stay away from that trench — you don't know who or what might be on guard out there. I mean it." He relaxed his grip a little. "If anything happened to you, buddy, what would I do?"

"Don't worry; I'll stick close," I said, patting his hand and pulling it off my arm. "What could possibly happen to me?"

THIRTY-ONE

Ten minutes of hunting in vain convinced me that all the asphalt in this circle was between the pits, and all the concrete was inside them — or over them, in the bridges. All the spans we'd crossed so far had been chipped and cracked, so I figured if I checked the base of the next one, I could find what I was looking for.

Then, too, no matter what Stone said, I wanted to get some idea of where the bridge was so I'd know if we really were close enough to see Miss C passing by. Just find it, I told myself, grab a little chunk of concrete or two and be back before Stone knows it.

I trotted up to the rim of the trench and looked down into the dim glimmer of low-watt lightbulbs, hanging naked from frayed wires attached in a line along the upper walls. About twelve feet below, thousands of doomed souls stood close together, dressed in heavy gold fabric — or at least I thought at first they were standing; after a few minutes I realized they were actually inching along at snail speed. Some whispered among themselves, and all were grunting and groaning while they trudged forward, as if the weight of the world were in their back pockets.

That is, for those who *had* back pockets. This was the first clothing I'd seen on the damned souls below Sheol, and the variety of styles reminded me once more that hell had been around a long time. Folks were dressed in everything from robes to hoop skirts, loincloths to bikinis, and all the outfits were made of the same thick, golden cloth.

I surveyed the pit and the pavement around it for any sign of demons but saw none. The souls themselves didn't look dangerous either; most looked down, and they were so wrapped up in their efforts that they didn't notice me. All in all, things looked safe enough, I reckoned, but I had one big problem: The bridge was nowhere to be seen.

At the speed they were going, those people might well have needed a thousand years or more to get all the way around the circle. But since some of them were dressed like they'd been there at least that long, somebody must have seen the bridge along the way. I didn't relish talking to them, but asking directions was the only quick way to find out what I needed to know.

I picked out an old woman creeping along directly below me in a gold, high-collared dress. "Excuse me," I shouted, crouching down. "Can you tell me where the bridge is?"

She looked up slowly, grimacing while she moved her head as if her collar were a fetter around her neck. "No," she said. "And even if I knew, what good would it do me? I couldn't climb it."

I was curious now; this trench hadn't rung a bell yet in my memories of Dante. "Tell me," I said. "What sin was it that sent so many people to this pit?"

The old woman snorted and gave me a long, hard stare. "I can tell you why everyone *else* is here," she said, "but I don't know why I'm here with them. These people are *hypocrites*."

Her words jolted my memory, and suddenly it all made sense. That wasn't gold fabric they were wearing after all. These wretched souls of the hypocrites, I remembered now from Dante, were condemned to walk around the circle of the trench in clothes made of lead — the gold was only paint on the outside. The clothing, like the lives they'd lived, looked pretty, but the glitter was deceptive.

They circled the abyss endlessly, toting a bear of a load. That's why it could take them hours to move a single yard.

"I haven't seen a doomed soul out of place yet," I said to the woman, more matter-of-factly than unkindly. "Where do you think you *should* be?"

"Why, in heaven, of course!" she whined, still crawling at a pace that would have had snails backed up for miles. "*I* was never a hypocrite. I went to church, paid my tithes, gave to missions. I even gave Bibles to the employees in my business."

That last statement *did* ring a bell. I looked closer at the woman's lined and sour old face and couldn't believe what I saw. It was Agnes Wolff, the owner of the portrait studio where I'd worked as a gofer when I was in high school. She'd given out Bibles to her new employees, all right — then treated them like dirt the rest of the time they were with her. I'd never known anybody so hard to work with, so stuffed with self-importance and so worried about maintaining the appearance of piety.

"I'm sure you don't remember me, Ms. Wolff," I said, "but I certainly remember you. I ran errands in your office when I was a kid."

She squinted to get a better look at my face. "Frankly, I don't remember you at all. You must not have made much of an impression."

"Well," I said, "I didn't stay around long enough, I guess. You went through employees like they came out of a Kleenex box."

"Just what do you mean?" she demanded. "I gave fair wages to anyone who met my standards of excellence. Obviously, you didn't."

"And how could I, the way you operated? Whenever you missed an appointment, you found a way to blame me for not reminding you — even though you never let me see the appointment book. When you made an error on the bank deposit slip, you always accused me of stealing the difference on the way to the bank. Nothing anybody ever did satisfied you, so you tried to do it all yourself, and when you blew it, you blamed everybody else. I hate to say it, Ms. Wolff, but I think you're in just the right place."

"How dare you judge me!" she hissed. "I was a charter member of our church!"

"Yep," said a male voice behind her, "and I preached a TV broadcast that went all around the world. Lot of good it did us in the end, huh?"

The man was dressed in suit pants, a loose necktie and a long-sleeved shirt with the sleeves rolled up. His hair was slicked back, and his scowling face, beaded with sweat, looked vaguely familiar.

"I spent my whole life preaching," he said. "Then one little slip with a call girl in Las Vegas, and that was all she wrote, boy. Don't seem right, does it?"

I remembered the story from the papers. "If my memory serves me well," I said to him, "it was more than a little slip. You were caught at it four or five times. How many times did you get away with it?"

He cussed me. "What I did in my private life was *my* business, and nobody else's."

"The people who supported your little empire with their hard-earned money, thinking they were giving to God, might not agree with you."

"Hmph," said Ms. Wolff, "I never did anything like *that*."

The preacher strained to move his left foot another centimeter. "Aw, shut up, Granny. We're all in the same boat now. Can't you move it along a little faster?" He sneered at me. "I'm getting mighty tired of the landscape here."

"Don't hurry *me*, you hypocrite," said Ms. Wolff. "I'm going plenty fast, and I'm wearing twice as much lead as you are."

"It doesn't make any difference," said a young woman grunting along beside her in golden lingerie. "Whoever put this place together made it so that a G-string weighs the same as a fur coat."

"Just how heavy is it?" I asked.

"Well," said a potbellied guy with a flattop just behind her, "it's like lifting up on the front end of a pickup with everything you got, straining every muscle till you think you're gonna bust — and holding it there for six hundred years."

"Don't you ever get a chance to rest?" I asked.

He looked at me as if I had six eyes. "Did you just get here, boy, or did your brain fall out on the way down? Chance to rest? This is *hell*."

"I don't see any guards," I said. "Who's to stop you from taking a break?"

"If you try to stop," said the flattop, "you've always got somebody pushing from behind, and that's just too dangerous. You might fall down — and if you do, you're so heavy you'll never get up again. There's no room for folks to go around you, so everybody else will be walking right over you in *their* lead duds till doomsday."

"Why don't you try to escape?" I asked.

They all laughed at once, bitterly. "Look, boy," said the preacher. "*You* try making a run for it in a two-ton toga."

"Besides," said a paunchy man with a grating New York brogue, "some of us are just waiting to get our day in court."

"You expect to get *out* of here?" I asked him.

"Hey — don't get smart with me. I was a governor, y'know, and a good one too." He grimaced and strained to move a quarter of an inch.

"So why are you here?"

"That idiot upstairs called me a hypocrite because I said I was personally opposed to abortion, but as a public official I supported abortion rights. We couldn't legislate morality."

"Did your state have laws against murder or rape or robbery?"

He scowled. "Of course, you fool. What has *that* got to do with it?"

"Then you were already legislating morality. In fact, most laws are just that: legislated moral codes. That's what lawmaking is all about. Admit it. You were just too cowardly to take an unpopular political position."

"Yeah," said the preacher, guffawing. "You *hypocrite*, you! Haw, haw!"

"Stuff it, buddy," said the governor to the preacher. Then to me: "By the way — you won't tell anybody else you saw me here, will you? I mean, I want the history books to focus on the good stuff, y' know?"

I made no promises. Instead, I stood up straight and pointed my finger down the length of the trench. "Doesn't *any*body here know where the bridge is?"

There was a murmur, then at last: "*Si, signore.*" It was a man in a long monk's robe, some distance behind the others. He gritted his teeth and peered out from a hood that must have weighed as much as a stone cathedral. "The bridge is out," he said simply, his accent thickly Italian.

"Out?" I asked. "What happened?"

"I was told it fell down in the Great Earthquake, long before most of us ever came to this place. The pile of rubble is a little farther down the trench, along the bottom of both walls."

I was so stunned I forgot to thank him. So this was the end of the road — unless we went down into that pit and squeezed our way through all these lead-wrapped sardines. It looked like Stone and I had probably camped in the right place after all.

Stone! I'd gotten so caught up in conversation with these characters that I'd forgotten all about why I was there. Stone would probably be worried by now, and I'd have to do some tall explaining about why I took the risk of coming to the pit after he'd insisted I stay away from it.

When I turned to go, a middle-aged man in a gold business suit about twenty feet ahead of the others called out. "Hey — you up there! How recently did you arrive?"

"Not long ago," I yelled, trotting up to where he was. "Why do you ask?"

"You sound like an American. Are you from California by any chance?"

"Shoot, no," I said. "Bred and born in Georgia — couldn't you tell from the way I talk? But what does it matter down here anyway?"

"I was a state senator there," he said. "I just want to know if some legislation I sponsored ever made it through. I died in a plane crash before it was voted on."

"Anything I might have heard on the national news?" I asked.

"Sure," he said and twisted his neck, chafing against his lead tie. "It was a hot topic, so they played it up in the media. I was trying to get the legislature to pass a law making it illegal for the state to hire known homosexuals. Those perverts were trying to take over the government, and we had to do something to stop it."

"I can't help you with that," I said, "but I've got a friend who might know. He lived in Hollywood, and I think that particular bill would have been of interest to him."

"Hollywood?" asked the senator. "I had a lot of connections there. Who's your friend?"

"You may have even known him from the movies," I said. "His name is Stone. Stone Jordan. Used to play in all those old teenage beach flicks."

The senator's jaw fell. "Stone? You know Stone? He's here?"

"Yes, he's *right* here," said an angry voice over my shoulder.

It was Stone. His fists were clenched, and the veins were popping out on his neck.

I was stunned. "How did you ever find your way here?"

"I followed the voices. You were certainly loud enough."

"But didn't you trip on the potholes?"

"I was careful." He looked straight into my eyes. "What are you doing here? You said you'd come right back."

I watched his face closely as I walked a few steps along the edge of the trench. His eyes followed me.

"So you can see after all," I said. "Did you have me fooled all the time?"

"Oh, I lost my vision, all right," he said, putting his fists on his hips. "It didn't come back till we were standing by the last pit."

"That's why you ducked when that demon swung his fork."

"You got it. I would have been crazy not to, even if it blew my cover."

I shook my head slowly. "You're a better actor than even I could have guessed."

"I played the role of a blind kid in a movie once. No big deal."

"But why did you feel you had to hide it from me? What was the point?"

He crossed his arms. "I could tell you still had some crazy notion about looking for Miss C. The only way I could keep you from doing that, I decided, was to let you think I was too much of a burden to come along and too helpless to be left alone."

"Well," I said, feeling my jaw tense up, "I guess you got just what you wanted."

"He *always* gets just what he wants," said the senator. "That's Stone's style. And he'll put on whatever act it takes to get it. Then he dumps you."

"*You're* one to talk, John," Stone growled through his teeth. "Talk about an act: You ran your whole campaign on a promise to pass that anti-gay legislation. You wrote it, you sponsored it, and if you hadn't died when you did, you would have pushed it through. Meanwhile, the whole time you were sleeping with me — and all three of your cute little male aides, too."

The senator's eyes were on fire. "I don't recall that you ever came out of the closet yourself, pretty boy. And by the way: Just who was it that made that highly publicized contribution to my campaign — the one that probably clinched the election for me?"

"People were beginning to suspect!" shouted Stone. "It was the only way I could get the tabloids off my case!"

Stone turned to me. "You!" He spat the word at my face. "It's all your fault! We were doing fine till you sneaked over here and started asking questions." He gave me a shove, and I lost my balance. Grabbing wildly, I latched onto his arm. We both went tumbling down into the pit.

The uncovered parts of the people below us cushioned our fall, but wherever we hit lead, it felt like a hammer blow. I was bruised but no worse, so I jumped up quickly and offered a hand up to Stone. He refused.

The senator was on the floor, having taken the brunt of my impact. I went over and tried to lift him, but it was hopeless. I might as well have tried to lift the Superdome.

"Get me up!" he screamed. "I'll be crushed!"

"He can't!" shouted the flattop, inching forward. "Once you're down, you're down for good!"

Just then Stone let out a yell. He was still sitting on the concrete, looking dazed and staring at his legs.

The pants he wore were turning gold.

I grabbed his hand to pull him up, but it was too late. He was already anchored to the ground by the tattered old trousers I'd given him.

"Let me up!" Stone screamed, pounding on the hardening folds of the fabric. "So it is willed where what is willed must be!" But the pants were gilded lead now and impossible to move.

He looked up at me as the other hypocrites continued their excruciating pace toward him. "*You* did it!" he shrieked. "You and all the other straights in the world! *You* made us live a lie. We knew if we ever came out of the closet, even to ask for help, you'd hate us and finally get rid of us. Well, you've succeeded!"

He was weeping now. "Your hate, your prejudice, your self-righteous idiocy did this to me. It wasn't my fault. It never was my fault. Damn the whole straight world and its smug hypocrisy! *You* belong here, not me!"

The doomed souls were pressing in on us like the jaws of a lead trap. My eyes were flooded and my heart was on fire, but there was nothing more I could do. Stone would never get out of the pit, and if I stayed any longer, neither would I.

"I'm sorry, Stone," I said. "I'm so sorry." Then I turned and began squeezing my way through the creeping thicket of dense metal and damned souls.

THIRTY-TWO

I scrambled up the far wall of the trench on the ruins of the bridge, numb and shaken, and ran off into the darkness. Strangely, my stomach was feeling better now, though you might have thought it would be hurting all the more. When I lost Stone, something died in me, down deep where memories haunt the heart as raw feelings instead of words or even pictures.

Sure, he had deceived me, had used me, had played me like a poker hand. But he'd also saved me from the slavers, just as a lifetime ago his red Chevy had saved me from despair. I loved him.

As a child I knew that the Stone on the screen was the man I wanted to become. Now I realized that the Stone in hell was the man I *could* have become. It may have seemed we'd been traveling the same road down through the fire and the pain, but the truth was that our common path had taken us to a fork long before we ever came here, and in the end he'd gone one way while I went the other.

What hurt and scared me most was knowing in my heart of hearts the terrible truth about that parting of the ways: Though you could call it a choice, I couldn't take credit for it. I hadn't sought and found the right way so much as the right way had sought and found me. In a thousand little circumstances — hell, I had begun to see, was not the only place void of coincidence — my weakness had been taken account of, my temptations blurred or blocked, my waywardness held in check by the teeth of heaven's own Pit Bull.

I remembered the drizzly morning alone in my apartment when the world seemed to have gone gray and the razor was already in hand, but the phone rang with a rainbow: It was Mama, calling to ask me to come visit. There was the night I jumped in my car, eager to find some flesh to dull the pain, and the car wouldn't start. And what about the friends who showed up again and again at my door just when I thought the leaden loneliness was about to crush my mind?

Did grace, in the end, always get its way? Could I have ever really turned my back and said no? Yet even now I knew I still had a choice. I hadn't yet died, the last chapter hadn't been written, and if I were to scribble *no* across the last page, even the best of beginnings couldn't make the ending turn out right.

But what about Stone? Had grace run out before it reached him? Had it reached him, only to be scorned? His last words left me trembling. Had the sins of his father been visited on the child? Did the self-righteous folks lurking outside his closet door, ready to jump him if he came out, have a share in his darkness? Those were *my* pants, after all, that had him riveted to the pit.

I had my own questions for God, though I was less confident now than Stone had been that I would ever get to ask them. In the meantime it was too much to sort out, and I had to plan my way — alone.

Alone. It hit me square in the face at last that I was totally on my own, and I collapsed on the pavement. The blackness pressed in around me, taunted me, told me it had won after all. Sunlight, moonlight, starlight were hollow memories now, swallowed up in the everlasting darkness of this place, ghostly recollections that only served to make the suffocating black air around me thicker by comparison. The terrible words I'd heard so long ago in Sunday school bellowed through my mind: *Cast him into the outer darkness, where there will be weeping and gnashing of teeth; for many are called, but few are chosen.*

Maybe I'd been called. But had I been chosen?

I laid my head down on my arms and wailed. Would I ever make it home again? And where was home, anyway? The firestorm of Gehenna had gutted my childhood and burned away the comfortable assumptions of my adulthood; what place on earth — or even in my own heart — could ever again feel secure enough to call home?

I wanted to run, but where could I run? I wanted to hide, but there was no place to hide in this God-forsaken funnel of asphalt and pain. I wanted to curl up in a ball and stay right here with my back turned to everything else. But at any moment a gang of devils could come along through the blackness, collecting stray souls like chipped marbles lost in the deep, dark crevices of an old couch.

Armed demon warriors, swinging guns and forks and whips. Tormented souls fleeing before them, their forms warped and their mouths twisted in cries of anguish. They rushed shrieking now, all at once, through my head — the predators and the prey, the diabolical claws of justice and the damnable quarry of hell.

Which of the circles had a place reserved for *me*? Which pack of devils had a list with *my* name? I couldn't deny that any one of them could stake some claim on me, no matter how old or trivial the claim might seem in my own eyes. Hell was not given to hair-splitting between fibs and lies, personal flattery and professional hype, one-night stands and full-blown affairs.

Nor did time in itself have any magical power to wash away sin. I might once have laughed or even boasted about the selfish ploys of my childhood, as if it were someone else who had pulled them off. But no, they were still stains on my soul, and the years since had only served to set them, not to leach them out.

My wails had faded to silence at last when I heard a footstep. Or was it the muffled thud of a demon's whip in a far-off pit? Maybe my ears were playing tricks, or the devils themselves were playing tricks with my ears.

I peered into the darkness around me, and even my eyes couldn't be trusted. The blackness swirled in hideous shapes, faces with fangs and horns and hollow eyes. Hell's mockery of a childhood pastime — the infernal version of finding pictures in the clouds.

No other sounds came, and the faces at last disappeared. What should I do? I was easy game no matter what; but a moving target had better chances than a sitting duck, so I pulled myself up off the pavement and started to walk again. There was nothing to do but keep my eyes wide open and stumble on somehow, looking over my shoulder as I went, listening for any little noise that might warn of trouble.

No doubt demons ate flying bullets for breakfast, but even so I was wishing again that I had that old gun Daddy had tried to give me. And if the truth be told, I was wishing I had Daddy there to shoot it.

The next pit looked like a long, dark, back alley in the scariest part of town. It was cluttered with brick bats and trash, abandoned cars and rusty garbage dumpsters. The faintest of light made its way through the clutter from some distant source down the length of the trench, and occasional orange flares, like the striking of matches, dotted the darkness.

From the bridge I could make out black shapes, some human, some reptilian. They ran or slithered from hiding place to hiding place, with the reptiles chasing the doomed souls in a wicked game of tag. Constant screams of human pain and fright tallied up the score: The reptiles were winning.

Snakes, gila monsters, gators, crocs. I hadn't seen that much serpentine leather since the last rattler roundup in Vidalia. Wherever I looked, they were slithering or creeping or coiling or chowing down. It would have been enough to send Indiana Jones back to the blackboard forever.

Just below me a wild-eyed man was running, his hands tied behind his back with a cobra's coils. The wide-ribbed hood around the snake's neck had slinked between his legs and was facing him, bare-fanged, as he ran. When the man tripped and fell, the cobra struck, sinking its teeth deep in his throat. His struggling body burst suddenly into flames, and within seconds the snake was slithering through a pile of smoking ashes.

I rubbed my eyes and looked again. The smoke had sucked up the ashes and was congealing now. As I watched, dumbfounded, the form of a man grew back again. He looked dazed with terror.

"Who are you?" I shouted down from the bridge. "What did you do to wind up here?"

"So I grabbed a few purses from some little old ladies with blue hair," he whimpered. "For that I deserve *this*? Even Miami didn't have snakes this bad, man!"

Nearby a sturdy woman with short-cropped hair was backed up against the trench wall by a grinning crocodile. "Leave me alone!" she shrieked. "The IRS was *supposed* to take money from people. So what if a few innocent taxpayers got ruined while we were trying to track down the cheaters? Who cares if I bankrupted a few nice guys and covered my tracks? That's the breaks. I was just doing my job!"

The crocodile swung its tail around against her ankles and knocked her down. Then it crawled up alongside her and pinned her against the wall. As I watched, both figures began to lose their form, like two crayons melting down and mixing together. Before long there was only one hideous shape with features drawn from each: human eyes and ears on a head with long, toothy jaws; four scaly limbs that ended in clawed fingers and toes; an armor-plate tail that twitched just above smooth, rounded buttocks.

By now I'd seen enough to remember what Dante's guide had told him when they'd come upon this place. It was the pit of the thieves.

Just then a gila monster leaped out of a dumpster on an unsuspecting little man crouching in a pile of trash. Its fangs caught him on the left side of his chest, then it fell to the ground at his feet. Oddly, the man only yawned and stared at it, as if he'd just been roused from sleep. Red smoke began to pour out of his wound, and from the lizard's mouth as well, the two clouds mingling around them. The man's legs began to fuse together into a thick tail; the lizard's tail forked and grew into two fat legs. The man's skin hardened into scales while the reptile's hide softened and smoothed into skin. The beady black eyes turned brown and puffy; the puffy eyes shrank into ebony beads.

In less than a minute the switch was complete. What had once been the little man was now a gila monster creeping through the trash pile, while the former lizard stood up and walked away, hissing and grinning from new-grown ear to new-grown ear.

I shook my head and turned away from the ghastly sight. Hell's irony twisted through this pit with a venomous vengeance. Those damned souls who'd once seized the belongings of others now found that they couldn't hold on to even the most basic possession of all: their own personal forms. The reptiles were stealing their shapes, robbing them of what made them look human — or maybe just exposing them as the low-down creatures they'd been all along.

When I started down the bridge, a noise at my feet stopped me dead cold. Only inches away, a six-foot rattler lay coiled and shaking its tail. Maybe I'd spoken too soon. All of a sudden those Zero candy bars I'd shoplifted as a kid jumped up and danced around my head, alongside the books — five years overdue — that I'd never returned to the public library.

The snake turned toward me to stare long and hard, as if it knew me, knew all about me, knew it had an excuse for striking me and stealing away my frame. There's something almost human about those unblinking eyes, I thought. Was it really a damned soul that had already swapped shapes with a serpent?

The sourpuss librarian who kept overdue records, if she'd arrived down here yet, was sure to be slopping around up in the oily swamp of the sullen. On the other hand, the old shop owner who sold the candy bars, I recalled, had once himself been accused of cheating the bread delivery man.

But the snake only stretched itself out and went its winding way down the other side of the bridge.

THIRTY-THREE

Pit number eight was easy to find: Deep red flames flickered along the whole length of the trench and licked its upper walls. The fiery concrete furnace echoed with agonized babbles of men and women who sounded anxious to talk all at the same time, though I couldn't imagine that anybody could actually be heard in all that racket.

I hurried up the bridge, not knowing just how high the flames might flare up. From the top of the arch I could see down into the pit clearly, and what was there perplexed me. I'd expected to see a solid blaze, roaring from a fuel bed of some sort — coal, wood, even oil. Instead, the fire shot up from the naked, sooty concrete floor in separate flames, like the little blazes around the rim of a gas burner, but with each one large as a man.

Meanwhile, there were no doomed souls to be seen. I knew they were there only by the maddening murmur of their voices.

A thin, raspy tenor with a British accent floated up from the pit above the rest. "You're headed the wrong way, my good man." Still no sign of a face that might have spoken.

"No one travels down," it continued. "Things only get bloody worse when you move lower. You'd better stay here or head back up again." By now I could tell that the voice was coming from one particular flame, skinny and about six feet tall, flickering slightly with each syllable it spoke.

A fire next to it snickered. "Don't listen to *him*, mate. He's the one who talked Chamberlain into appeasing Hitler with chunks of Czechoslovakia. Thought a wretched 'peace with honor' would assure his own move up the diplomatic ranks — maybe even into Parliament."

"And what about you?" I asked the second flame. "Why are you here?"

"I'm still not sure, to tell the truth. This is the pit of the evil counselors, so they say, but I think someone in charge just has it out for us psychoanalysts. From what I can tell, just about everyone here who's not a barrister is a shrink, including old Freud himself. Whoever's in charge needs his head examined."

"That could be grounds for a libel suit, you know," said an American voice from a flame several feet away. "If we could only find out who *is* in charge."

"I will tell you not *who* is in charge, but *what* is in charge," shouted a gruff voice with a German accent. It came from a sputtering red flame some distance away. "History is marching on under the relentless control of economic laws. Even here the dialectic operates; we are destined to overthrow our bourgeois oppressors and build a classless society!"

If I could have seen his face, I would have known it from his picture in all the history books; but his words were just as easy to tag as his wild-haired mug. Who could it be but Karl Marx, the "evil counselor" who had talked half the world into living the communist madness, leaving whole nations in shambles? Here he was in hell, a pathetic diehard, still peddling his economic fantasies while Marxist empires upstairs were crumbling and Eastern children were free at last to dance on his grave.

He shouted, but no one listened. "Workers of hell, unite!"

The analyst's voice hissed with sarcasm. "Well, old chap," he said to Marx, "go find Lenin, Stalin and Mao, and maybe you can have yourself a little revolution over tea!" The flames around him flared up a bright orange, roaring with laughter.

Standing apart from the others, conspicuous by its silence, was a dark, brooding flame, the color of an ember almost gone out. I turned to it now and asked how it got there.

The fire stood erect for a moment, then at last it spoke. "I was a U.S. Supreme Court justice. I shared in the *Roe v. Wade* decision. And I would do it again."

"I'm with you," said a female flame next to him. "You opened the door for my family-planning organization to do what we'd wanted to do all along."

As the words left her mouth, both she and the justice turned from dull red to bright white to searing blue, till they screamed and sputtered in agony. Even the surrounding flames moved away from the intense heat.

"Let's take a vote," said a voice that reminded me of some talk-show host, though I couldn't remember which one. "Who says he should turn around and go back?"

"Go back!" they screamed in unison. "Go back!"

"It's certain doom down there!" said one.

"It's all a trap!" said another. "They'll turn you into a popsicle for the Devil. He's waiting for you!"

They joined now in a chant. "Go back while you can! Go back while you can! Go back while you can, you fool! Go back...."

I covered my ears with my hands. They were calling out the rabid doubts that until now I'd kept chained and frothing in the cellar of my mind. What if they were right?

I still didn't think Miss C could be deceiving me, but what if she herself was deceived? What if a demon horde was waiting for me at the end, paying up stacks of damned souls to the Devil because they'd lost a bet that I couldn't make it all the way down?

My head began to spin and fill with black smoke. Gathering together below the bridge, the flames flared up to lick their edges around me, and one stretched all the way across my path like a barricade of fire. "You must go back!" it murmured. "If you're not careful, you could do worse. Much worse."

Where had I heard those words before? The sudden memory of Stone's attempt to stall me came like a slap in the face. I shook myself and pointed at the flame. "I know that voice," I said. "You speak through different people, but it's all the same voice."

The flame ignored me. "You're a pinball ricocheting around God's infernal little machine, and He wants to see how far you'll bounce before you end up in the hole —"

"No!" I shouted. "Shut up! This is the *real* trap. I almost fell into it once, but not this time."

The voice droned on. "...Satan himself is just waiting for you right by that hole at the bottom — ready to chew you up and spit you out...."

"You can't hold me," I said. "So it is willed where what is willed must be!" Then I closed my eyes and ran through the flame.

The blaze singed the whole front of my body, and I yelped with pain as I passed through it. But it didn't stop me. When I turned to look back at the pit, the flames had all shortened again, flickering dark red. They whispered as I trotted away, "You'll be sorry. You'll be sorry. You'll be sorry...."

Once I was out of earshot I sat down, panting, and closed my eyes. What now? Another pit crossed, and still no Miss C. Maybe I could make it past the demons and the damned after all, with the formula and a little gumption. But could I find my way to the end? The bridges were easy enough to locate, if not always to get across. But how would I get down to the last circle, and how could I possibly chart my way there across a sea of ice?

Worse yet, what would be waiting for me when I got to the exit? The farther I went through Gehenna, the more I was remembering from Dante; each horrible scene was like another session of shock treatment that jolted my memory. But I'd never even read his last few chapters, so when it came to the exit, there was nothing to recall.

Maybe letting Miss C find me out here on the open asphalt wasn't so bad an idea after all.

In my mind's eye a picture slowly formed out of nowhere: I saw myself as a toddler walking down the street with Daddy, my chubby little hand in his. My brothers were all following behind. We were on our way to the neighborhood barbershop.

I loved that regular trip to "get our ears lowered," as Daddy called it, an ancient male rite in the days before unisex hair salons. Men and boys only — women wouldn't come near the place — sat on their swivel thrones surrounded by a glorious mess of hair clippings, smoking cigars or blowing bubble gum from the penny dispenser, hopping down when the final splash of cheap aftershave had christened their necks. The magazines scattered across the cracked vinyl seats where we waited our turn were all about hunting, fishing and bodybuilding; the comic books were jumping with macho superheroes who made the world right.

I hated the haircut itself. The cold blade gave me a close buzz that made me look bald and big-eared — a "Samson scalp," I called it. But I felt my maleness sharply in that barbershop ritual, and it was the only place Daddy ever took me except the woodshed.

I could see his face clearly now, younger than I last remembered him but no less stern. He trudged along silently, yanking me so fast that I thought my arm would come off. But I was glad anyway just to be holding his hand.

The picture faded. I felt a sudden pull inside to get up and get going, and I knew that somehow Daddy was still yanking me along. *You gotta do something, even if it's wrong.* But this time, I told myself, it wouldn't be wrong.

I stood up and looked around. Sitting around waiting for Miss C to show up was too passive a plan, though I knew it would be just as useless to go out looking for her. There was nothing to do but forge my own way across the last two bridges and find a passage across the ice myself. How much worse could it be than what I'd already survived?

If on the journey I met up with Miss C, it would be no coincidence; and if I didn't, well, that just might be part of the plan too. But everything inside me hoped against hope that I'd see her again.

With a deep breath, I stuck my chin out, threw my shoulders back and started walking. As I went, the words of an old hymn began sifting through my brain, resurrected somehow from the old Wednesday night prayer meetings of my childhood. Try as I might, I couldn't get the melody to come out, but I said the words aloud, and knew it was a prayer.

Abide with me; fast falls the eventide; the darkness deepens; Lord, with me abide! When other helpers fail and comforts flee, help of the helpless, O abide with me....

The darkness was deepening, all right. Ahead of me, space stretched out like the deep blackness between stars, the darkest I'd seen yet — so thick I half-expected it to rub off on me like soot. Somebody could have been standing ten feet ahead of me, and I wouldn't have seen them.

For the second time I'd come to the end of the verse; this time I hesitated, trying to remember the words that came next. In that second of silence I heard a footstep on the pavement behind me.

I stopped dead still. Scared to move even a finger, much less to turn around, I kept my head straight but swung my eyeballs from side to side. Nothing. No more sounds either.

An eternity passed, and still nothing. With my heart trying to hammer my stomach back down into my gut, I pivoted slowly to face the ebony emptiness.

Must have been hearing things again. Hell was still up to its old tricks.

I turned again to go on — and out of the shadows a cold hand grabbed my arm.

THIRTY-FOUR

They could hear the scream all the way to Sheol.

I leaped up like a toad and fell down like a dead man to the pavement.

"Thomas! Thomas, are you all right?" I thought I was hearing things again, but I wasn't.

It was Miss C.

I didn't know whether to laugh or cry. That black pearl of a face was the most beautiful thing I'd ever laid eyes on, upstairs or down.

"It's *you!*" I bawled, jumping up again and throwing my arms around her. "I *found* you!"

"*Who* found *whom*?" she asked, pushing me to be precise, as always. But she was hugging me close and grinning.

"All right, all right," I said, "you found me. But how did we ever get separated?"

"That is quite a long story, Thomas. Let me tell you on the way down. I fear that we may not have much more time to complete your journey."

I didn't like the sound of that at all. "But meeting up with you again means I haven't yet run out of grace. No coincidences in hell, remember?"

"Well, Thomas," she said as she took my arm to walk, "grace never runs out, but in some cases it can wear thin, and if we tear in it a large enough hole, we can fall right through it."

"What do you mean?"

Her face was sober again. "I mean that in hell as in the upper world there is a limited time and space given us in which to find our way. We have nearly reached the end of ours; the delays have cost us dearly."

"You mean we have a deadline?"

"I cannot explain now. But time is running out."

"Why did you have to go in the first place? I was terrified."

"I am truly sorry, Thomas. It was my only chance to gain a clue about what had happened to my sister. I expected to come right back and find you on the bridge."

"But we couldn't stay on the bridge. Stone was in danger."

She shook her head slowly. "Stone *was* the danger. His presence with you was what worried me most about our separation. And where is he now?"

I looked down at my feet as we walked. "In the sixth pit with the hypocrites."

She patted my back. "I know it must have grieved you. But he could have done worse — much worse."

I stopped and grabbed her shoulder. "Don't say that. I don't ever want to hear those words again."

She started to speak, shrugged and held her peace.

"We didn't go far," I said. "We were looking for you, but we couldn't find you anywhere. What happened?"

She sighed. "The woman in the pit was one of my master's mistresses. She claimed to have information about my sister's whereabouts, but she only threw out little bits of a story one at a time, stringing me along like a fish on a line while she walked the great circle of the trench. By the time I realized she was only mocking me, we had traveled a great distance. I came back to the bridge as quickly as I could, but it was too late. You were gone."

"Did you look for me?"

"Everywhere! Along every bridge. Down the edge of every trench."

"And no one bothered you?"

"I was careful not to be seen in most places. But the devils caught me at the fifth trench and almost threw me into the boiling vat."

"How did you get away?"

"Just when I thought all was lost, one of the demons whistled and pointed at a soul trying to escape from one of the vats. At once all of them let go of me and went after the man, shouting something about a 'Boss Tweed.' I lost no time in escaping while they were occupied."

I squeezed her arm. "I believed you would search for me, whatever the cost, though I have to say that when things looked darkest, I had my doubts too. Most of all I worried that you'd never find me again no matter how hard you searched."

"There were certainly no guarantees, Thomas. But now we must turn all our energies to getting into deep hell as soon as possible." She hurried her pace, and I had to work hard to keep up with her.

"So you found out nothing about your sister?"

She stopped in her tracks. "I did indeed find Apangela."

"You found her?" I was thrilled, but Miss C wasn't even smiling. "Is something wrong? Where was she?"

"She was standing by the pit of the evil counselors, weeping. She had been searching for me, and they had told her I was held captive there. They said the only way she could ever be with me again was to join them in the flames. So Apangela was preparing to throw herself down."

"But if you stopped her in time, where is she now? Why didn't she come with you? Wouldn't it be better for her not to travel alone?"

Pain washed across Miss C's face. "Yes, of course. To travel alone in hell is utterly dangerous. But we had different destinations."

I grimaced. "You left her just because you had to hunt for *me*?"

"That is only part of the truth." Miss C looked down at the pavement. "You see, Apangela was headed all the way down alone. She is convinced that the time has come when she can leave Sheol and escape hell."

"Didn't she ask you to come along?"

"She did not think it my time yet." Miss C began to cry. "And *I* do not think it *her* time either. None of us in Sheol are destined to escape. I fear...I fear she will be imprisoned forever in the lowest dungeon of Gehenna."

She was wailing now. I wrapped my arms around her and held her close. When her tears at last slowed down, I said gently, "You already know I disagree with you about that. Can't you find it in your heart to hope that she may be right? Even Lakshmi — "

"It was Lakshmi who convinced her!" she shouted, her voice quaking with anger. "Lakshmi believes she hears from heaven. She heard a voice in her head saying it was Apangela's time to leave. And she has persuaded Apangela to obey that voice!"

I took her hand. "I saw Lakshmi again myself."

Miss C grabbed me by the shoulders. "Lakshmi? When? Where?"

"By the pit of the false prophets."

"The false prophets? Have mercy!"

"No — wait," I said, taking her hands off my shoulders and holding them together. "She had traveled all the way down from Sheol to give us a message."

Miss C looked skeptical. "And what message was that?"

"She said that under no circumstances were we to separate, and I was to trust no one else but you."

"She was speaking of Stone?"

"I know now that she was. And she was right."

"I find it difficult to trust these messages heard inside her head. My instructions have always come from a messenger."

"Maybe this time Lakshmi *was* the messenger."

"But my sister is risking everything on her message. What if Lakshmi is mistaken?"

"All I can say is that she was right on target in what she said to me. She even knew exactly where to find us because the voice in her head told her where to go."

Miss C turned away and rubbed her hands across her face. "The demons could have told her as much."

"That's true." I took a deep breath and let it out slowly. "Tell me, Miss C. How well do you know Lakshmi?"

"As well as anyone in Sheol, except for Apangela."

"Have you always trusted her until now?"

"Yes. Without reservation."

"Both her motives and her wisdom?"

She nodded slowly. "Yes, both."

"And what about Apangela? Does she often act foolishly or on impulse?"

"No. She has always chosen her path with discretion, and only after much deliberation."

I put my arm around her. "Then I guess you'll have to trust them both this time as well, won't you?"

Miss C began to cry again. "I will try. But I fear that her name prophesies her destiny after all: *She who intends not to finish her journey*. Oh, Thomas, Thomas, she is my only sister, the apple of my eye, and I can do nothing to protect her...."

We stood a long time there, both of us spilling tears till they reached our feet: She wept for her sister, and I wept for her. When the tide of our grief ebbed at last, I asked her one more question.

"Did Apangela have anything else to tell you? Did she say when she thought your time might come?"

Miss C's face went flat. "We spoke of many things. Now, however, is not the time to talk about them." I could tell she was hiding something important from me. But I'd learned long before that when she wasn't ready to talk, you might as well try to pry words out of a fencepost.

"We must hurry along now," she said. "But we must be quite careful. The pit of the schismatics is next, where breeders of hatred and discord are punished. They are a ferocious lot."

"When we talk about schismatics in a seminary classroom," I said, "we mean religious sectarians who split the church apart. Is that who you're talking about?"

She shook her head. "Sectarians are only a fraction of the population there. Much more numerous are those who spent their lives pitting people against one another without so noble an excuse as religion for their behavior."

"You mean the hatemongers — racists, sexists, bigots who stir up ethnic strife?"

"They are the worst, yes. But you will also find in that pit the habitual gossips, the journalists who sowed public scandal and the lawyers whose greed pressed their clients to fight friends and family in court."

"Why," I asked, "do we have to be so careful?"

"Remember what happened when we traveled near the slavers, Thomas. Many in this pit despise the color of my skin as much as they did. We must hurry past them as quickly as possible."

She smiled and took my arm to go on, but the smile was brief and only a brave show. Her hands were cold and clammy, and her eyes were wide with fear.

If the schismatics were ferocious, their fate was more ferocious still. We could hear the screams of agony far off, long before we could make out the faint line of the trench in the distance. And when we stood above them at the edge of the concrete wall, I gagged.

Down below, one at a time, the damned souls were filing by from our left to our right. Each one was horribly scarred in one sickening way or another, and their bodies were encrusted with dried blood. I could see terror in some faces, grim resignation in others; a few fought among themselves as they trudged along the bloodstained concrete floor, wearing it down into potholes and a rut. They all stumbled along like the dazed survivors of a grisly battle, still not sure they had escaped the holocaust.

When I looked farther down the trench in the direction they were facing, I realized that they *hadn't* escaped the holocaust. It was waiting for them ahead.

Maybe half a mile down the line, a crimson demon in a butcher's coat stood in blood up to his knees, wielding a chainsaw. He divided each soul that came along differently, as if he were laying out choice cuts of meat, lopping off heads and limbs, sawing torsos in halves or quarters. But no matter how many pieces they ended up being, somehow the souls held themselves together when he was done, and they kept walking.

"They heal as they make their way around the abyss," said Miss C in a low voice. "The scarring is complete by the time they get here — just in time for the butcher devil to cut them up all over again."

"I think this one's the most gruesome yet," I said to Miss C, holding my hand to my mouth.

"Perhaps," she said gravely, "you now have some idea of how deeply heaven detests the selfish sundering of human bonds of charity."

A man with mounds of fat flowing down his sides like lava arrived at the slaughter station. The devil sawed off his head and handed it back to him. Then the man stumbled on, carrying his head by the hair.

"Henry the VIII of England," said Miss C. "He wanted to break the bonds of matrimony, and when the church refused him, he broke the bonds of faith instead. He shattered the peace of the church in his nation, not for the sake of conscience, but to indulge his own lusts and political ambitions."

Behind Henry came several middle-aged men with sour, pinched faces — all with wrist scars that showed their hands had been lopped off more than once.

"They must have scattered their scandals through the written word," said Miss C.

I could guess who they were: tabloid writers, muckraking reporters or maybe a few radical leftist pamphleteers who'd tried to stir up a revolution.

I was wrong. As they walked by, I could tell from their talk that they were preachers, clubbing each other with their scarred fists and keeping up the fight they'd started upstairs.

"All I did," shouted one, "was refute all you charismatic heretics!"

"Refute us?" said another, boxing the first one's ear. "You never even took the time to find out what we really taught! You're an old gossipmonger who repeated rumors and twisted what we said, and you know it."

"I was proclaiming the hard truth when no one else would."

"Gimme a break, you pompous old jackass! You weren't interested in the truth at all. You just wanted your fans to think you had all the answers, and you wanted to keep them away from us so they wouldn't find out you were really full of bull."

"You fools deserved whatever you got!" shouted the first one, punching the other in the gut. "All that tongues stuff was splitting the church. And all those fake faith healers had to be exposed."

"Fake? Your own *sister* was healed when somebody laid hands on her. You knew it had to be a miracle because you knew that tumor was real and she was dying. But did you tell all your followers? Of course not! You'd have had to admit you were wrong, and you'd have lost fans, and your little ministry kingdom just might have crumbled."

The first preacher wasn't listening. "Some *real* theologian had to lay it all out on the table," he said, sniffing. "Now, for doing the church that service, I wind up *here*."

"Sure you're here," said the second one. "That's what you get for messing with God's anointed. But what *I* can't figure out is what I'm doing here *with* you."

"Well," said the first, "I remember your preaching that all Catholics were going to hell. I believed it too, but at least I didn't preach it."

"What are you talking about? All I ever preached was *pure Bible*, boy, and if that meant putting Catholics in their place — or any other of those idol worshippers — well, then, so be it!"

"Just admit it, you old fool. You preached in a city where everybody hated Catholics, and your anemic little church wasn't going to grow unless you bashed them."

"You think you know something about bashing? I'll teach you about bashing, bucko. And when I'm done with you, I'm gonna find me a few Catholics to beat up too." He swung again, and this time all the others around them got in on the brawl.

I was close to laughing at the craziness of it all, but Miss C tapped me on the shoulder and pointed to the left, without comment, to a short man with straight black hair and a little black mustache. He was followed by a long line of young white men with shaved heads.

After them came older white men and women, then a line of mostly young blacks, then racial and ethnic groups of every type. In some groups the women were clustered together.

Hell, the great equalizer, had lined them all up for a common fate. But even in hell they still segregated themselves, leaving large gaps in the line as their territorial boundaries. They cussed and jeered one another as they plodded along.

I had no desire to view the details of their wounds; I was close to heaving again. Every time I watched the butcher devil rip through another soul, empathetic pain washed over me and nearly made my knees buckle.

It's high time, I told myself, to get out of here. Miss C is looking more scared than ever, and I'm sure that whatever I'm supposed to see on this part of my tour has already passed by. I took her by the arm to go.

Way down the line, somebody started shouting. "Hey, boy, wait!" shouted a wiry old man, the last white in line before the black group started. "What you doing hanging around with that nigger woman?"

The blacks behind him all turned to look up at us. "Yeah, Grandma," said the first one, a young man. He jabbed his finger in the air at Miss C, his eyes smoldering. "You better quit messing around with that white devil, you old Tom."

A female voice jumped in too, calling to Miss C: "*All* men are devils, sister. We don't need any of them. Dump him!"

I pulled Miss C back away from the trench wall. All those bloody heads were only a few feet below us, and I didn't know how high they might still be able to jump, no matter how many scars they had.

Suddenly an old man's voice bellowed from somewhere down the line of whites. "Tommy! Is that you, boy?"

My heart fell out of my chest and rolled down into the pit. It was Daddy.

THIRTY-FIVE

There was no mistaking the voice, and when I ran down the line to find him, there was no mistaking his face either. He looked just the same as the day he died — but with a mess of hideous scars, one crisscrossed right on top of the other, stretching from his chin to his belly.

"Tommy!" he said again, his face wild with surprise. "What are you doing here, son? I always reckoned if *any*body would make it to heaven, *you* would — teaching religion and all."

"There's a lot more to it than that, Daddy. They've got preachers here too."

"Well," he said, "I knew a few of *them* myself that ought to be all the way down in the cellar by now. But tell me, boy — why you still running 'round in your shorts? Everybody else here's buck naked."

"I'm not dead yet, Daddy. I still have a chance to make it out of here."

He frowned. "Say what? Folks can get out of this hellhole?"

"I've been told I can. Maybe you can too, Daddy. Come on with me."

His brow was furrowed. "How am I gonna get out of this old

227

pit, Tommy? I'm too old to climb." He pointed to the scars. "I'm scared I could rip all this right open again." I winced to think how many times he'd already been around the circle.

Then he looked again at the devil up ahead and panicked. "You gotta help me out of here, son. Don't let him cut me again! Please don't let him cut me...."

My eyes were burning. "I'll get you out, Daddy. Don't you worry. I'll get you out."

A couple of stout-looking whites with scar rings around their bellies moved over and grabbed his arms. "We'll heave you up, Grandpa," said one. "Maybe you can get out, and maybe you can't. But you gotta swear to us that if you find a way to get out, you'll come back and tell us so we can run too."

"I swear on a stack of Bibles," said Daddy. "But you got to hurry. That chainsaw fool just might look this way, and then we'd all be in trouble."

They put their hands and shoulders together and gave him a lift up. I grabbed both his hands and pulled. He grunted and puffed and panted, and between the four of us we finally got him up on the pavement.

"Much obliged," Daddy said to the men below, trying to catch his breath. "If there's a way out of here, we'll find it, and you'll be the first to know. I swear it."

They nodded, sober-faced, and went on, dragging their feet harder — like everybody else — the closer they got to the butcher.

We moved back about ten feet from the edge of the pit and sat down so the demon couldn't see us. Over Daddy's shoulder I could see Miss C near where I'd left her. She was standing about as far back from the trench as we were, shifting her gaze back and forth between it and us.

She must have known we'd have a lot to talk about, so she was giving us our privacy just now. But the look on her face told me we didn't have much time, and I knew already what she thought about the chances Daddy would have to escape. Even so, I had to try.

"Bless your heart, son, you're a sight for sore eyes," said Daddy. "I sure never thought I'd see your face again."

My eyes filled up. "Same here, Daddy."

"I swear, boy, looking at you makes this place all the worse, 'cause your face brings back so many memories." He looked up in the air just over my head, as if he could see them all in the distance.

"It's the same for me to see you again, Daddy."

"What would I give right now for just one more Sunday dinner, with all you boys licking up every last smear of gravy on your plates, and Mama coming back from the kitchen with a perfect pecan pie — rest her soul."

"Yessir," I said between the tears, "rest her soul."

"I suspect when she left the planet all those years ago, she went on to higher ground, don't you suspect, Tommy?"

I nodded. "Yessir. No way Mama's gonna be down here. A finer woman never walked the earth."

"That's right, boy. That's right. And I wonder what she's doing right now."

I wiped my nose on my arm. "Maybe she's praying for us, Daddy. We need all the prayers we can get for what's ahead of us."

He frowned, but it wasn't stern. "Let's not talk about that right now, young 'un. Just let my eyes get a fill of you for a minute. It's been a long time, son. A long time."

He was sniffling now too. We sat there, just staring at each other. It made him uncomfortable; he fidgeted with his hands and looked away.

Finally he looked back, then down at my feet. "Is that what's left of my old shoes?"

"I'm afraid so," I said. "It's been kinda rough on 'em down here."

"I can see you've had a scrap or two." He pointed to the three marks on my belly. "You always did get that funny kind of scar when you got cut. I remember how even your vaccination looked bad."

"Well, let's say I've had a few close calls," I said, rubbing my hand across the burns on my arms that had healed. "But it looks like you've been through a whole lot worse."

"Nah," he said, "it ain't so bad." Of course, he was lying, but Travis men weren't used to letting on that they hurt. "Tell me, Tommy, what's happened since I left?"

"Not much to tell," I said. "Jimmy and Billie Jo had another little girl. Looks just like Mama."

"I'd like to see that," he said. "But it's a shame he still ain't had no boys."

I grinned. "Maybe he had his fill growing up. A day never went by when the rest of the brothers didn't gang up on him about something."

Daddy nodded, smiling. "What about Sammy?"

"Still delivering babies and making more money than he knows what to do with."

"And Bo?"

I shook my head. "Bo's as ornery as ever. Gets in a brawl on the job and gets fired just about every other month, from what I hear — though I haven't seem him in a while. Keeps to himself a lot; you know Bo."

"Yep, that's Bo," he said. We sat in silence again, both looking down at the pavement.

Finally I spoke again. "You know, Daddy, since I've been down here, I've missed a lot of things about home — blue skies, moonlight, the breeze rippling on down the water. But you know what I've missed most?"

He smiled a far-off, dreamy kind of smile and started to rock a little back and forth, crossing his arms in front of him. "Sure I know. You miss sitting on the front porch in a thunderstorm."

I nodded. He went on.

"You miss feeling the wind slap your face, and the raindrops bouncing off the porch rails to tickle your bare feet. You miss the lightning bolts splitting open the sky like a new chick cracks the egg; the roll of the thunder bumping down the back steps of heaven; and that musky smell, sweet and wild, like no other smell on earth."

It was the one thing in the world we'd always agreed on: the beauty of a summer thunderstorm. Even in hell the memory of one was enough to bring out the poet in Daddy that had never had a chance to blossom.

All of a sudden I had an urge to hug him. But in my family, men didn't hug.

"Daddy," I said at last, taking a chance, "we don't have much time. We've got to get going. But before we go, do you think that maybe just for once..."

I choked up and didn't know if I could even get the words out of my mouth. I swallowed hard and went on. "Maybe just for once you could put your arms around me and give me a hug?"

You'd have thought I asked him to speak Chinese. He stared at me blankly.

"Why?" The word hung in the air, hard and lonely.

"Because I need to know that no matter what happened in the past when we were both back upstairs, you still love me. Please, Daddy?" My tears were streaming now.

He sat staring at me. Then his eyes got misty, and at last he raised one arm awkwardly and propped it stiffly on my shoulder without saying a word. He looked angry, but I knew he was really just plain scared.

I didn't wait any longer. I got up on my knees, threw my arms around his chest and pulled him to me, squeezing as hard as I dared with those new scars running down his middle. "I love you, Daddy," I said for the first time since I was a child.

The stiffness in his arms melted. He was holding me tight now, pressing me against his scarred chest in a way he'd never done before. But he couldn't get the words out I wanted to hear. He'd been taught for a lifetime that men just didn't talk that way.

I couldn't leave it at that. "You love me too, don't you, Daddy?" I asked, shaking all over now. "Don't you?"

He still couldn't say it. But he pulled my chin up to face him and nodded, his face all twisted and wet. That was enough for me.

Suddenly embarrassed, he let go and pulled back. "I didn't mean to act like a plumb baby, son." He rubbed his eyes. "I reckon we'd better get on our way."

I nodded and wiped my nose on my arm again.

"How do you know the way out, Tommy?" he asked. "Got a map or something?"

"No, Daddy, a guide. She knows the way because she's been down it lots of times before."

"She?" Shock swept over his face. "You mean you got a *girl* leading you around?"

"Not a girl, Daddy — a woman."

A smile cracked his face. "Is she pretty, Tommy?"

I sighed. "Daddy, this is hell, and I'm not out looking for pretty. Besides, she's probably old enough to be your grandma."

The smile fell off his mouth. "Well, boy, you had me excited for a minute. You know I never gave up hoping you'd give me some grandbabies. So how'd you get hooked up with her?"

"She came to meet me when I first got down here."

"Come to think of it, son, you never really told me how you *did* get down here in the first place. If you didn't die, what happened?"

"Well, it's a long story, Daddy. They were having race riots in Atlanta, and I happened to be in the wrong place at the wrong time when a gang came along and — "

"Niggers?" he said, standing up. "Niggers came after you?"

I knew right away, but a second too late, that I'd brought up the wrong subject. "Daddy," I said, "they never even touched me. But when I tried to run — "

He wasn't listening. "Blasted niggers. Did they hurt you, boy? I'll kill 'em. I'll go back to haunt 'em. I'll..."

At the worst possible time, Miss C came walking up.

"Thomas," she said firmly, "we can delay no longer. We must go on."

Daddy looked at her as if she just broke out of jail. "What's *she* doing here? What's this nigger woman doing, talking to you like that?"

"Daddy," I said, "you're not gonna like it, but we don't have a choice about it: This is my guide. Her name is Capopia, but I call her Miss C. Miss C" — I turned to her — "this is my daddy, Homer Travis."

"I am pleased to meet you," said Miss C and stuck out her hand. It stayed there, hanging in the air, while Daddy just stared at her with his jaw hanging halfway to his chest.

"No," he said, wagging his head violently. "No sir. Not her. I ain't going nowhere with her."

"It's our only chance, Daddy. She knows the way. She can get us out."

He was looking ice picks at me. "You're just fool enough to believe that, aren't you, boy? You're just fool enough to think you can trust a nigger. After what they did to you in Atlanta, you still think you can trust 'em? You got a watermelon for a brain, boy?"

"She's already proved too many times to count that I can trust her, Daddy. She saved me from the demons more than once."

He was breathing heavy and punctuating his words with short jerks of his hands. "Redbirds don't hang around bluebirds. Doves don't mess with crows. Whites ain't supposed to mix with niggers. That's just the way the world's put together, boy. She don't belong with you and me."

"Daddy," I said, pleading now, "you've got to forget all that stuff. It's not true. It's not right. It won't work. Can't you see that's what brought you here in the first place? If you want to go to heaven, you can't take along any souvenirs from hell."

"I don't know any other way to live, boy. That's just the way things are, and the way they're supposed to be. I won't let you go with her. Send her on her way — now."

I looked him square in the eye, my whole body shaking. Forty-two years of love, fear and rage were heaped up on that single moment, pressing down like a great leaden finger on my heart, and the weight was about to break me.

"Daddy," I said slowly, barely able to squeeze the words out, "you always said a man has to find out what's right, and when he knows he's right, he can stand his ground on it, come hell or high water. This time, Daddy, I know I'm right, and come hell or high water or even you, I've got to stand my ground. She's coming with me to show the way, and if you don't want to come too, then I can't make you. But you won't stop us."

His eyes flashed, his fists clenched, his lips turned white and his jaw began to quiver. I'd seen him like that ten thousand times, and I knew what was coming. So I stepped back out of swinging distance, wondering what to do next.

Then I froze. Past Daddy's shoulder I could see in the distance the butcher devil, peeking over the edge of the pit right at us. Then he went back to his bloody work. I opened my mouth to warn Daddy and Miss C, but before I could say a word, Daddy swung.

He didn't swing at me. He turned to Miss C and boxed her on the jaw. She went down hard on the pavement.

That was more than I could take. In a second I was on him, shoving him to the ground and trying to grab his fists so I could hold them fast to the pavement. I couldn't bring myself to slug him, but that left me wide open — he was swinging wildly, punching me in the face, the ears, the gut, even the groin.

I grabbed him by the shoulders and tried to knock the breath out of him against the asphalt, but instead he threw his arms around me and tried to roll over on top. We went twisting and rolling, first one way and then another, closer and closer to the trench. I'd never known Daddy to be so strong, even before his heart attack; he seemed to have the power of three men raging in those shriveled-up arms. Something more than Daddy was wrestling me, I knew, and it wanted me in that pit.

We were close enough to the edge now that the doomed souls could watch us. They took sides and cheered; if they could have sold tickets, they would have.

"This is a *good* one!" shouted an old man with a face full of scars. "A daddy 'gainst his own boy — they're fighting their own flesh and blood!"

Our feet were hanging over the edge of the pit now. The damned were calling for blood, and a crowd of young black men were jumping up to try to grab our ankles. They knocked off what was left of my old shoes.

I saw bloody hands come within an inch of Daddy's foot, and I yelled, "Look out!" When I did, he landed a punch right in my nose that knocked my head against the pavement. It dazed me, and while I lay there, my head spinning, he jumped to his feet and took a few steps back.

"You gonna do as I say now, boy?" he snarled, out of breath. "We ain't going nowhere with no nigger."

Right at that second one of the black men finally got ahold of my ankle. He hung on it, cussing and swinging. Daddy dropped to his knees next to me, leaned over the edge and started swinging his fist at the guy's face, trying to knock him off.

I tried to shake him off at the same time, but it was no use. So I turned over on my knees to try crawling farther away on the pavement. When he jerked down with all his weight, I could feel my shin bone cracking against the corner of the concrete.

"Daddy!" I screamed in pain. "Daddy, he's breaking my leg!"

Just then several other black men grabbed the body of the one hanging on me and started pulling. I was beginning to slip over the edge now, and I knew it was all over.

When Daddy saw what was happening, the look on his face shifted from rage to fear. He looked me in the eye for a fleeting second, as if to say good-bye. Then before I could stop him he leapt off the edge of the pit down onto the young man holding my ankle and smashed a fist into his nose. The man let go, and he and Daddy went rolling across the concrete floor with the others. Five more black men jumped into the fight, then half a dozen whites piled on top.

The pain in my leg had my head swimming so fast I couldn't even stand up, so I lay down and tried to roll over and throw myself into the pit. But somebody had me by the legs, pulling me back from the edge. I looked back to see Miss C, bleeding from the mouth and tugging with the strength of a mule.

"No!" I screamed. "Don't! *Daddy! Daddy, come back!*" Then I felt myself drowning in darkness, with the savage roar of the damned ringing in my ears.

THIRTY-SIX

When I came to, I was lying out on the asphalt somewhere far down slope from the pit. Miss C was sitting by me, nursing a swollen jaw.

I sat up, but too quick. My head spun around, and I had to lie back again.

"How do you feel?" she asked.

"Pretty sore all over," I said. "My leg hurts the worst."

"You must rest a few minutes more," she said. "I think you may have fractured it slightly. But it will heal quickly. It must. We have so little time left."

"How about you?" I asked. "Daddy sure packed a wallop in his punch."

"It too will heal," she said, but when she tried to smile, she winced with pain.

"I'm terribly sorry for my father's behavior. I had no idea he'd go so far as to swing at you."

"Hatred makes people irrational," she said. "I received much worse than that many times when I was a slave."

I didn't know what to say. How could Daddy have done what he did?

"I would have fully understood if you'd just left me then on the spot," I said. "Who could have blamed you? But why did you pull me away from the pit? You know I had to try to help my father. Why did you stop me from getting in?"

I started to cry. She reached over and patted my hand.

"You were losing consciousness, Thomas. You might have gotten yourself into the pit, but you could have done nothing to save your father once you got there, and you yourself would have been captured."

I sat up again, slower this time, and then tried to stand up. But my leg gave out under me.

"I have to go back," I said, pleading. "Don't you understand, Miss C? That's my *father* back there. I can't leave him."

"You cannot even walk on your leg, Thomas. And after what just happened, the demons are sure to have the entire length of the trench heavily guarded. They do not take kindly to attempted escapes."

"I don't care. I'll fight my way through them on one leg if I have to. Not even devils can stop me from rescuing Daddy. You'll see."

Her face was grim. "Even if you could get him out of the pit again, he would not come with us. I do not think he would change his mind about me."

"Then you can give me clear directions for the rest of the journey, and I'll go back for him alone. He'll come with me then."

She shook her head sadly. "Thomas, Thomas, you must face reality, son. It is a terrible truth, I know, but you cannot change it. Your father cannot be rescued — not by you, not by other souls, not even by a troop of heaven's own messengers."

"Why not?" I shot back, my voice rising. "If he wants to come, and I can get him to the exit, what's to stop him?"

"What is to stop him? His entire life on earth, Thomas. He made his choices, and when he died, the choices were sealed. The die is cast, son. His soul has been ripped in two by hatred, and no one can ever sew the two together again. You yourself heard the words of bitterness that poured out of his heart."

"But what if he repented?"

"Have you seen anyone here repent yet? It is too late, Thomas, just as it was too late for Stone. Despite the good in his heart, the evil inside your father has conquered, and it will anchor him in hell forever. Even if he escaped that pit for a season, sooner or later he would return of his own will to be among those who share his hatred — or else he would end up farther down than before, as Stone did."

I sat in silence for a long time, gathering together the crumbles of asphalt from a pothole near my leg and then scattering them again, over and over.

"You just don't understand," I finally said. "You don't know what it's like to leave your father struggling in a pit of hell."

"I know all too well," said Miss C softly. "Every time I make this journey I must pass by the ice where my own father lies frozen."

Her words rattled me. "*Your* father? You mean you know where he is?"

"He lies in the lake of ice — where justice has buried alive those who were treacherous to their kindred."

"What did he do to deserve that?"

"I suppose I never told you how I came to be sold into slavery, Thomas." Her eyes were deep with sadness. "My mother died when I was young. My father remarried soon after to a wonderful woman whose kindness to me was boundless. She treated me not as a stepchild but as one of her own. Yet she could not protect me from the drunken rages of my father."

"Did he beat you?"

"Many times. But the worst of all happened one night when he got drunk and called for the services of the village harlot. He was low on money — so he sold me to the slavers that very hour for the price of an evening's pleasure."

My anger drained out all at once, and my heart broke over her words. "I'm so sorry, Miss C. I didn't know...."

"Of course. You could not have known — I never told you. But perhaps you can believe me now when I say that I know the depths of your anguish in leaving your father behind. Your present struggles were once mine. But I have learned since then to forgive and to accept what I cannot change. That is my name, after all: *I do not dispute God.*"

She hung her head and sighed. In that moment I realized how wrong it had been to call her Miss C.

"Capopia," I said softly. "I'll call you Capopia from now on. Forgive me for failing to appreciate just how rightly you were named."

"You make a good Thomas as well," she said, without looking up. "Always doubting, always questioning, always wondering how things could possibly be the way they are." This time I hung *my* head.

"But that is not all bad," she added. "As long as you do not expect to find all the answers."

I took her hand. "There's one answer I wish I could know for sure even now."

"What is that?" she asked, looking up again and holding her free hand against her jaw.

"What happens at the last judgment? Do the torments of the damned finally come to an end? I could live with a little less anguish if I knew that Daddy would someday be free of that pit — even if the only way out was for him to cease to exist altogether."

"Those questions have been asked for as long as people have known about hell, Thomas. I fear there are no certain answers."

"What do *you* believe?"

"Those of us in Sheol who know something of the Scriptures believe that when the Last Day comes, every physical body will be resurrected to be joined again to its soul. Then the judgment of every soul will be made public, and at last every knee will bow and every tongue confess the Name — even the demons and those who now continue, despite their torments, to deny God's rule."

"And then?"

"For those who live in Sheol, I cannot say, though I suspect we will simply be left to ourselves forever. But the blessed will enter into the full joy of their Master, while the damned fulfill the prophecy of the Apocalypse: *Whosoever was not found written in the book of life was cast into the lake of fire.* Hell itself with Satan and his demons, the Scripture says, will be thrown down into that terrible lake — a torment unimaginably worse than anything you or I have yet seen."

I shuddered. "So will that final fire destroy them at last? Or will they agonize forever in conscious torment?"

"The Apocalypse also says that those in the lake of fire will be tormented day and night forever and ever."

"But why forever?" I asked. "What would it accomplish? It

239

seems to me that punishment can serve either to cure or to prevent evil. But if the flames of hell are final, they accomplish neither purpose. Is it purely retribution, then? Is God, after all, a vengeful God?"

Capopia stood and began to pace slowly. "Punishment also involves making criminals face up to their crimes, Thomas. Justice is more than rehabilitation, deterrence or confinement. It requires the unmasking of the criminals' self-deception, a making plain of the truth about who they are and what they have done. The damage done by evildoers must be brought home to them — a morally ordered universe requires at least that much. And so does God's love."

I frowned. "I haven't seen anyone here yet who's fully faced up to that kind of truth."

"I have no doubt that if such a self-reckoning has not taken place by the final judgment day, it will happen then."

"So let's say they *are* unmasked at the last judgment, and they recognize at last the truth about themselves. Is it still necessary at that point for them to continue in torment forever? Why should even a whole lifetime of sin deserve as punishment an eternity of pain? It seems out of proportion."

Capopia shook her head. "Time is not the proper standard of measurement for the appropriateness of punishment, Thomas. Think about it. Even on earth we do not measure out the length of punishment according to how long the crime lasted. A man may commit murder in less than a minute, yet be imprisoned for the crime for a lifetime."

"But is any sin so terrible that it deserves *everlasting* punishment?"

"It seems extreme to us, and yet our own standards of good and evil have been marred. If we could see as God sees, perhaps we would agree that even what looks to us like small sins are far worse an affront to His holiness than we had ever dreamed."

I didn't have a quick reply to what she said, but I wasn't convinced she was right either. I thought a minute, then asked: "Don't you think that in the end everybody — even the folks in heaven — would be better off if the ones in hell were gone altogether?"

She let out a long, deep sigh. "No doubt it would satisfy my heart to think that some day the impenitent wicked would simply cease to exist, that their misery would finally come to an end and the universe at last would be done with them. And yet..."

"And yet?"

"The terrible words remain," she said. *"Their fire is not quenched, their worm dieth not."*

"The fire may be unquenchable, but are the wicked indestructible?" I asked. "Think of all the other words of Scripture that speak of the wicked being utterly destroyed. The psalmist said they would be cut off and be no more, that they would perish and vanish like smoke. The apostle Paul said that their end is destruction. Peter said they would be like Sodom and Gomorrah, condemned to extinction. And those are only three of the places where you can find that kind of statement."

Capopia nodded. "You are right, Thomas; I have heard them all. The words of Scripture can be argued both ways. But the tradition of the church leans strongly toward a conviction that eternal torment is the final reality."

"The tradition can be wrong," I said. "What about simple moral reasoning? How could a God of love allow His own creatures to suffer everlasting torture?"

She sighed. "I fear that the reality is less simple and more severe than you and I can reason or even imagine, Thomas. Perhaps justice is also some matter of cosmic balance — that a moral universe would be twisted, left with a gaping void, if the damned were simply extinguished. Perhaps in some terrible way eternal punishment serves forever to right the scales."

I threw my hands up, exasperated. "I just can't see it. Justice defined in that way would seem to leave no room for mercy."

"I cannot say, Thomas; it is too deep for me. I think we may find in the end that we are dealing with a mystery — the mystery that lies in the word 'eternal.' Does it mean 'everlasting,' or something else?"

She had a good point. "Somebody," I said, "once jokingly described time as God's way of keeping everything from happening all at once. Maybe eternity will be when God finally *lets* everything happen all at once. I've always thought that eternity was outside time — or better yet, that it was the culmination, the ripened fruit, of time. Don't you think that to enter into eternity will mean to leave behind the experience of existing moment by moment? That in eternity all the moments will be caught up together and experienced all at once?"

"If that is true," said Capopia, "then no wonder those who are promised eternal life will know perfect bliss. The blessed ones would experience all possible moments of joy in heaven at once."

"And the damned," I added grimly, "would experience all possible moments of torment at once. Is it any wonder if I suspect that such an experience would annihilate them?"

Capopia stopped her pacing and turned to face me. "We must leave our discussion there," she said. "And if you can possibly walk on that leg after so short a rest, we simply must go on now to cross the last bridge."

What I really wanted to do was dive deeper into our talk about eternity. But for the time being we were still living from moment to moment — and the moments were fast running out.

THIRTY-SEVEN

As we made our way toward the tenth pit, Daddy was never far from my thoughts. My heart was shattered, though quiet now; I'd given up on trying to be at peace and settled for numbness instead. In my mind's eye I kept seeing the butcher demon with his chainsaw, bearing down on Daddy's throat. But each time my mind rebelled against the picture, and my imagination never went any further.

The last pit soon turned my thoughts to other things. Shrieks, bellows and even growls came from it — you'd have thought it was feeding time at the Atlanta zoo. I half-expected to see bars across the top when we got there. But instead the concrete trench looked and smelled more like a makeshift hospital ward in a war zone.

The floor was lined with souls who were gasping and choking and writhing in pain. Many were covered in pus and scabs, and they raked their skin off with their own filthy fingernails. Some were swollen into human balloons; others were little more than skeletons. Palsied arms twitched helplessly next to gangrenous legs. And over it all like a putrid blanket lay a thick, gut-twisting stench.

"The pit of the falsifiers," said Capopia, trying in vain to wave the odor away from her nose. "Liars, alchemists, forgerers, counterfeiters, imposters — and all the other kinds of charlatans you can imagine."

A pack of wild men and women, foaming at the mouth, came leaping like dogs on all fours across the other souls, biting every limb they could get their jaws around.

"We had better hurry to the bridge," Capopia said, pulling me in that direction. "These are mad with rabies, and you never know what they might do."

"Are the rabid ones all here for the same reason?" I asked.

"Most often they were unscrupulous journalists who falsified information to discredit their enemies."

"I know the type," I said as we reached the bridge. "They're what I call the media attack dogs. Whenever some public figure falls out of favor with their editor, he yells, 'Sic 'em,' and they go for the jugular like riled pit bulls."

"Your generation has been especially plagued with them, I think," Capopia said.

"Yes, and nobody's safe from them. They can blow trivialities all out of proportion to make a vice president look stupid, or twist the reasonable comments of a pro-lifer till he sounds like a fascist."

Just under the bridge lay a brown-skinned man, emaciated and struggling to breathe. He saw us, moaned and lifted his head a few inches to speak. "I don't deserve this," he rasped in a Spanish accent. "I was a doctor. I tried to help people. I was straight, and I never touched drugs."

"What is your illness?" asked Capopia.

"AIDS. I am wasting away now with pneumonia and a dozen other infections."

Capopia looked unmoved. "Did you ever deal with AIDS patients in your practice?"

"You better believe it," said a woman beside him who looked even worse. "He put the word out in the gay community that he'd discovered a wonder drug — one that could stop the spread of the HIV virus. People came to him from all over the world. He shot them up with a saline solution and took their life savings. And since he operated just across the Texas border, the FDA couldn't touch him."

She bent double and coughed till I thought her lungs would fly out. "See that old geezer next to him with the skin peeling off?" she said, then straightened out again and pointed at an old man scratching himself furiously. "He falsified military documents to try to cover up the effects of Agent Orange."

"And what about you?" I asked her.

"Charity fraud," she said weakly, holding a bony hand to her forehead. "Told people we were raising money for starving kids in Africa, and pocketed it ourselves. Now I've got scurvy, cholera, parasites, TB, leprosy — every Third World plague in the book."

Capopia tugged at my arm. "The most virulent diseases known to humanity are circulating through this pit, Thomas, and you have no recourse to medicine if you should get ill. I believe you have seen all you need to see; we had better go quickly."

She wasn't going to get an argument out of me. The stench alone was enough to drive me away, and I knew that any air that could carry a smell could just as easily carry a germ. In any case, my leg was throbbing, and I needed to rest it.

I was limping badly now. So as soon as we'd gotten out of the smelling range, Capopia helped me sit down.

"I see that your hair is growing back," she said, looking at my arms and chest. "I am relieved. The worst effect of the radiation sickness is to destroy defenses against disease. If you had not recovered by now, this last pit would have been for you the most dangerous of all."

"I'm just glad not to have a bellyache anymore," I said, patting my middle. "But you know, I never could understand why it didn't go away as soon as we got out of the seventh circle. I didn't expect to take it with me."

"My guess," she said, "is that your relief began as soon as Stone left you."

I chewed on that for a minute. "You're right. Come to think of it, that's just what happened. Was Stone some kind of carrier?"

"No, not a carrier, though he himself was certainly ill. But as long as you submitted to his influence, you were still breathing the poisonous atmosphere of the seventh circle. In that regard, Lakshmi's message was certainly true. The more you trusted him, the more fragile was your destiny."

I snickered. "It still looks mighty fragile to me, considering how this leg feels. How far to the last circle?"

She bit her lip. "Under any other circumstances, much too far for someone in your condition. But we have no choice. Take my arm and lean on me if you must; the time has almost run out."

That next sloping stretch of asphalt was in fact the widest we'd crossed yet. The air here was not as black; it was a twilight of sorts, though still much darker than the gray of the Cosmic Parking Lot. As we walked, the space around us grew thick with a cool mist. The sudden drop in temperature reminded me of how much I'd been dreading the lake of ice.

Each step was pain, though not agony. My worry wasn't so much about whether I'd make the trip, but about what condition my leg would be in by the time we got there. I'd have given my eyeteeth for a pair of crutches, or even for Granddaddy's old walking cane.

Almost as bad was the feel of that rough asphalt, potholes and all, against my bare feet. Capopia knew what she was talking about when she warned me to hang on to my shoes, miserable-looking as they were. They'd saved my feet a thousand deaths, and now that they were gone my toes were already curling up, cringing at the prospect of a trek on ice.

Worst of all, I guess, was the churning in my stomach. The radiation sickness was long since gone, but this time I could feel the fear flowing up my spine and filling my gut with turmoil.

No doubt I'd already survived more close calls in hell than in my whole lifetime on earth, and I was grateful. But Capopia had said in the beginning that a soul might slip through one circle only because they were waiting for it lower down. And everybody seemed to agree that the lowest circle is the most horrible of all.

I couldn't help feeling that everything up to now had been the cat playing with the mouse. How many times had somebody down here warned me that Satan himself would be waiting for me at the end? What did they know that I didn't know?

Capopia was looking more troubled than ever. You'd have thought from her face that she was on her way to a funeral, and just maybe she was. What wasn't she telling me?

"We are almost there," she said suddenly, as she pointed ahead. Far off in the mist a jagged, black silhouette appeared, like a cluster of skyscrapers rising out of the plain.

I turned toward her as I limped along. "Is that some city out there?"

"So it appears from this distance," she said. "But those are not buildings you see. They are the giants."

Giants? I'd seen a lot here already that I once thought haunted only nightmares and fairy tales. But giants *that* size? Who designed this circle — the Brothers Grimm?

"I didn't know such things really existed," I said. "Are they from some other planet?"

"You know less of the Scripture than I realized," said Capopia. "No. The giants once lived on our own planet, in the time of the ancients." She closed her eyes to recite while she walked. "*There were giants in the earth in those days; and also after that, when the sons of God came in to the daughters of men, and they bare children to them.* So says the Scripture."

"But I thought those words meant oversized men the size of Goliath. If *that* kind of creature walked the earth, why haven't we found any remains?"

"They were exceedingly wicked, terrorizing humankind and claiming they would overthrow heaven itself. But the great flood in Noah's time cleansed the world of them, sweeping even their bones into the depths of the sea."

"Were they demons of some sort, then?"

"No one knows for sure — no one in Sheol, at least. Even in hell the tales about them have multiplied. Because of the words I just quoted, some think perhaps they are a hideous half-breed, with women for mothers and fallen angels for fathers."

"That's hard to believe even for somebody in hell. But the more immediate question is this: If they're as mean a clan as you say they are, why are we headed right for them?"

"Because we must climb over them to get down to the next circle."

Maybe it was finally time to think about turning back. "Capopia — how can we possibly survive climbing over something that could stomp us like cockroaches?"

"Because they are buried up to their bellies, and the rest of their bodies are bound with great chains. We need only avoid their teeth."

I took her by the shoulder. "Is that the *only* way down?"

"Please trust me, Thomas. It is the only way. And it is actually one of the safer legs of our journey. What we will face *after* the giants is of much greater concern."

This was sounding even worse than I'd expected. "You haven't told me much about the last circle except the temperature," I said. "What kinds of sins are punished there?"

She took a long time to answer, and I knew she was weighing her words. "Circles seven and eight, where we have just been, hold sinners guilty of simple malice — that is, those who injured strangers or mere acquaintances through violence or fraud. But the souls in circle nine are much guiltier still."

"How's their sin worse?"

"The difference lies not in how they injured, but in *who* it was they injured. The frozen souls we will soon view all committed the same kinds of crimes as you have seen in the last two circles — murder, theft, seduction and the like. But the stain on their souls is much deeper because the people they injured had a special relationship with them. These wretched souls betrayed someone whose trust they held — family, country, friends or benefactors."

The distinction made sense. What would be worse: to steal from a stranger or to steal from your own mother? to beat up some jerk in a bar or to beat up...

...*your own father.*

The realization hit me like a kick in the groin. My knees buckled, and I had to sit down on the pavement right where I was.

"Thomas!" Capopia shouted, kneeling down beside me. "Thomas, are you all right?"

I opened my mouth, but the words wouldn't come out.

I saw it all now. The chainsaw devil hadn't tried to stop me from getting Daddy out, hadn't even come over to stop the fight, because he knew what was waiting for me below. Now his gruesome face filled my mind, and he was laughing, laughing, laughing....

Daddy was back there being butchered in the ninth pit because I'd jumped him. I'd betrayed my own father, and now I was about to go where traitors of kinfolk were punished — in the lowest circle of all.

Finally I got the words out. "Daddy...I betrayed my daddy. They're waiting for me, Capopia. I can feel it. What am I going to do?"

Her brow was furrowed as she shook her head sharply. "No,

Thomas. You do not understand. That was no act of treachery. You were defending me and taking a stand against the evil that gripped your father, not against your father himself. You would have betrayed the truth to do otherwise."

"But the demon saw us," I said, "and he didn't try to stop me. He let me go because he knew...he knew I was doomed."

"Do not curse yourself with those words. We must go on, Thomas. The ice will have no claim on you simply because of what happened at the ninth pit. Please — stand up now and hurry. We have so little time."

I felt too stunned to argue, so I stood up and followed her like a dumb sheep. But I didn't believe her. It had all been planned. She couldn't see it because she was the one I'd defended. But I could see it clearly now.

It was *my* funeral we were walking to. And strangely enough, I didn't have the strength to run the other way, or even the inclination. I felt guilty. I deserved to get what was coming.

Already I was beginning to feel stiff and cold and damned.

——————— THIRTY-EIGHT ———————

When we got close enough to the giants to see them through the mist, I began to have my doubts that we would even *make* it to the ice. They were as big as King Kong, and twice as hairy.

The brutes stood tightly packed, shoulder to shoulder, buried in the asphalt up to their bellies all around the circle of the abyss. There was no room at all to squeak between them — a strategy I'd planned to suggest to Capopia — but at least they were facing away from us, toward the abyss, so maybe we could sneak up on them.

It was going to be a climb, all right, one nasty fistful of fur at a time. No doubt they were chained, as Capopia had said they would be. But they looked hungry, and I wasn't excited about playing Fay Wray. Meanwhile, I wondered whether giant fur like that just might be infested with giant blood-sucking fleas.

We chose one with long, straight gray hair on his back, each strand as thick as a rope. Capopia showed me how to wind a few hairs around my fist and pull myself up on them, using my good leg against his body so the other would be spared most of the weight.

I was wishing I had an extra hand just to hold my nose; he smelled like a herd of hogs grubbing in a garbage dump. But there were other things to think about as we climbed his back, slipping on the grease in his fur: Beneath my foot I could feel his muscles tensing up until his whole body began to twitch.

"Do not be afraid," said Capopia. "He can move no further. The chains are tightly bound, and they only cut into his hide when he tries to break them."

The chains weren't especially thick, I noticed with some uneasiness, but there were plenty of them. Even his head was held in place by bonds on both sides. So at least he couldn't bend his neck to bite at us as we rounded his shoulders.

When we finally reached that point and could rest a minute, I didn't know whether to celebrate or panic. Heading down was sure to be easier than climbing up, but now we'd be facing the beast — and I didn't want to see his face. Maybe I could make it all the way without looking up.

We started down his chest, passing a brown nipple the size of a manhole cover. His breathing was ragged; the uneven rise and fall of our climbing surface made us slip all the more. I kept my eyes either straight ahead or pointed down so I could see the next clump of fur to grab. Soon we'd made it to the upper curve of his belly; it wouldn't be much farther now.

"*Rafel mai amech zabi almi.*" He was speaking to us, but in a language I'd never heard before. The babbling growl buzzed my ears like the roar of a low-flying jet, and his whole body vibrated beneath us. Though I didn't understand his words, the meaning of that ferocious tone was clear.

I hurried over the great bowl of his gut and was almost to the pavement below. Suddenly he let out a hideous howl that echoed across the abyss. Startled, I forgot to keep my head down, and I looked up at his face.

At first the sight surprised me — not because he looked monstrous, but because he looked so surprisingly human. His features, though they were the size of a face close up on a large movie screen, were nevertheless well proportioned; not handsome, but not brutish either. I hung there a moment, fascinated.

"Thomas!" said Capopia, now standing on the ground below me. "No time to lose! Come down!"

I wasn't paying attention. My eyes were locked into his; I was mesmerized. Slowly, he started to smile.

Capopia grabbed the ankle on my good leg and yanked me down, breaking my fall with her own body. The spell was broken. I scrambled up again, pulled Capopia up beside me and turned to run.

"Keep your back to him," she said firmly, and this time I listened.

He spoke again. *"Rafel mai amech zabi almi — Tomee."* That last word he added — was it "Tommy"? Did he know my name? I limped along even faster, and the ground below me began to shake like the first tremors of an earthquake.

The giant was laughing, laughing, laughing....

In a minute we'd reached the edge of the pavement. It made a sheer concrete cliff, like the one Geryon had flown us over, but there was no Geryon to help us out this time. Instead, a narrow, rusting staircase, like a fire escape ladder, ran straight down and disappeared into the gray mists below.

"I know it will hurt your leg terribly," said Capopia, "but I cannot help you as you climb. We must go down one at a time, and I will go first. But perhaps you will be encouraged to know that this will be your last climb."

Yes, I thought; my last climb and my last journey of *any* kind. I wasn't encouraged at all.

The pain was close to agony now, made worse by the continued chilling of the air as we went down. Once again I was glad for the mist; it kept me from seeing how far I had to go, or how far I'd fall if I slipped. Thank heaven, as Mama used to say, for small favors.

We reached the bottom just when I thought my leg would give out altogether. I plopped down on the ice to rest, but that was a mistake. I was up in a hurry, stunned to feel just how cold it could be. Maybe it wasn't even frozen water — it could well have been dry ice or something colder. Whatever it was, it was hard as iron; I don't think even bullets would have chipped it.

I looked out anxiously over the wide open spaces ahead of us. Big relief: no devils in sight.

The gloomy mists still swirled, pushed along now by a slight breeze that only made the air colder. The ground was solid ice as far as I could see — which wasn't very far — as if we were back on earth and the sun had died, so that a whole ocean had been cast into a dark, deep freeze.

The ice was mostly flat, but there were places where holes had been carved out. Scattered in the distance, too far away to be seen clearly, were the tips of mysterious objects half-buried.

In a few places I could make out rectangular frames of some sort standing out on the ice. They looked like clothing racks that held pants and coats, frozen stiff and swinging in the breeze. More costumes for the demons?

"Stay as warm as you can for as long as you can," said Capopia. "If we do not move quickly, the air will freeze us where we stand."

That was easy for her to say. She was still wearing shoes and a dress, though she was missing a sleeve and the fabric was ragged now with large holes.

I, on the other hand, was still sporting boxer shorts. Staying warm was going to be about as easy as shoveling fleas across a barnyard. If only we'd thought to bring along one of those flaming evil counselors.

She must have been reading my thoughts. "Take my shoes," she said bravely. "And I will rip off part of my skirt so you can wrap it around you."

"No!" I said, almost insulted by the offer. "I wouldn't think of doing that."

"We must do whatever is necessary to help you finish your journey," she said soberly. "If you fail, I fail as well."

I still refused. "Look, Capopia" — I patted my belly — "I've got a lot more natural insulation than you do, and the shoes wouldn't fit anyway. But thanks all the same."

The wind began to rise as we walked, sharp and frigid and sucking out of us even the memory of warmth. My breath turned to frost in the air and fell to the ground; crystals were forming at the corners of my eyes. Meanwhile, my bare feet stuck to the ice with each step, and each time I pulled them free I left a little more skin behind me.

I wondered if this was what it would feel like to fall overboard naked in an arctic sea, or stand in the shadows of the moon's dark side.

This was the most open space I'd seen yet in hell, and the most lonely. The emptiness should have been comforting, considering what had filled the other circles. But instead it was eerie, and the vastness of the place made me feel like a speck of dust waiting to be carried off into oblivion by the wind.

"Where are all the souls?" I asked, trembling from more than the cold. "Are there so few traitors in the world?"

"You will see them soon enough," said Capopia. "First we will pass over those who betrayed family; then, traitors to their country; third, those treacherous to friends; and at the very center of hell, those who broke trust with their benefactors."

So family traitors were first. At least I wouldn't have to suffer through the rest.

Capopia could see the fear all over my face, blue as it was. "I told you, Thomas," she said. "You need not fear that what you did in the ninth pit has damned you. If you still do not believe me, look around you. Even now we are passing among those who betrayed family, and there is no demon in sight to arrest you."

I was about to ask her where the souls were when I tripped over something sticking out of the ice. I bent down to look closer. It was the scalp of a male human head; the rest of him was purple and frozen within the ice. His knees were drawn up to his chin, with his arms wrapped around them in fetal position.

"A father who had his child aborted," said Capopia. "The aborting mother cannot be far away."

She was right. The mother was curled up in the same position, only a few feet beyond him. Both of them had their eyes open.

"Are they conscious?" I asked.

"Of course. The damned never have the mercy of losing consciousness." There was no pity in her voice, but no satisfaction either.

I looked around. Scalps were sticking out everywhere. "This place is filled," I said.

"Your generation has filled it."

"All of these are aborting parents?"

"All those in the fetal position," she said. "But there are others as well — those who committed incest, abusers of child and spouse, parents who failed to pay child support, adulterers."

I stepped back from the grisly scene and bumped into a frozen female head, cracking the ice across her lips. She cussed me, then screamed at me to knock the ice off her eyes too. I did.

"It's about time somebody came along," she said, no hint of gratitude in her voice. "I've been wanting to cry for a long time now. But the tears froze up my eyes, and the rest of it just backed up inside."

She was no more than a teenager. "Why are you here?" I asked.

"My mother wouldn't let me stay out all night, even though I was fifteen, y' know? Lots of other stuff too that really bugged me. So I wrote a story about how I was gonna get even, and my English teacher loved it. Then one night while Mom was sleeping, y' know, I held a pillow over her head while my boyfriend cut her throat. We drove her car across the country trying to get away, and I dumped my boyfriend in Reno 'cause he was getting scared. When the troopers found me a few weeks later on the highway, I tried to outrun 'em, but I didn't make a curve. Next thing y' know, I'm a popsicle."

"Is your boyfriend here?" I asked.

"No — it wasn't *his* mother, y' know. Besides, I heard he got religion right after I dumped him. Turned himself in."

I was stunned. As gruesome as her story was, she was empty of remorse. In fact, she'd probably have done it again if she could.

Capopia pulled me away as the girl's mouth and eyes began to freeze shut again. "I only let you talk to these so you would see that I am telling the truth — this is the place of the traitors to family, and you are still safe. But there is no more time now for conversation."

I couldn't argue with her. No doubt about it: These frozen folks had betrayed family members, yet here I was on top of the ice, walking free.

It was sinking in now. Capopia was right. What happened at the pit didn't count. I was safe. *I was safe.*

I would have cried, but the ice around my eyes wouldn't let the water out. Even so, I started to shake, and soon I was delirious, jumping up and down on my good leg and shouting like a man who'd just slipped off death row.

"I'm gonna make it!" I shouted. "I'm gonna make it!"

THIRTY-NINE

In the middle of my celebration, a sudden, pointed thought hit me like an ice pick in my gut. I turned to Capopia. "Who is it you said we pass by next?"

"Traitors to country. Surely you have nothing to worry about there."

"That depends," I said, suddenly panicked. "I got out of fighting the war in Vietnam by going to college. Some folks called me a traitor for it."

"Did you think it an unjust war?" she asked.

"Yes, I did, though the rest of my family didn't understand. But I have to admit that my motives were mixed. There was a lot of fear there too. I'd never been athletic — didn't have much physical strength or endurance — and I was sure that if I went, I'd come back in a body bag in a month. Or worse: I'd heard stories about those Vietcong rat cages and hotboxes."

Capopia shook her head. "I do not understand all that, nor can I judge it," she said. "But if you were acting in good conscience — and if your conscience was well-informed and not deceived by willful ignorance — then I think you will be safe enough."

I looked back the way we came. "I still think they've let me through this far just to snare me up ahead. Didn't you hear that giant laughing? Didn't he know my name? That's been my fear all along. The mist is so thick we wouldn't know if a whole horde of demons was waiting for me."

I was losing my nerve. "We've been through a lot to get here, Capopia...but maybe I'd better go back after all."

Capopia frowned, near the end of her patience. "Back to what?" she said. "The boiling blood? The butcher devil? You have never had a guarantee of completing your journey, Thomas, and you have known that all along. Why do you falter now?"

"Call it an intuition, a voice inside, whatever. Down in the pit of my stomach is a feeling that this is it — that I've been set up, and that you've been set up to get me down here. Can't you feel it too?"

"No, Thomas, I cannot. And I see no alternatives. The only way out is down."

"Why couldn't I just stay on the asphalt between the pits — or better yet, go back to Sheol with you? It's not so bad there."

She sighed and pulled her ragged dress closer around her thin, trembling frame.

"At this point, Thomas, even that is not possible. The regions of ice are narrower ahead, so the distance we still have to travel is much less than the distance we have already come across the lake. I believe you can make it to the end. But with your leg so badly hurt, you would not survive a trek back."

She gripped my numb shoulder. "Think of it, Thomas: If you froze out here on top of the ice, you would be no better off than those frozen below it. What you fear most would have come upon you anyway."

There was no winning. I felt like a gambler who'd lost all his chips but one and couldn't get out of the game unless he played that one too. Worst of all, I had no idea what kind of hand I was holding.

"Let's go," I finally said to Capopia. "If I lose, I lose."

The souls we passed by now were all lying in the ice face up, so I had to be even more careful not to step on anyone. But doing that had become more of a chore: The mist had turned black like smoke, more dense, more eerie, more threatening — more capable, I knew, of hiding devils.

Just then Capopia pulled me to a stop and pointed off to the left to a distant hole in the mist. There was a movement. Then nothing. Then another movement. Then the black swirls parted like curtains.

Demons. They were busy shuffling around one of those racks we'd seen, maybe half a dozen in all. Could they see us?

They could. The whole gang turned around in our direction and stared, their eyes glowing blue like gas flames. But they didn't come toward us. They didn't even speak. They just stood and stared.

My feet were freezing to the ground, and my heart was freezing in my throat. Without a word Capopia tugged on my arm, and I followed her silently. The blazing eyes continued to turn our way as we walked, but they never came any closer.

I kept watching them over my shoulder, letting Capopia guide me around any faces in the ice. Then at last the disturbing figures disappeared in the blackness behind us. Why did they let us pass without a fight?

Before long the wind had become a gale, furious like the frenzied air in the circle of the fornicators. My teeth were chattering so fast I could barely speak. But at least the wind had blown away the mist. Though the space around us was still vast and dark, we could see much farther now.

Not far ahead stood a mound of huge ice blocks, stacked to form a windbreak of sorts. Did the demons get cold too?

I noticed that we were no longer stepping around faces. "Where have all the souls gone?" I shouted, trying to be heard over the wind. "Aren't there any more traitors?"

Capopia leaned over to speak in my ear. "Come with me and stand behind the wall of ice to break the wind. We will not be so cold there, and we can hear each other better."

I didn't realize till we stood behind the wall how much a difference the windchill factor was making. After pressing through the kind of cold that could make your nose and ears fall off, this sheltered little spot was a spring garden by comparison, and we didn't have to shout to be heard.

"We have passed the region of the traitors to country and to friends now," Capopia said. "The devils we saw were their guardians." I could feel the relief spreading from my stomach outward, like the warmth from a bowl of soup.

She pointed between her feet. "Look closely and you will see that the damned are still imprisoned here. But these lie fully beneath the ice."

I bent over to look. There they were, all right, blue and stretched out in weird positions: some upside down, some spread eagle, some bending to touch their toes. One woman was arched backward so that her feet came up to the back of her head.

"Are these souls of a different type?" I asked.

She nodded. "These are the souls who betrayed their benefactors. They abused the trust of someone who had shown them unmerited favor — kindness that was not an obligation of kinship, or citizenship, or even friendship, but rather a gift of grace. Theirs is the most reprehensible crime of all."

I couldn't think of any benefactors I'd ever betrayed. Hope began to dawn again. "So are these the last of the damned? Is this the worst that hell has to offer?"

She turned away from me suddenly and didn't answer. I was confused. Why wasn't she hugging me with joy? Wasn't this the last stop before the exit?

I gripped her by the shoulders and turned her back around. "What's the matter, Capopia?" I demanded. "What is it that you're not telling me?"

She broke the ice from around her eyes and began to cry. I pulled her to me and held her, but that only made it worse. She was wailing now, like a mother who'd just lost her child.

My stomach was knotting up again. I leaned toward her and said, "You've got to tell me." It was a command.

She pulled back slowly and looked into my frozen eyes, wiping away her tears before they could crystallize. Then she pulled me back close to her.

"Thomas," she said, sobbing now, "I can go no farther than this border. From here on you must finish your journey alone."

My mind exploded. "No," I said, pushing her away. "*No*. I can't possibly go alone. I want you to come, and I want you to escape with me. We can make it together."

She shook her head violently. "You do not understand, Thomas. I *cannot* come. I have never traveled through this last region of ice; the ones I escort have always had to finish alone. If I went any farther, I might be caught, and I would remain frozen here forever."

She wasn't making sense. "What do you mean? How could you be at risk? How could you possibly be guilty of betraying a benefactor?"

"There is no time to tell the whole story. But this much you must know: The night the slavers took me away, and my father watched from the shore with his harlot, I screamed to him a terrible truth that until that time had been kept a secret from him. I told him that his only son, the child of my stepmother, was actually the bastard of another man. I meant it as a vengeance, to pierce his heart, though I later repented of what I had done."

"But he was your father, Capopia. If you really were liable to be punished for such a thing, you'd be in danger in the first region of the ice, not here."

"No, no," she said, her face twisted in pain. "The one I betrayed was not my father, but my stepmother, my greatest benefactor. When I tried to wound my father that night, I betrayed the secret she had entrusted to me. Because of my treachery, she was put to death for adultery."

Capopia buried her face in my chest, weeping. I cracked the ice off my eyes and cried myself, resting my chin against the white wool of her hair.

For a long time I'd secretly hoped I could talk her into escaping with me. Now that hope was shattered. She had to return to Sheol once more, and I had to face the last region of ice alone.

We couldn't stand still much longer, even behind the shelter; our feet were freezing to the ice, and our limbs were getting numb. "Then you must tell me quickly, Capopia," I said. "Where is the exit?"

She looked up at me, her eyes wide with fear. "It is a hole in the ice — right next to the belly of Satan himself. He guards the final exit, Thomas. Don't you remember Dante's final chapter?"

"No," I said weakly. "I never read it."

I couldn't believe what I was hearing. How many times had the damned warned me that Satan was waiting at the bottom of Gehenna, ready to pounce on me? They hadn't been lying after all. In their own perverse way they'd been prophesying my fate.

"Capopia," I said, "why would Satan be in this region? Why isn't he in some kind of administrative headquarters at the top?"

"You forget, Thomas. Satan began as a leader of the hosts of heaven, blessed by God with every good and beautiful gift. But he rebelled and tried to take heaven's throne for himself. He is the prince of those who betray their benefactors, and so he is imprisoned with them in the ice."

"Then he's bound? You mean he can't get ahold of me, just like the giants?"

"He is buried in the ice up to his middle, where the exit lies. But his upper half is free to move, including his hands. And his pleasure is to chew on the damned like so many plugs of tobacco. The demons supply him with souls by chipping them out of the ice."

She pointed to the ice wall beside us. "This is a stack of blocks they have carved out, each with a soul waiting to be brought to him."

I rubbed off some ice shavings for a closer look. Sure enough, each block held a frozen man or woman. Shivering all the more, I stepped back from the "windbreak" and looked away.

"No matter how many other souls Satan may torment," she added, "he chews perpetually on Judas Iscariot. But he can chew on more than one at a time."

Somehow I wasn't surprised. If you'd asked me to name the most despicable crime in history, I'd have told you it was Judas's treachery. Once again hell's architecture made sense: The ultimate human traitor of the ultimate Benefactor suffered the ultimate punishment in the ultimate dungeon.

"Why didn't we talk about this before?" I asked.

"I thought you remembered your Dante — and if you did not, I certainly did not want to bring up the subject."

"Because you were afraid that if I knew Satan guarded the exit, I'd turn back."

She nodded. "I am sorry, Thomas. But I could not risk it."

I rubbed my head, though by now my scalp was too numb to feel it. "How can anyone possibly get by him?"

"If you have not betrayed a benefactor, Thomas, he has no right to hold you."

That was no assurance at all. "But what if he tries anyway? Some of the other devils haven't played by the rules."

"You are right. But there are certain seasons when Satan seems to have his fill, and he leaves the damned in the ice while he himself broods over his fall from heaven. That is why I have been so anxious to hurry — I knew that he was in his brooding season, and that the time was fast ending. We have had so many delays, I fear he may be taking his pleasure again. But perhaps he is even now still lost in his bitter thoughts."

I took her hands. "Then I must be going right away."

"Yes, you must," she said. "But there are still three more things I must tell you quickly. The first is that I gave Apangela's necklace back to her. I thought perhaps it might help her in some way on her journey. So if you should see in this region a woman wearing it who resembles me" — she paused and blinked back a freezing tear — "please do all you can to help her escape."

"Of course, Capopia. I'll do for her everything I would do for you, if you could only come with me."

"Good," she said, satisfied. "The second thing is this: If you make it back to the upper world, you must tell what you have seen. That is one important reason why you were allowed to come here. On your story will hang the fate of thousands of souls; for many, only the fear of hell's clutches will drive them into the love of God's embrace."

I nodded. "And the third thing, Capopia?"

She looked down at the ice. "I do not know quite how to tell you this, Thomas. It is something I learned from Apangela when we last met, something told to her by one of the messengers. You do not have to know, but I want you to know."

I waited, growing drowsy from the cold and wondering if we were unwise to keep talking.

She touched the scars on my belly. "Thomas, are you aware that this kind of scar — this raising up of the wounded flesh — is a trait most often found in people of *my* race?"

I nodded. "Yes, I read it once somewhere, but I never thought much about it. Why?"

"Thomas, your ancestry is not all white. You have this trait because there is a drop of black blood in your veins. And that drop came from me."

My jaw dropped open, but it was too cold to leave it open. I closed it and shook my head. "That's impossible, Capopia. My great-aunt traced our family tree on both sides all the way back to eighteenth-century England. It's all European."

"Thomas...." She hesitated. "Thomas, you were adopted."

"*Adopted?*"

"Your parents never told you, but you were born out of wedlock to an acquaintance of theirs in New York. Your birth mother had planned to abort you, but your father pleaded with her to let him take you — though she demanded as payment everything he had saved for years."

"But what does that have to do with you?"

"Your birth mother was a descendant of mine through a child by my second master, born late in my life. Rather than kill the child as my first master did, he gave us our freedom and sent us north. Thomas, I am your great-grandmother's great-grandmother. That is why I was chosen to be your escort. I wanted you to know before we parted ways."

I stood there, trembling, for what seemed an eternity. Then I bent over, kissed her on the forehead and threw my arms around her. We both cried again.

I had so many other questions now, so many things I wanted to say. But time, as she had told me so often, was running out, though only now did I understand how precious the moments had been. "I love you, Great-Grandma," I said and smiled through the freezing tears.

"And I love you, son. I...I will pray for you. Perhaps the prayers of Sheol will yet be heard."

"Remember my promise," I said stepping back. "If the day ever comes when at last I see God face-to-face, I'll beg Him to come back for you."

Then I turned and limped away, pressing my way into the gale. I looked back over my shoulder one more time, and in my last glimpse she was standing erect, shaking with cold and grief, crying and waving good-bye.

F ire and ice; ice and fire. Scenes of Gehenna from every
circle flashed through my mind: the damned souls, the
demons, the faces of three people I'd loved and lost forever. I was alone now, walking through the frigid valley of the
shadow of death. What kind of table was being prepared by my
enemy?

I felt more numb than ever, though whether from the cold or
from Capopia's revelations, I couldn't tell. My mind was pulling
in from my surroundings, trying to disconnect to protect itself.
The air was the blackest I'd seen, and the howling winds blew
with hurricane force. But maybe the dark and the noise would be
my best defense after all: Could even the Devil himself see or hear
in a place like this?

As my thoughts retreated, they settled again on Daddy, and I
was full of questions. What would he say if he knew I had kinfolk
in Africa? And why did he and Mama keep the adoption a secret
all my life? Did they worry that I'd be ashamed of my bastard
heritage or that I'd love them any less?

If only I'd known years ago what I knew now. Daddy's gruff-
ness, his impatience, his distance wouldn't have felt so much like

rejection. I'd have been able to tell myself in the worst of times that no matter what he said or did, he'd still chosen me, paid dearly for me, snatched me from the butcher's knife and taken me home. I wanted to thank him, but it was too late now.

There was one more thing I wanted to tell him. All my life I'd wrestled with trying to forgive him for the hurt he'd caused me, for making me feel like an orphan in my own home because I hadn't met his expectations — I hadn't been the rough-and-tumble, football-toting, girl-chasing boy he thought I ought to be. Knowing what Capopia had just told me, I could forgive him at last.

Maybe he just hadn't known how to show his love; his own father sure hadn't been any model for him in that way. Maybe he was just afraid to show his love; most of his friends would have called him a sissy for hugging me. In any case, now I knew the depths of his love; at last I could let go of all the hurtful memories, knowing they could never outweigh what he'd done while I was still in the womb.

At the same time, somewhere down deep I felt my own guilt; the street hadn't run just one way. You can excuse a child for fleeing the pain, or even striking back at it. But a big part of growing up is laying down the burden of childhood and going on.

Though I should have laid it down years before, I hadn't. Instead, like the damned souls sitting on the edge of that oily swamp, I'd rehearsed the hurts, maybe even exaggerated them. The bitterness had swollen like a boil inside me till all my soul was one big sore spot, too tender for Daddy to touch even in the kindest of ways. Is it any wonder he finally gave up trying?

Now that I was letting go of what he'd done to me, I wondered if Daddy had ever let go of what I'd done to *him*, and if God had let go of it all. Though my father would never hear me say it, maybe God would listen: *I forgive you, Daddy. Please forgive me. And God forgive us both.*

Despite the numbness, I could feel it: A weight like a mountain quaked and slipped off my heart. Only in that moment did I know just how heavy was the lead that had wrapped my own soul for so long.

The wrap had covered my eyes as well. Daddy's face filled my mind now, and it was as if I were seeing him for the first time. It had taken me most of my life to discover an unlettered poet down inside my father; now here, in this wretched place, I'd finally uncovered an unsung hero as well.

Now I knew for sure what I'd long suspected. His harshness was only the defense thrown up by a man scared of his own lion-hearted tenderness. The story of my adoption bordered on fairy tale: Who else, I asked myself, could say he'd been saved from the slaughter by a total stranger who gave nearly all he had for the rescue?

Then it hit me, and I stopped dead in my tracks.

God, please, no — it couldn't be true. But it was true.

Daddy was not my kinfolk after all. He was my benefactor.

No wonder I'd made it, unmolested, through the region where family traitors were frozen. No wonder the butcher demon and the blue-eyed demons had let me pass. I could hear the giant again, calling my name and laughing. They all knew. They had it all planned.

Down in the lowest bowels of Gehenna, where traitors to their benefactors lay in icy stacks to be chewed up and spit out, Satan himself had a claim on Thomas Travis.

Capopia was sure that the fight with Daddy at the pit was no betrayal, that even the Devil couldn't make a case for that. She thought she'd been proved right when I made it through. But she was wrong. It was all a trap. Though she couldn't have known it, she'd been the bait to lure me down for a dinner with the Devil.

There was no place to hide and no way to turn back. My only chance, impossible as it seemed, was to slip by Satan somehow, whatever his claim might be. And if he just happened to see me anyway and caught me, what then?

It would be no coincidence, after all. If heaven had guaranteed justice — and the grace for my journey, as Capopia feared, had at last worn through — then so be it. There was nothing I could do. *I do not dispute God.*

The cold had finally numbed my limbs all the way through, and though I could hardly move them, at least the pain in my leg was dulled. Stacks of frozen blocks were everywhere now, and I knew the exit could not be far. For the first time I passed close by one of the racks I'd seen scattered across the ice all along.

My darkest suspicions were confirmed: Those weren't clothes hanging on them. They were frozen souls, chipped out of the blocks, swinging in the wind like so many hog carcasses in a slaughterhouse deep freeze.

From the rack I turned my gaze back again to the ice ahead, and I saw some kind of movement, immense and steady, far up in the air. I kept walking, and as I did, the lines of what was in motion slowly came clear.

Bat wings. Or more nearly, pterodactyl wings. Three pairs of black, leathery pinions, big enough to dwarf the wings of the world's greatest jumbo jet, rising and falling in a restless but regular motion. From the angle of the wind, I could tell that their flapping created the gale.

In a moment I could make out as well the lines of a head and shoulders — no, *three* heads on shoulders. The figure towered above the ice, taller than even the giants. It had to be him.

Then the features of the three faces came into view, and I froze at the sight. No medieval painting of the Devil, no descriptions of demons from the ancient accounts of exorcism, could have prepared me for what I saw.

The middle face was as hideous as all the old tales made him out to be: the skin deep scarlet and gruesomely scarred; the teeth huge and sharp, but crumbling like ancient mountain peaks; the eyes murky, yellow moons, bloodshot with red foam that dripped down onto the matted hair of a shaggy chest.

But the other two faces — one male, one female — were hauntingly beautiful.

The female face was richly black, draped in stunning jewels. Massive earrings of ruby and emerald set in gold hung out from under a sweep of shiny, ebony hair, and a string of sapphires wrapped around her forehead. Her deep brown eyes were seductively half-closed; her lips curved in a sultry smile.

The male face was white though tanned, surrounded with waves of long blond hair. His features were perfectly proportioned — square-cut and strong — and his eyes were a pale, dreamy blue. The long line of his mouth twisted somewhere between a smile and a sneer.

All three heads were chewing on the damned, the legs of each soul draping out of their mouths like half-smoked cigarettes.

The brooding season was over.

Slowly the male face turned toward me and gazed down. He spit out his wad of soul and spoke in a voice so deep it sounded almost synthesized.

"*Tommy. Tommy, I've been waiting for you so long now. Come closer, son. You're a sight for sore eyes. I want to get a good look at you before you join me for dinner.*"

He laughed wickedly, and the bellow rolled across the ice like arctic thunder.

I gathered up all the guts I could muster and shouted back in defiance. "You can't keep me. So it is willed where what is willed must be."

This time all three faces began to laugh, nearly choking on the soul stubs in their mouths.

"But I have a claim on you, Tommy," said the blond head. "Surely you know that by now. I've already had them carve your name in the ice where I keep a roster of who lies where."

I edged a little closer toward him, and closer to the exit. All I had was Capopia's argument, but maybe it would buy me a little time.

"When I fought with my father at the pit," I shouted, "that was no act of treachery. I was defending an innocent woman and taking a stand against the evil in my father, not against my father himself. I would have betrayed the truth to do otherwise."

He snickered and looked at the other two faces. "So we have an ethical expert on our hands."

Then he turned back to me. "You want to argue ethics? I can quote you every sniveling, sophist twist in the book. I *wrote* the book."

Suddenly he pounded his fist on the ice. "Fool! Who cares about that stupid little spat by the pit? I'm talking about a lifetime of betraying your benefactor."

My heart was pounding, but I slipped a little closer to the exit. "What do you mean?" I asked.

"Can't you see it now, idiot? From the time you were young you learned to take vengeance on your father in a thousand ways. If he wanted you to ride to town with him, you stayed home to spite him. If he wanted you to toss a softball, you ran to your room to read. If he wanted to watch an old war movie, you whined until he switched it to the public station for a symphony concert."

He was right, and we both knew it. He was grabbing all the things I'd finally let go of, the things I was hoping God had let go of, and throwing them up in my face.

"That's over now!" I shouted. "Let me by."

He wasn't listening. "When he needed you to help him work on the car, you said you didn't feel well. When he hoped you'd fight for your country, you went off to college to flaunt your independence. When he begged you to choose some practical major so you could have a decent career, you thumbed your nose at him and majored in religion."

The fierce blue eyes were looking right through me. "Whatever you did," said the blond head, "you did to hurt him. A whole lifetime of rebellion, Tommy. You betrayed your precious daddy at every turn. And now you'll pay for it."

I had inched even closer to the hole by now. The opening was small — only wide enough for one person to enter at a time, and then only if you raised both hands over your head to slither down. It would be like jumping inside one of those utility poles of the suicides and hoping I didn't get stuck.

But if I was ever going to make it out, that was the only way, and this was the only time.

I dashed toward the Devil's belly. His response was awkward and slow, as if he couldn't quite make up his mind how to stop me. Even so, with my cracked shin the sprint took too long, and he slapped his hairy left hand flat across the hole. The blond head grinned; the other two looked irritated.

I turned a sharp right and hobbled around his side. He lifted the same hand and swatted at me, but again his motion was hesitant, uncoordinated. The hand missed and struck his own flank instead. I made it all the way behind him just in time.

He snarled. "You'll never get away from me, moron. You might as well just give up."

All three heads were twisting around on their necks now, looking around all those wings, trying to spot me. He couldn't move his waist, so I had a bit of an advantage. Both arms flailed behind the monster's back, but I dodged them, staying only inches ahead of ten pointy fingernails while I slipped and slid on the ice.

When the two hands were stretched down behind him as far as they could reach, scratching at the ice to find me, I made a limping run for it around his right flank. The black head looked down and saw me.

"This side!" she screamed to the others. "This side, you bumbling idiots!"

"No!" huffed the red face. "He's still back there!"

"Fools!" shouted the blond. "He's on *my* side!" The two hands were jerking angrily, unable to coordinate a move.

Then I saw it. Satan kept bungling the chase because that unholy trinity of heads was nothing but an unruly mob, a house divided against itself. Maybe, just maybe, I could play them off against each other.

One more time I made it around his torso, close to his hide so the faces couldn't see me as easily. The hands were spastic now, slapping his own belly, and the heads were cussing three ways at once. With more guts than I'd ever even dreamed I had, I grabbed a fistful of fur on the Devil's back and crawled up as we had on the giant.

All three mouths roared. The arms swung around to the front again and reached backward over his shoulders, with elbows bent up in the air. But they were too stout to get beyond the shoulder blades, and the wings kept getting in their way.

His back was twisting now, trying to shake me off. I held on and climbed steadily, one long clump of hair at a time. When I finally got within his reach, I darted between the bases of the wings to confuse him.

Just as I crawled to a spot a few yards below his right shoulder, the arms pulled back forward over his head. He was going to try reaching around sideways instead of from above, and if he did, he'd get me.

No time to lose. I climbed up on his right shoulder, ran across the black neck and between the red and black heads. The ice hole was directly below me, next to where a navel would have been if Satan had a birthday. A jump through the air was out of the question — the exit was too far down and too small for a bull's-eye. But the Devil had been chewing on souls for millennia now, and he had quite a paunch.

Before I could tell myself it was too risky, I leaped from his neck and went sliding on my backside down the oily curve of his belly. When I hit the ice on all fours, I was only a few yards from the hole.

I scrambled to slide in, but this time the Devil had his act together. Down came his left hand on the hole again, knocking me flat on my back on the ice, only inches from his thumb.

All three heads laughed again. "Here," said the blond. "Let me make you a little more *comfortable.*" Then he bent down and breathed lightly on the ice where I lay — a hot, putrid breath that smelled like week-old road kill. The ice beneath me melted a little, soaked into my shorts and began to freeze again.

"I suppose that place will do as well as any," he said, gloating. "You can lie there and get hard all the way through while we decide who gets first chew." Then the three heads began to argue.

My shorts were frozen solid to the ice now, heavy as the leaden pants that had anchored Stone to his doom. I pulled in my belly and squirmed to tear myself out of them. The skin ripped off as I did, but I stuffed the howls of pain that tried to bust out.

One last jerk, and I was naked and free.

But all too late. The blond looked down at me and cussed, then the right hand grabbed me and pinned me down only inches from the exit.

"We've played long enough," he said with a snort. "You're not frozen, but well-chilled will have to do."

"Wait!" came a shout across the ice. "You have better prey than that!"

I turned, dumbfounded, to see who it was.

───────────── FORTY-ONE ─────────────

It was Capopia.

"*No!*" I screamed. "Go back! It's too late!"

Capopia ignored me, her gaze fixed on the middle face. "Surely an escort is a greater prize for you?"

She walked closer as she spoke. "You know you have a claim. Catch me if you can."

"I want her!" shrieked the black head. "Drop the man and grab her!"

"Fools!" said the red face, spitting the words at Capopia. "Now we'll have you both. One for each of the other mouths, while I continue my pleasure with Judas."

He held me too tightly for me to wiggle out. All I could do was watch in horror as Capopia ran into the reach of his other hand. As he grasped for her, I couldn't bear the sight. My head jerked away toward the ice near my shoulder.

A glint of silver flashed at the edge of the hole. What was it? I reached out and pulled it to me.

It was Apangela's necklace.

I gripped it in my right hand and looked at Capopia again. The Devil had stretched her out on the ice. Her arms, pinned down by his fingers, extended out straight from her sides.

"Capopia — the necklace!" I shouted, swinging the silver cross in the air. "I found Apangela's necklace!"

She lifted her head from the ice just high enough to see for herself, and all three devil faces turned toward me as well.

A blood-curdling scream in trio shook the ice. The hairy hand dropped me at the edge of the hole.

"Where did you get *that*?" shrieked the black face, turning away.

The other hand still had Capopia pinned down. "Escape down the hole!" she shouted to me. "Now!"

"I can't leave you!" I shouted back.

"You cannot save me now!" she said. "But if you go, you can tell your story and keep your promise — go find God, and beg Him to come back for me!"

All three faces had closed their eyes to the cross, but that free hand was only inches away from me and groping around to catch me again. Suddenly the blond head bent over toward me, bellowing. His jaws stretched out over me, and there was only one place to go.

I clutched the cross, threw my hands up over my head, closed my eyes and cried out, "God help me!" Then I jumped into the hole.

I could feel myself slithering down, down, down a narrow, slippery pipe. It closed in on me, wrapped around me, squeezed me from every side. The walls were hot and slimy, and the friction of its slide across my face, my chest, every nook and cranny of my body, burned my skin like liquid fire until I was numb all over and I couldn't really tell whether I was sliding anymore or whether I was stuck.

I panicked. Maybe I *was* stuck, right in the middle of the pipe — just like the suicides, with no way out for eternity, no way to open my eyes, no way even to scream. Maybe what I'd feared most had come upon me.

The questions exploded in my mind. Did Satan get me after all? Did he swallow me whole, without even stopping to chew? Am I stuck in a crease of the Devil's gut, waiting to be digested like a rat in a rattlesnake's belly? Or am I buried alive at the bottom of the abyss, with the weight of all hell crushing down on my face?

The only answer was a suffocating blackness that squeezed

through my eyelids till it filled my head. I slipped away into a silent oblivion.

A distant babel of voices — some crying, some shouting, some only murmuring — stole softly through the darkness and called to me. When at last my head cleared enough to listen, I found that they spoke in tongues I couldn't understand. Shafts of bright light pried open my eyes and blinded me. I sat up, holding my head and marveling: *I'm alive.*

When I could look around, I saw a room cluttered with yellowed papers, filthy rags and sticks of wood. The window where the light shone through was shattered, its glass scattered across the dirty concrete floor. A rusty pail of water sat in a corner, and Apangela's silver necklace lay beside me.

Next I dared to look at myself. My naked body still carried the scars of fork and fire, and its hair had all grown back. But my skin was a dark brown all over now, as if the final slide through the exit had burned every part of me.

Afraid to see more, but afraid not to, I crawled over to the pail of water and looked at my reflection. What little hair I'd had on my head and face when I started the journey was all there, but it was bleached white as wool.

Where was I? Before I stepped out the door to see, I wanted to cover myself in some way. Among the piles of rags on the floor I found a long, soiled cloth of white cotton and wrapped it around me like a toga. Then I stepped out to study the noisy scene that had called me to rise up from the blackness.

Thousands of brown-skinned people wrapped in ragged loincloths and saris surged down a long dirt street, its yellow dust mottled by the shadows of crumbling buildings on either side. On every corner I could see gaunt, grim faces — many begging, and many more dying.

A sea of pain and despair. Was it just another miserable region of hell Capopia never knew about?

Only one way could I know for sure. I fell on my knees to whisper the word I'd wanted to say for so long, but couldn't: *"Jesus. Jesus. Oh, Jesus..."* And I wept to know that grace at last had triumphed.

Standing up and stepping inside again, I went to the water's mirror to glimpse my face once more. The old Thomas was dead, purged away forever in the fires of Gehenna. I hung the silver cross around my neck, pulled the white rag tightly around me and limped back out into the sunlight, feeling at last a ravenous hunger that demanded to be fed.

Beside the door of the building I exited hung a rusty sign, clinging to the wall sideways by a single bolt. It was written first in a flowing script — Hindi, I guessed — and then in English: AUTHORIZED PERSONNEL ONLY.

Where was I? Where would I go? How would I stay alive? God alone knew. But of one thing I was sure now: A destiny was waiting for me out in those screaming streets.

I had a story to tell — and a promise to keep.